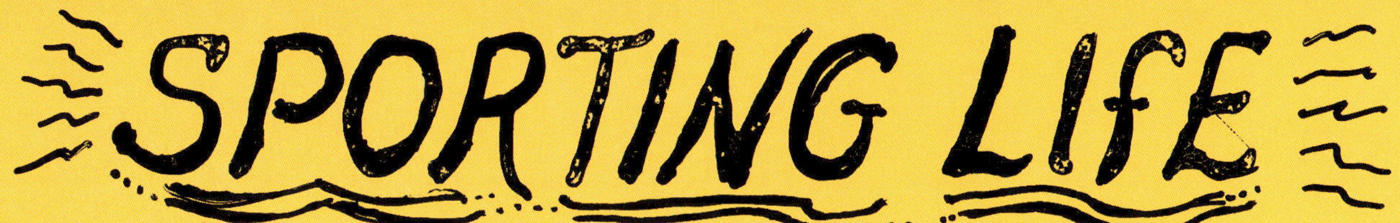

...THE JOURNALS...

WALTER IOOSS

CEO & Creative Director: B. Martin Pedersen

Editor: Michael Porciello

Art Director: Lauren Slutsky
Design & Production: Nicole Recchia

Luis Diaz, Joanne Sullivan, Alexia Leitich

Published by Graphis Inc.

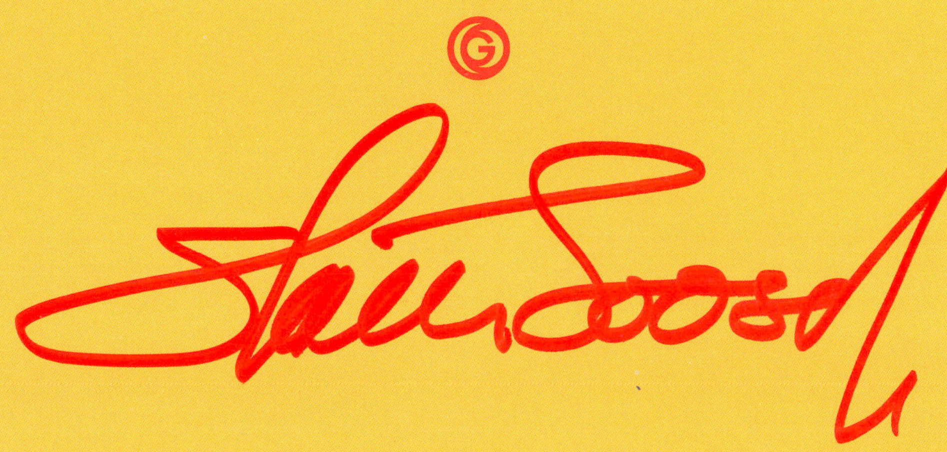

Copyright © under universal copyright convention copyright © 2002 by Walter Iooss, Jr. Jacket and book design copyright ©2002 by Graphis, Inc., 307 Fifth Avenue, Tenth Floor, New York, New York 10016.
No part of this book may be reproduced in any form without written permission of the publisher. ISBN: 1-932026-00-2 Printed in Hong Kong. Distributed by Publishers Group West

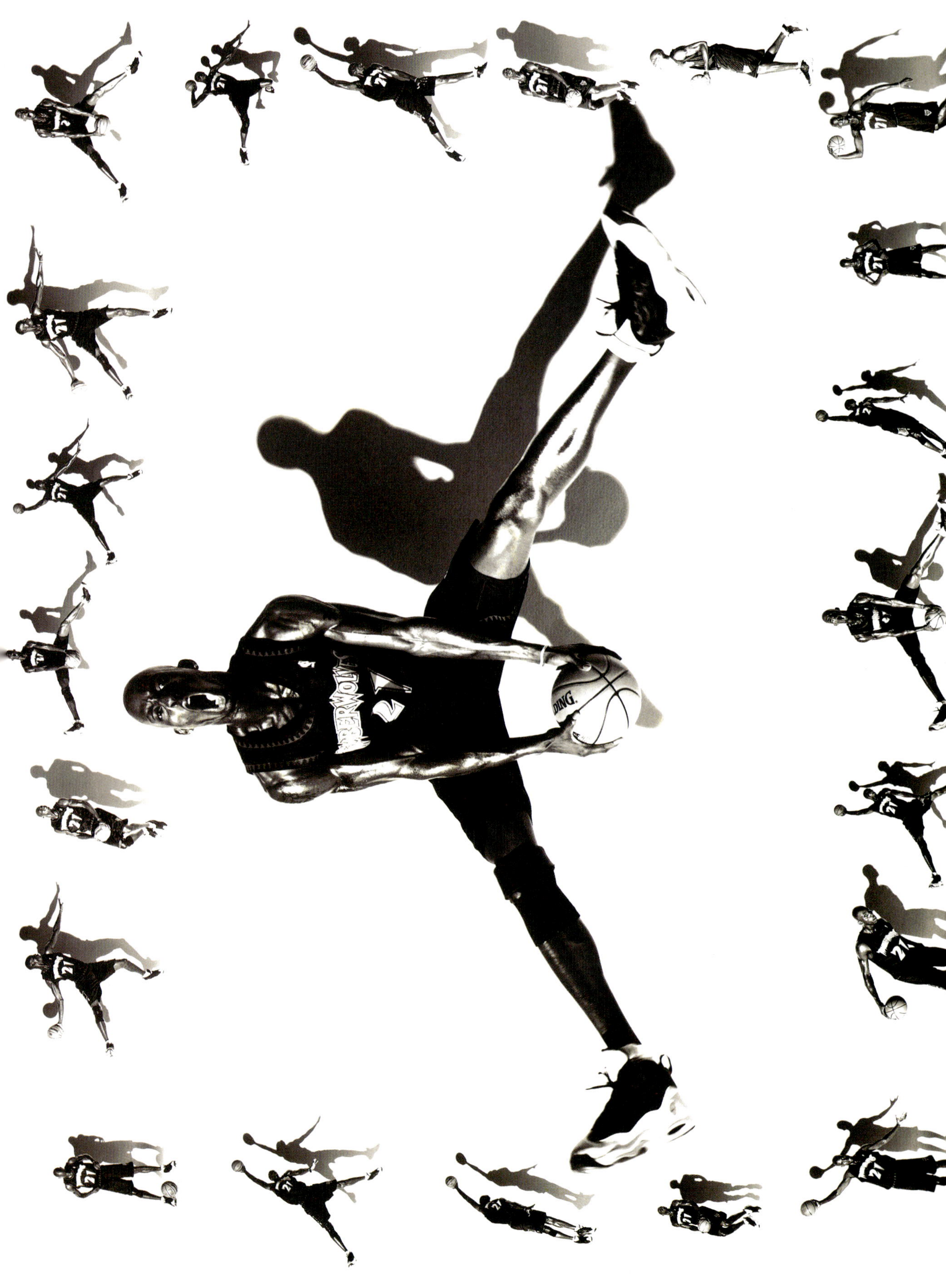

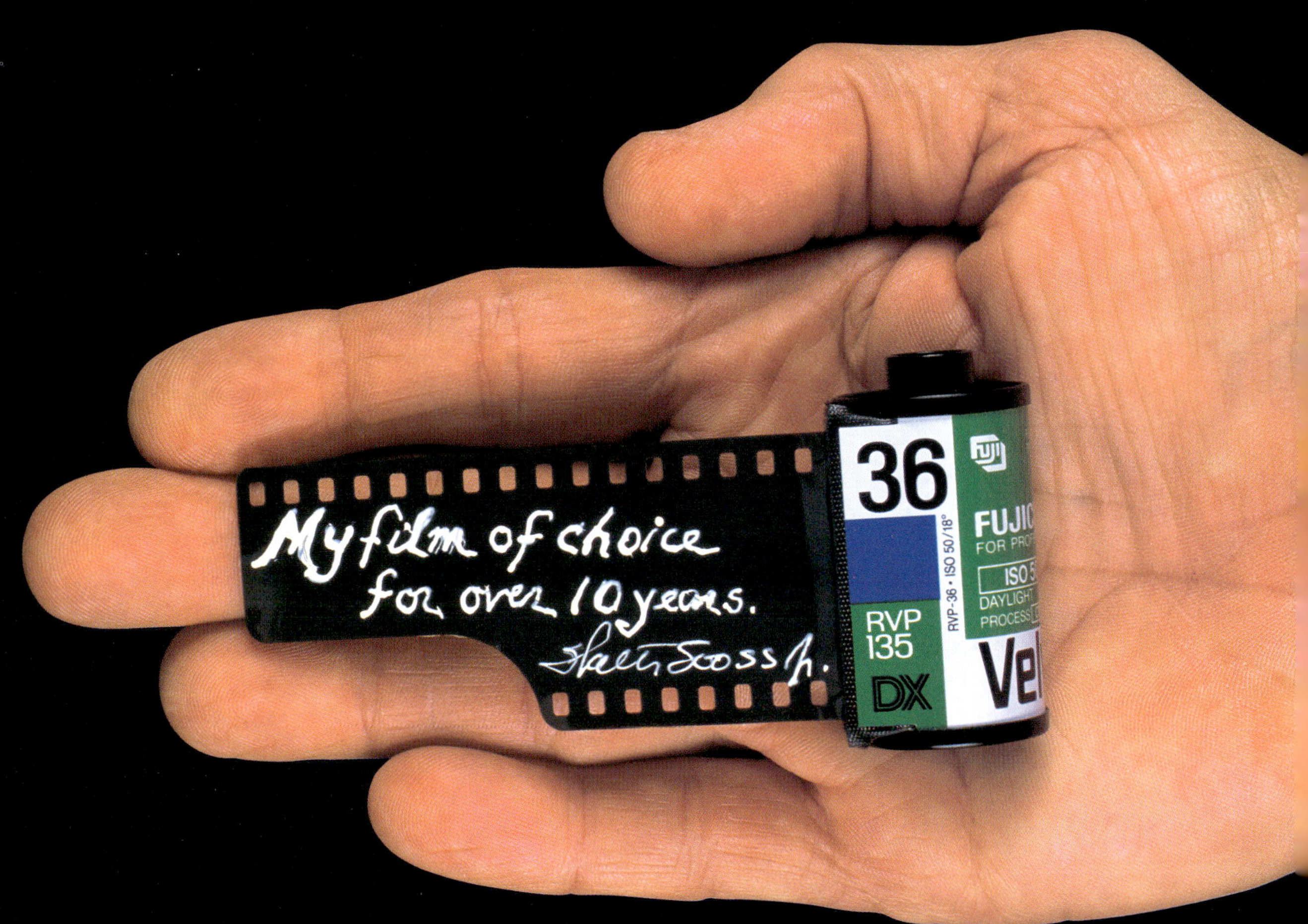
My film of choice
for over 10 years.
36
RVP-36 • ISO 50/18°
RVP
135
DX

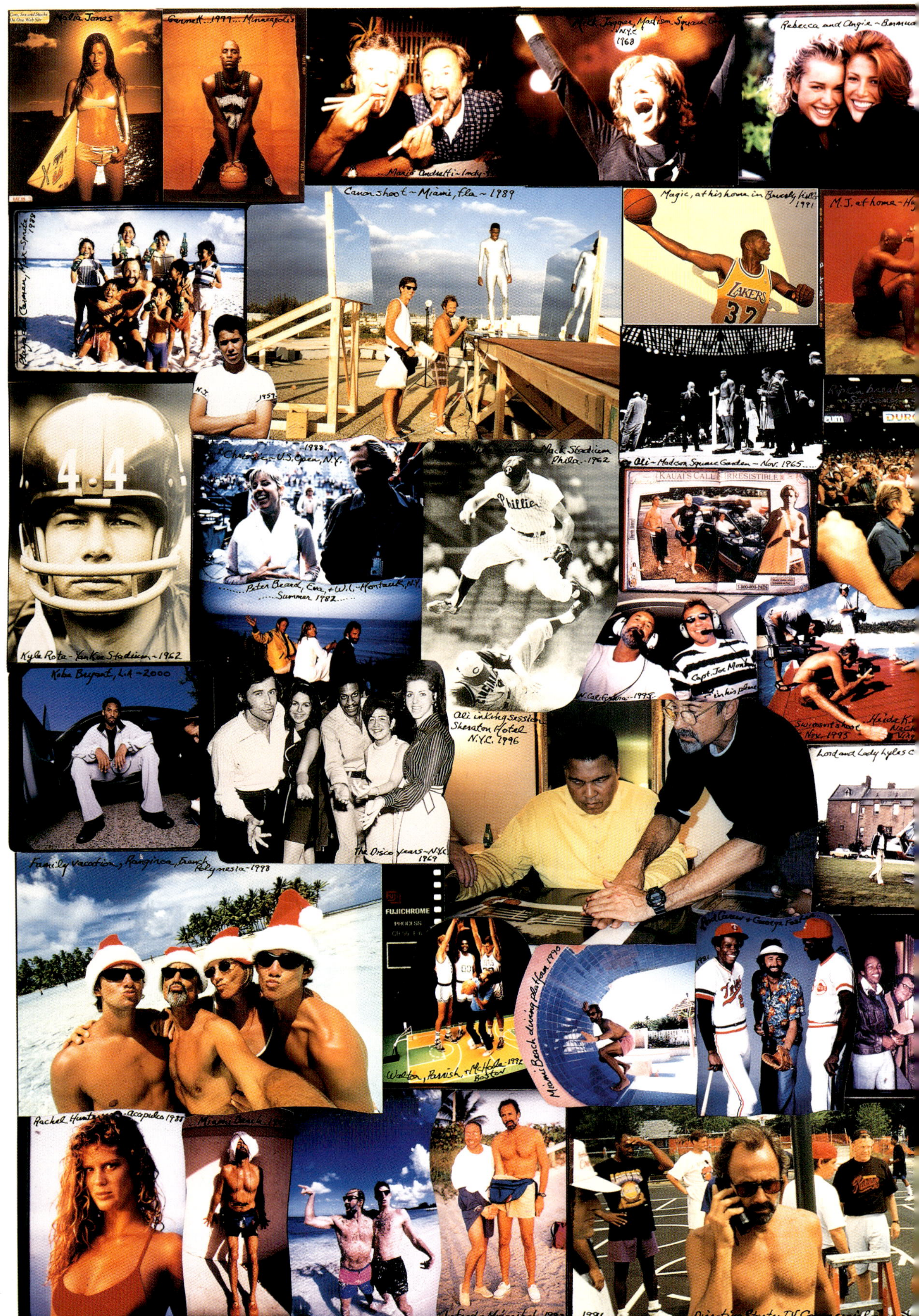

Montauk Pt, N.Y.

~ S

g Life ...

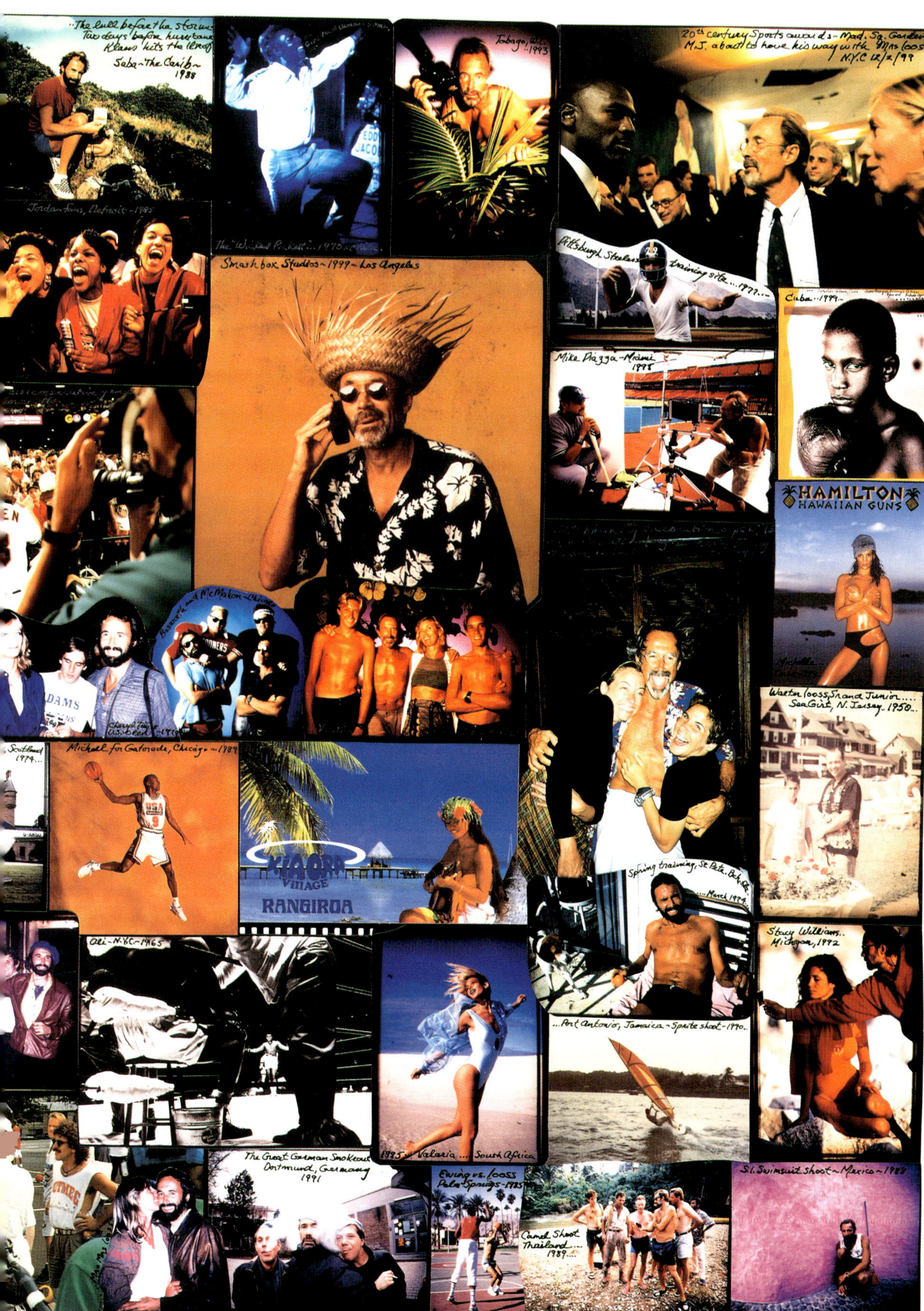

2000 ~

Patty Iooss

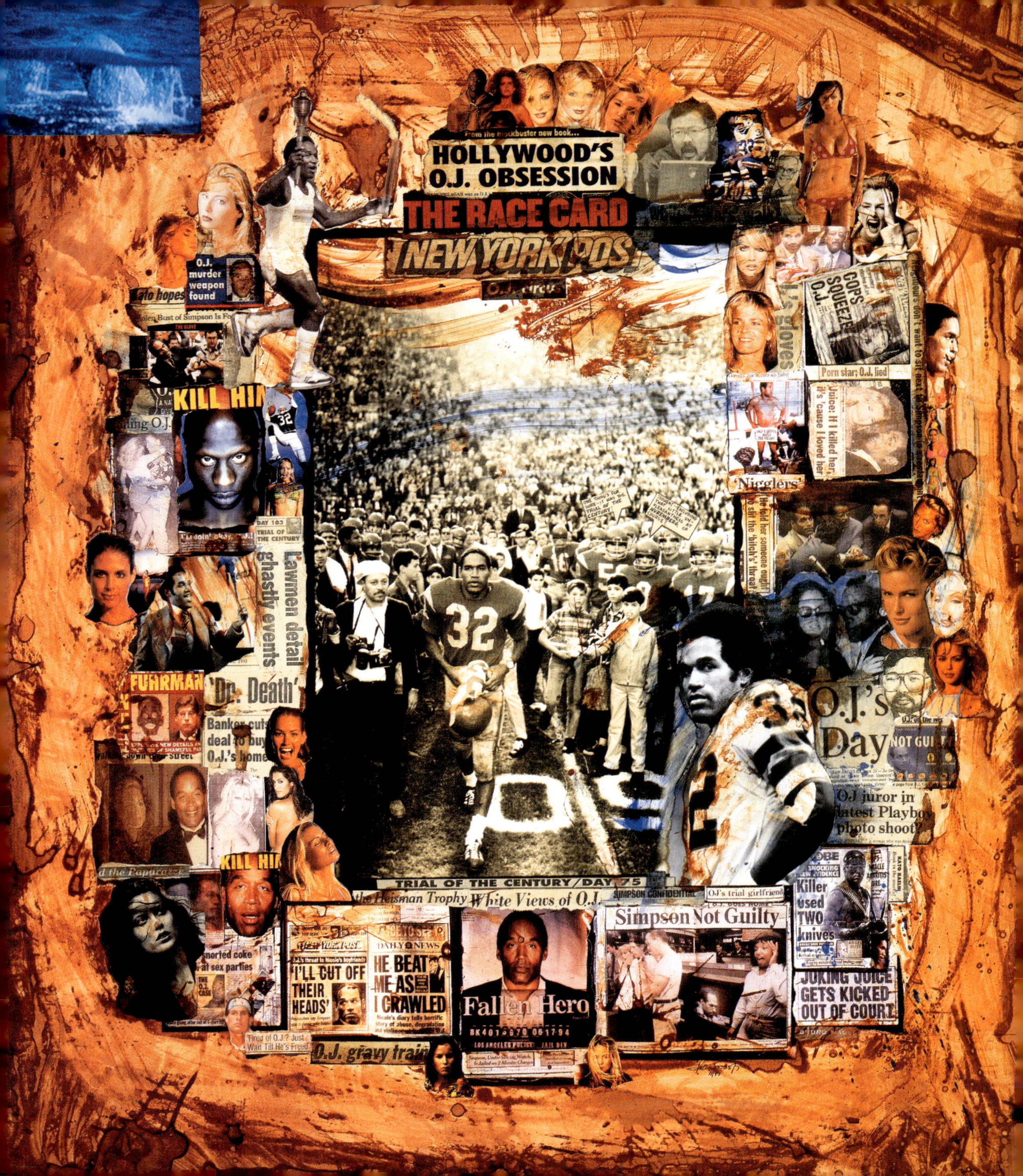
HOLLYWOOD'S O.J. OBSESSION
THE RACE CARD
NEW YORK POS
O.J. murder weapon found
KILL HIM
COPS SQUEEZE O.J.
Porn star: O.J. lied
Juice: If I killed her, it's 'cause I loved her
Nigglers
Lawmen detail ghastly events
FUHRMAN
'Dr. Death'
Banker cuts deal to buy O.J.'s home
O.J.'s Day
NOT GUILTY
OJ juror in latest Playboy photo shoot
TRIAL OF THE CENTURY/DAY 75
the Heisman Trophy
White Views of O.J.
SIMPSON CONFIDENTIAL
OJ's trial girlfriend
Simpson Not Guilty
Killer used TWO knives
JOKING JUICE GETS KICKED OUT OF COURT
I'LL CUT OFF THEIR HEADS
HE BEAT ME AS I CRAWLED
Fallen Hero
LOS ANGELES POLICE JAIL DIV
snorted coke at sex parties
O.J. gravy train
Tired of O.J.? Just Wait Till He's Freed

In 1981, I started keeping the diary. It was simpler back then, containing SX-70 Polaroids of my wife Eva and my young children, Christian and Bjorn. More a family album than journal.

The idea came from the model/actress Carol Alt, while on a Sports Illustrated swimsuit shoot. She would paste Polaroids of the jobs she worked to have a yearly record of her life.

My diaries started to evolve into something more interesting in the mid- to late '80s, with exotic trips, over five years, to the Philippines (four times), Thailand, Malaysia, Tahiti and Hawaii. I started mixing Polaroids from my 35mm camera with prints I could make at home from a Polaroid printer, clippings from newspapers, magazines, and anything I might find that would add some local color to the spreads.

By now another piece of machinery called a Fuji Pictrostat came into the Time/Life photolab in New York. It enabled me to make beautiful prints, of any size (up to 8 1/2 x 11") in two minutes. Now I had a variety of technical resources to choose from, and assignments that began to make them more intriguing.

I started to realize how much enjoyment people got from looking at my diary. The quirky headlines from newspapers were often amusing and proved that fact is stranger than any fiction you could imagine.

In the mid '90s I began to put more thought and design into the diary spreads. I started to photograph the diary pages and use them, rather than a simple sequence of individual images, for self-promotion in advertising source books. I felt that there was more spirit and humor in the diary then in a single image on a page. My portfolio is now all diary spreads printed on Iris prints.

I also began to use a variety of inks to tone the pages and write on the prints.

My assignments continued to provide rare and rich opportunities. No doubt that the shots I brought back from Bangkok of kids kickboxing, of children's sports in Cuba, of Sports Illustrated swimsuit shoots around the world made for more exotic spreads than my previous efforts. They were no longer just a dry record of the what, where and when of my career.

The diary process has pushed me into other areas in photography as well. I now use a variety of camera formats, papers and films—up to the 20 x 24" giant Polaroid. In 1996 I started making collages which pushed me into other uncharted areas; large pieces up to 3 x 4', with one containing 142 images.

In August 2001, I went to Brazil to shoot youth soccer and the SI swimsuit issue. Not only was I shooting for the magazine, but I photographed and collected everything I could that would later help me in assembling the spreads. Twelve spreads took me a month to complete. I sat in Bjorn's room with the diary, inks, prints, contact sheets, double-sided tape, Polaroids, postcards and collected trivia spread across his desk and onto his bed. He was away at school and it was the only place in the house I could leave the materials out.

I played the same two pieces of music repeatedly; Beethoven's 5th piano concerto (the Emperor) and Mozart's piano concertos #20 and #21 (with Rudolf Serkin at the piano). Listening to this hypnotic loop of sound, I would sit for hours working night and day. When I completed these spreads there was a great relief, but after a week I realized that it was a special period of time and I missed working on them. I also felt they were some of the best work I had yet done.

I'm fortunate that Eva is a painter of botanicals. Her knowledge of colors and their combinations has been a great education.

Bjorn, at 21, is studying photography at the Rhode Island School of Design, and he's also been keeping a diary for three years. His edgier eye has opened mine a bit wider, and influenced my composition. I have been trying to take my subjects farther from the center of the frame to the edges, where he lives as a photographer.

And Christian, also a good shooter, is now picture editor of Golf World Magazine, and another eye to honestly scrutinize my photos.

We all feed from each other, which has been wonderful for all of us these last five years. I thank them for their criticism and love. I'd also like to acknowledge Peter Beard for his influence over the last 20+ years. He is the master recycler, collagist and diarist, and a fountain of inspiration.

Walter Iooss

Montauk July 17, 2002

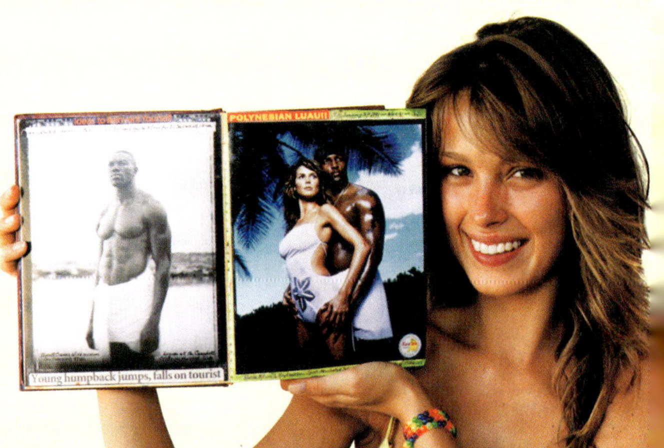

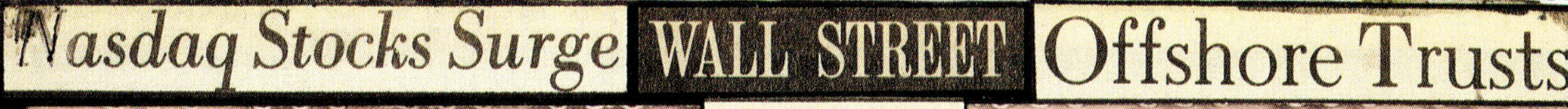

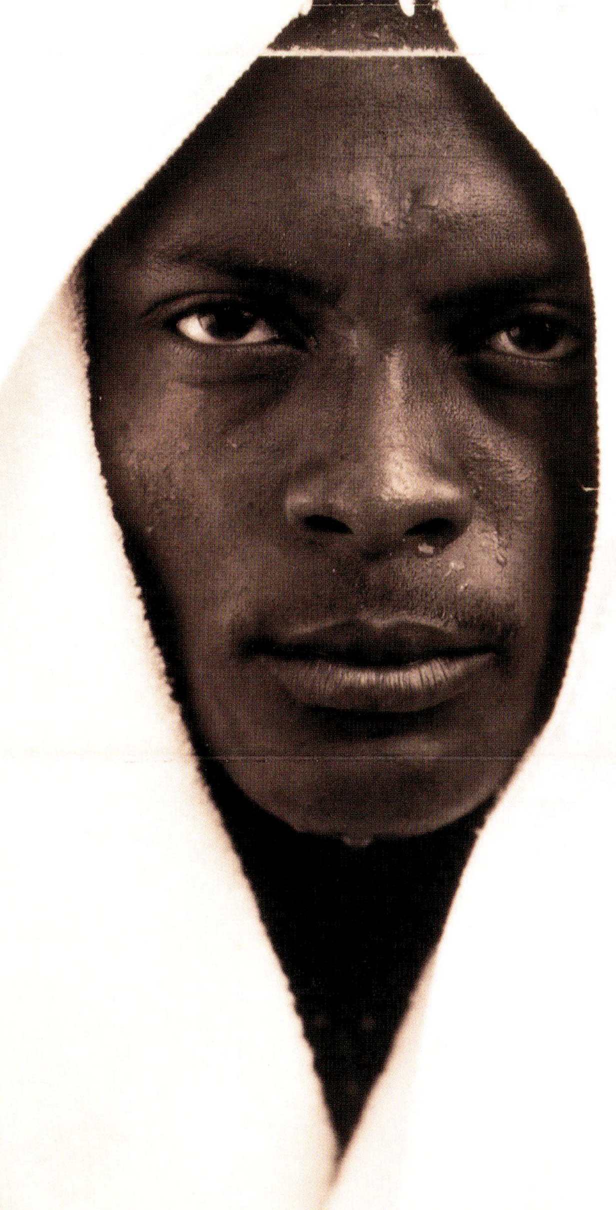

Nasdaq Stocks Surge
WALL STREET
Offshore Trusts
JUNK-BOND ISSUES
....7/12/97.. SANTA MONICA, CA... 5:00P.M.... EDDIE GEORGE for ADIDAS... SANTA MONICA COLLEGE...
Greenspan Bites Tongue
"This Is Bullish"

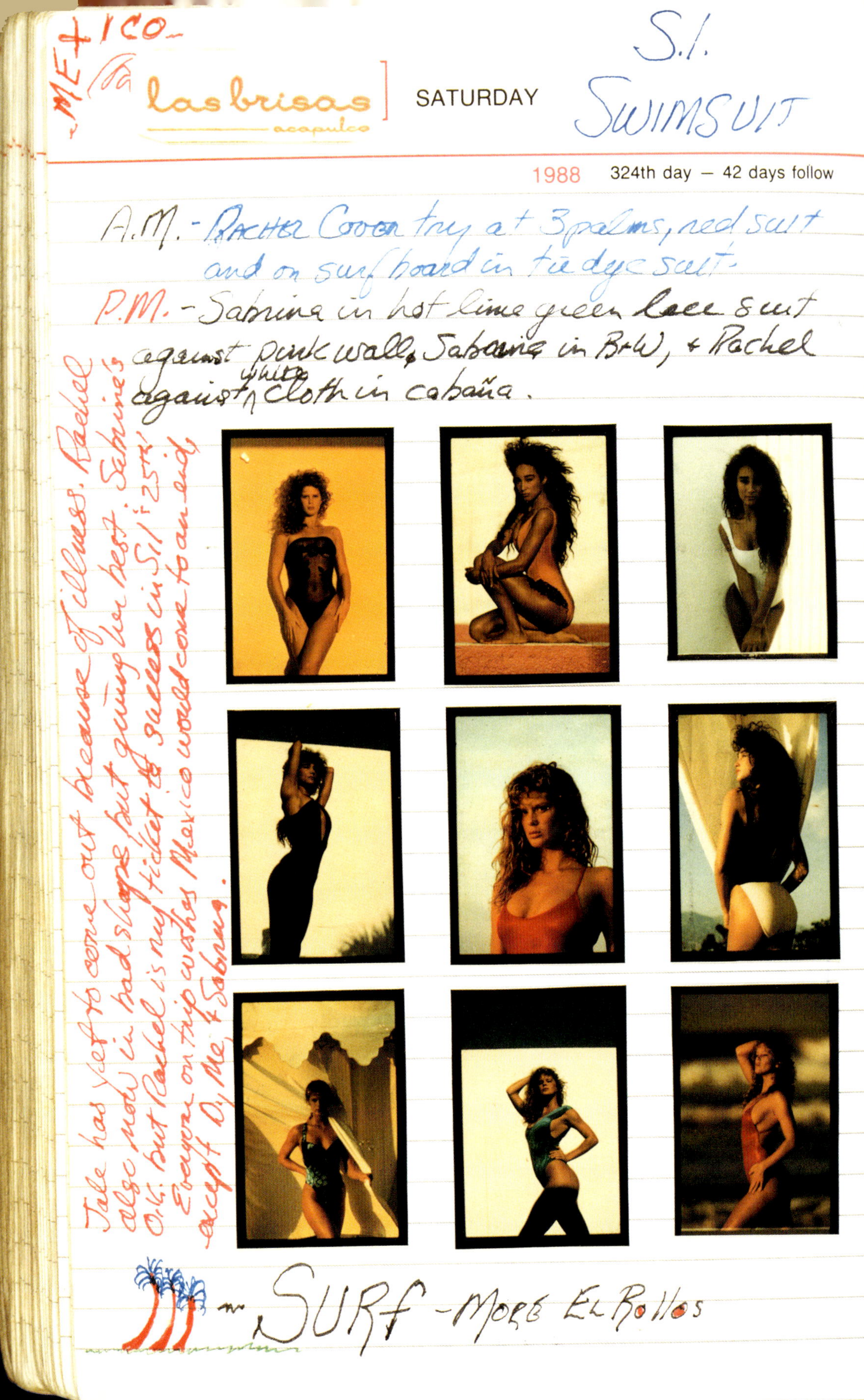

MEXICO-
las brisas
acapulco
SATURDAY
S.I.
SWIMSUIT
1988
324th day — 42 days follow
A.M. - Rachel Cover try at 3 palms, red suit
and on surf board in tie dye suit -
P.M. - Sabrina in hot lime green lace suit
against pink wall, Sabrina in B+W, + Rachel
against white cloth in cabaña.
Jale has yet to come out because of illness. Rachel
also now in bad shape but giving her best. Sabrina's
O.K. but Rachel is my ticket to success in S.I.'s 25th.
Everyone on trip wishes Mexico would come to an end,
except D, Me, & Sabrina.
SURF - MORE EL Rollos

S.I.
Swimsuit

ACAPULCO

SUNDAY **20** NOVEMBER

1988 325th day — 41 days follow

A.M. Rachel + Sabrina performing ballet like leaps. Rachel crawling on all fours "hate this fucking pose".

P.M. Sabrina all afternoon. Very hot set of pics against all white backgrounds with brilliant light.

Julie still has not been able to make it on the shoot as her illness continues. Rachel can not make the afternoon session as splitting headache K.O.'s her.

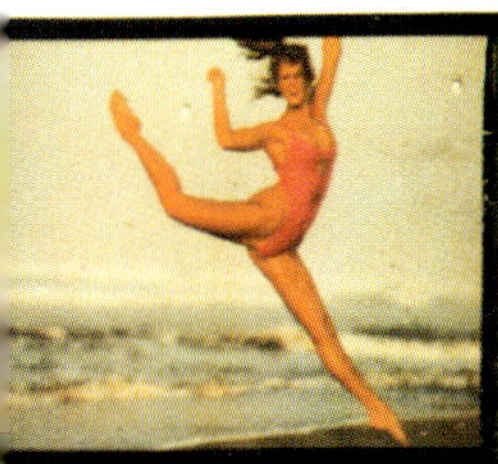

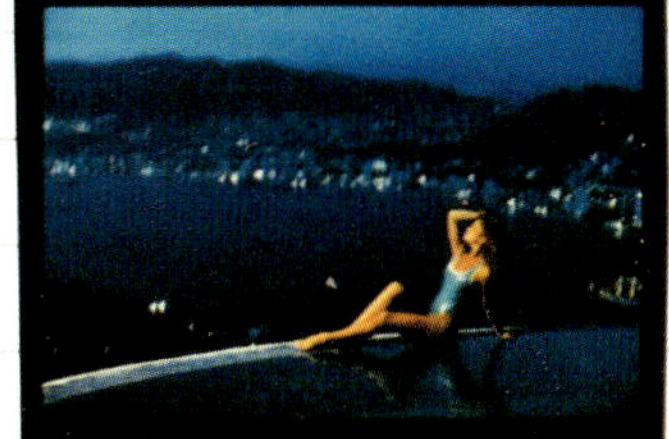

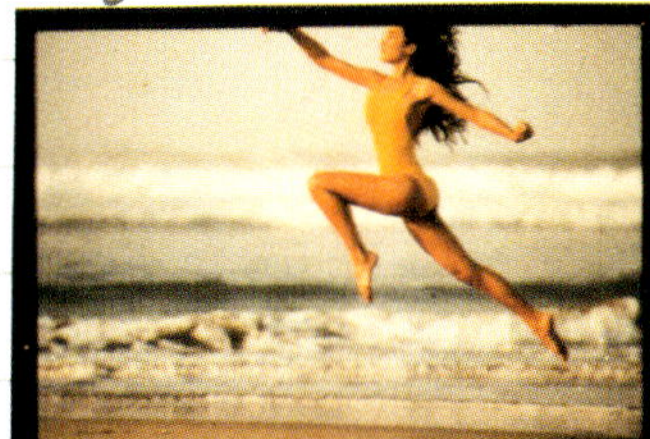

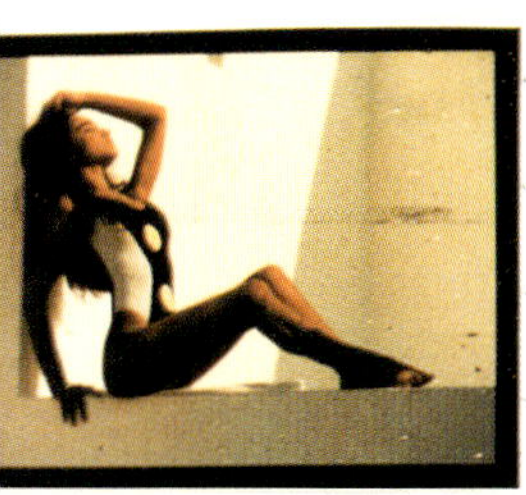

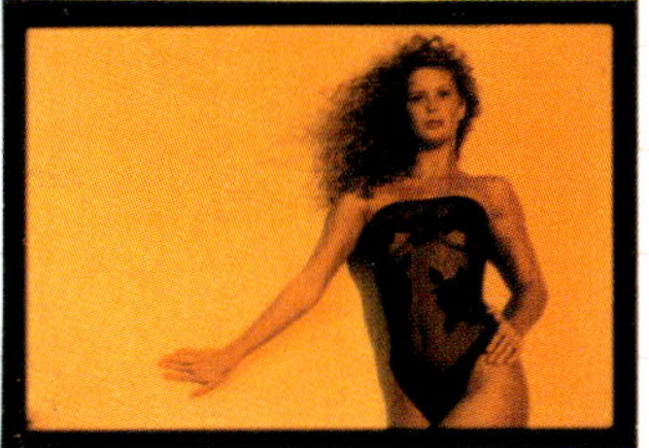

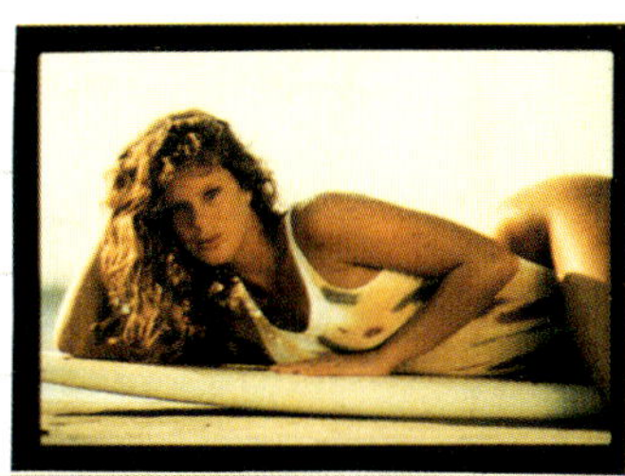

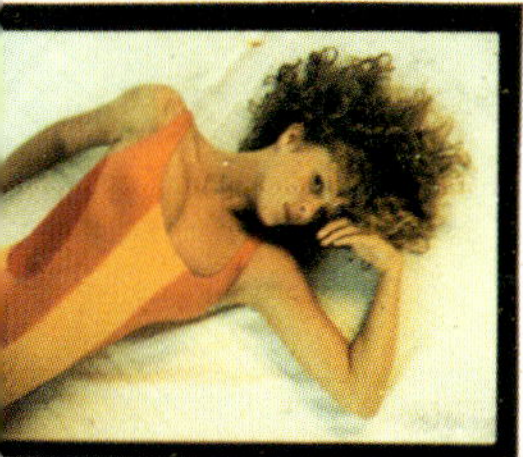

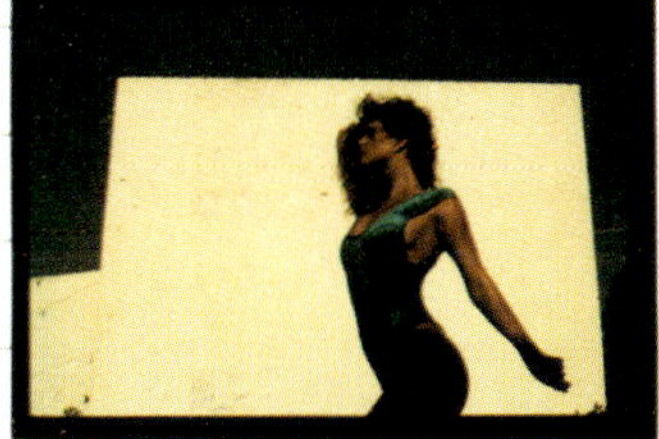

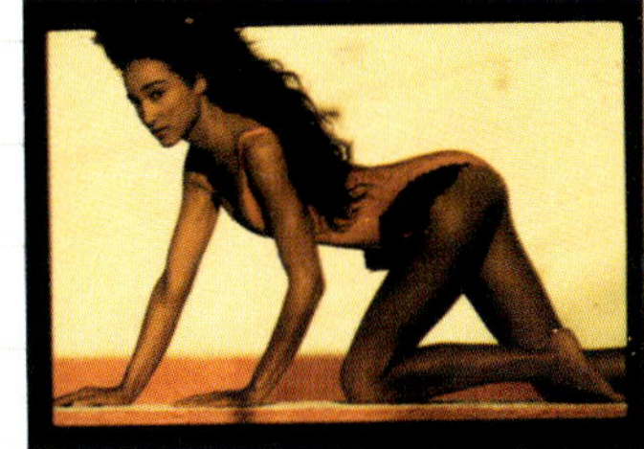

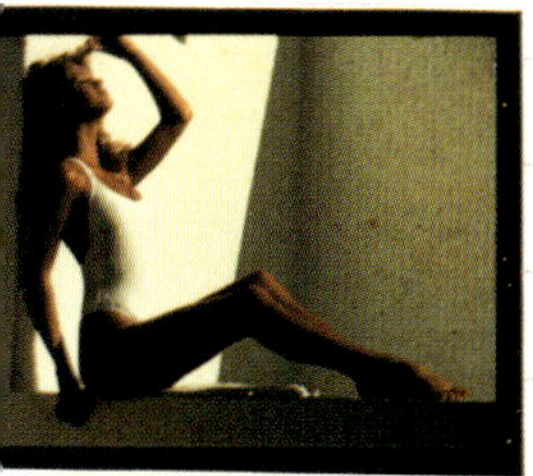

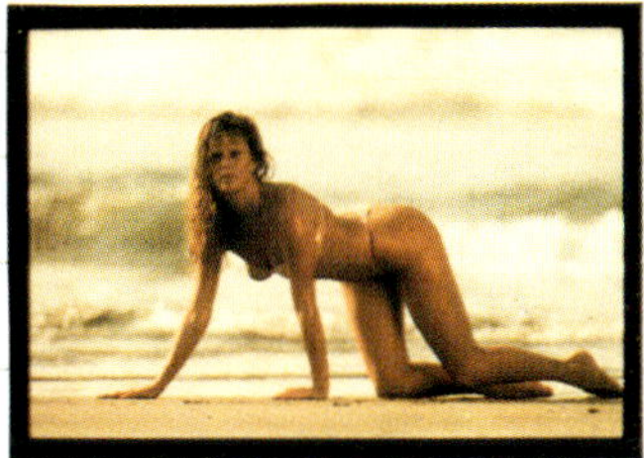

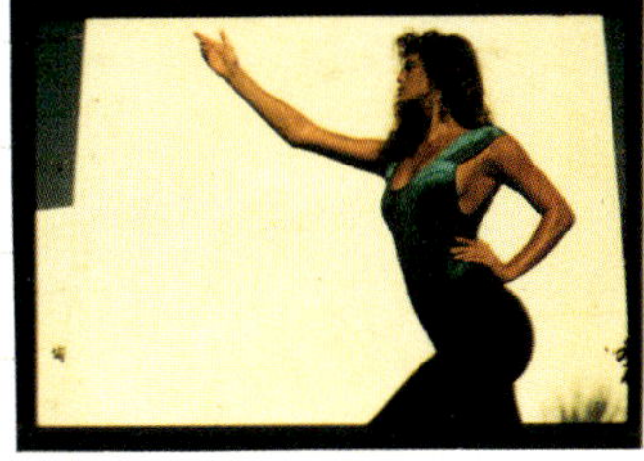

SURF

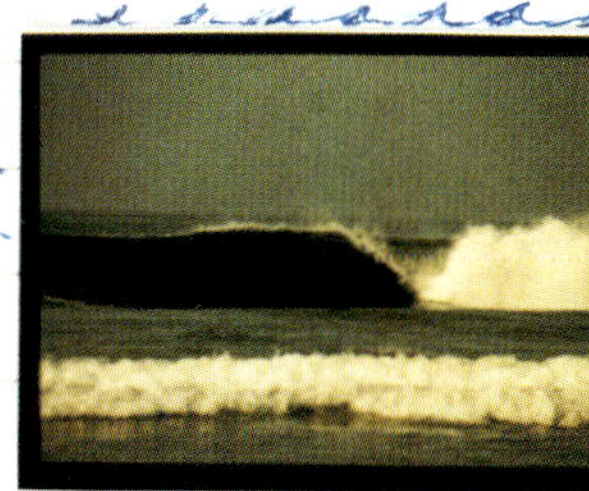

— find Syringes on Beach —

but lousy, tide too high and closing out with bad currents

·PREP DAY·

··#7·· SEPT

··SAN FRANCISCO··

Montana

Sports Illustrated

Very anxious today. Concerned whether I can keep Joe occupied while I try to delay shoot for an hour. Upon meeting Joe he states "let's get started," I have to go to dinner. I start to talk to Joe, while he's sipping on a Corona, and we fall into a wonderful 45 min. conversation. Joe stays until dark....

~SUSHI~

"LIVING LEGENDS SERIES"

'ZANOLER + WELSH ASS'T.

TUESDAY **10** SEPTEMBER

- CAÑADA COLLEGE - SHOOT DAY -

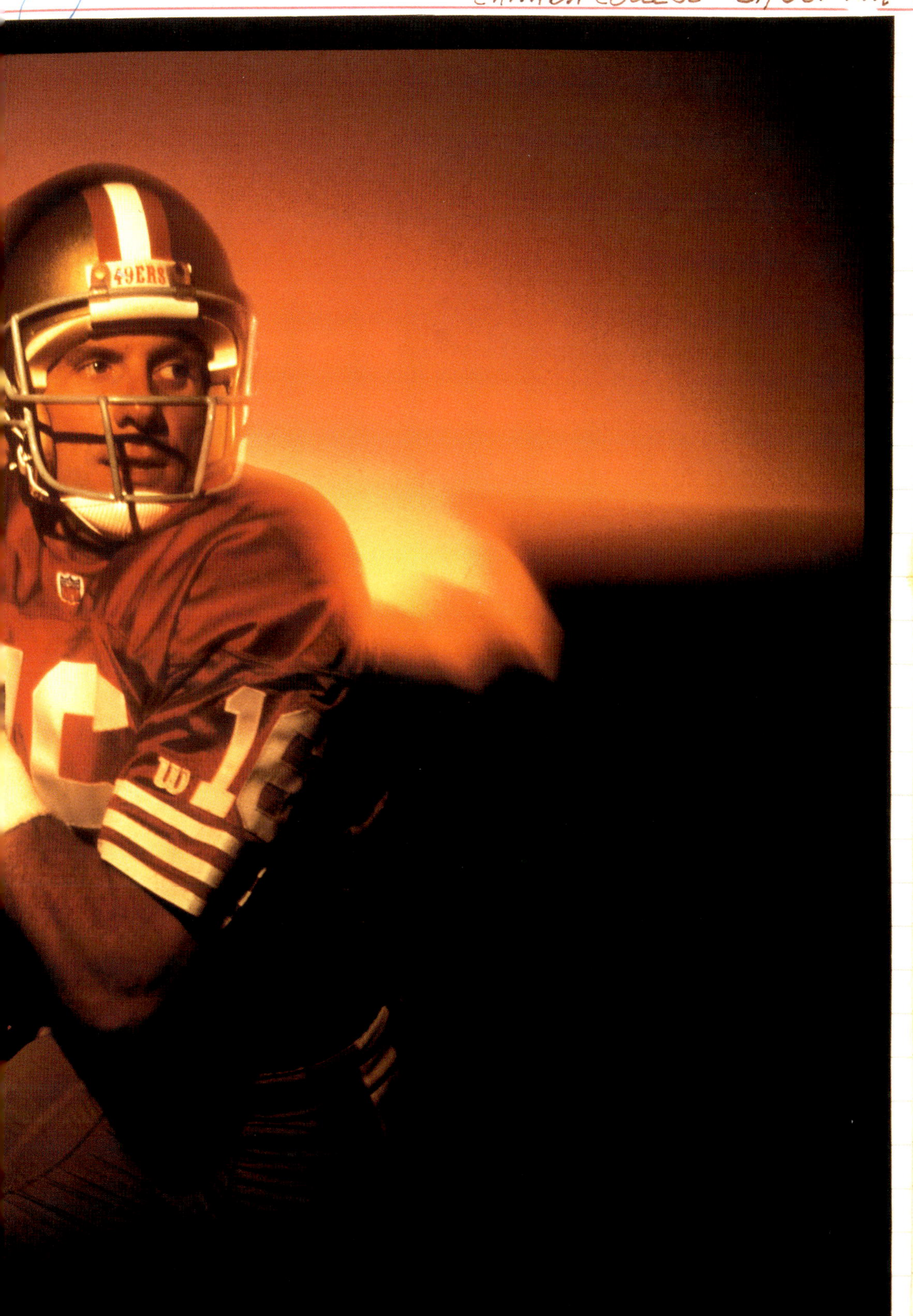

#9

Magical Michael

SUSHI

Zander, 2 carpenters and Caz all assist over 2 days in Deer, Ill.

LV FOR CHI

1991

288th day—77 days follow

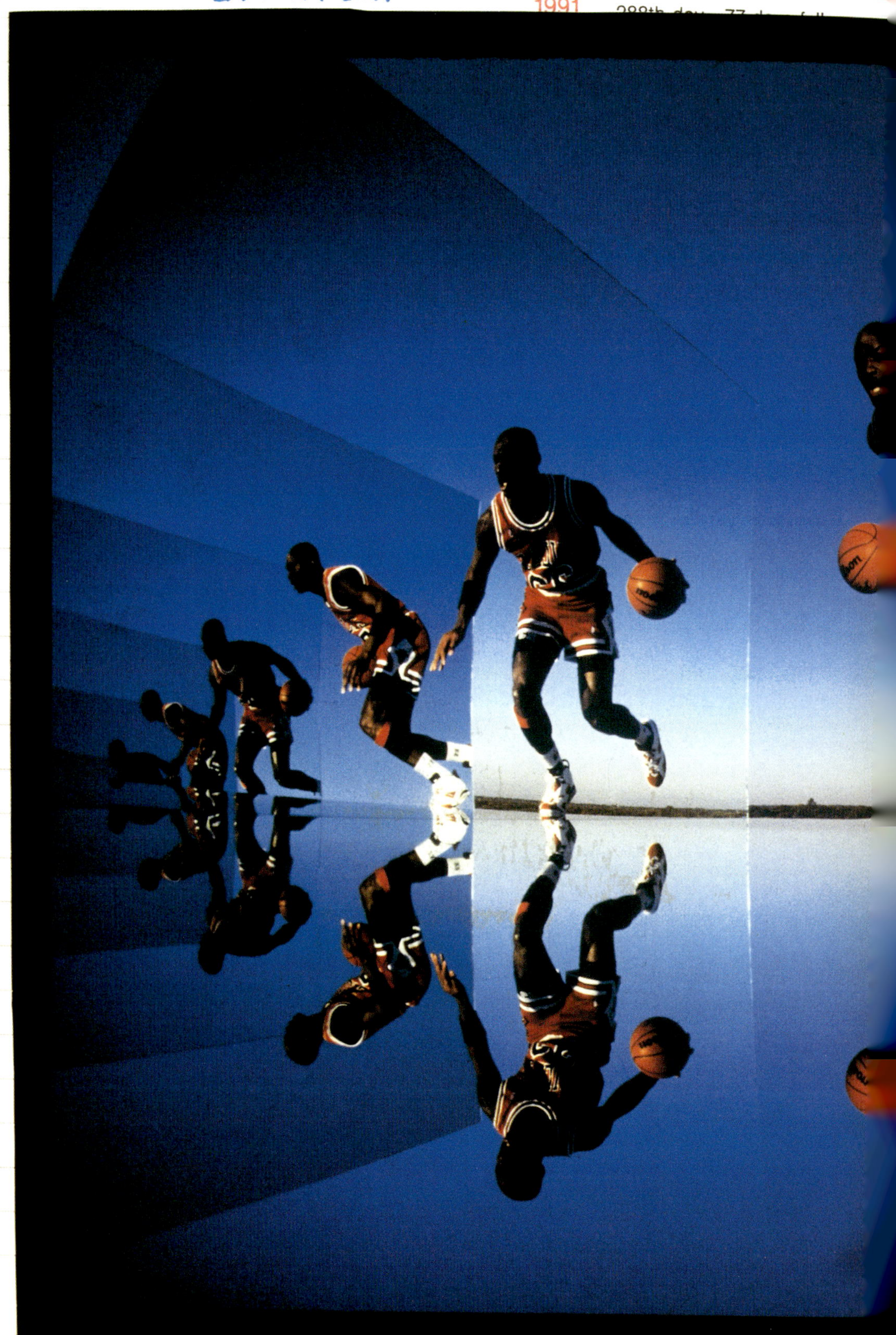

WEDNESDAY **16** OCTOBER

Deerfield, Ill.

14mm - Fuji 100 +½ - H.S. CAMERA.

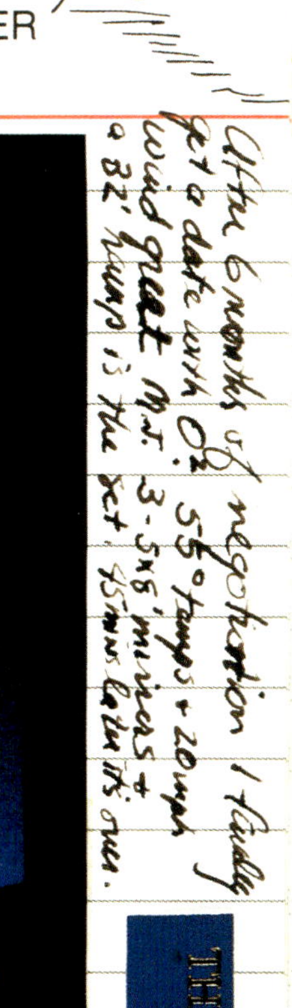

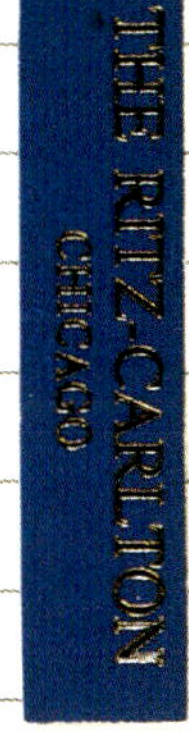

Sports Illustrated

LV. FOR N.Y.....

#6

Magic Act

...BEVERLY...
Hills.
90210

Shoot Magic at his house. Use tennis court, white seamless, and Gobos. Magic is wonderful, concentrating on the job, making Chris + Bjorn at home. Have more equipment here than at any other location shoot.

F. Schaffer + Welsh Go LIGHTLY asst. // 1 hr with EARVIN-

Earvin Magic Johnson #32

"LIVING LEGENDS"

WEDNESDAY

Sports Illustrated

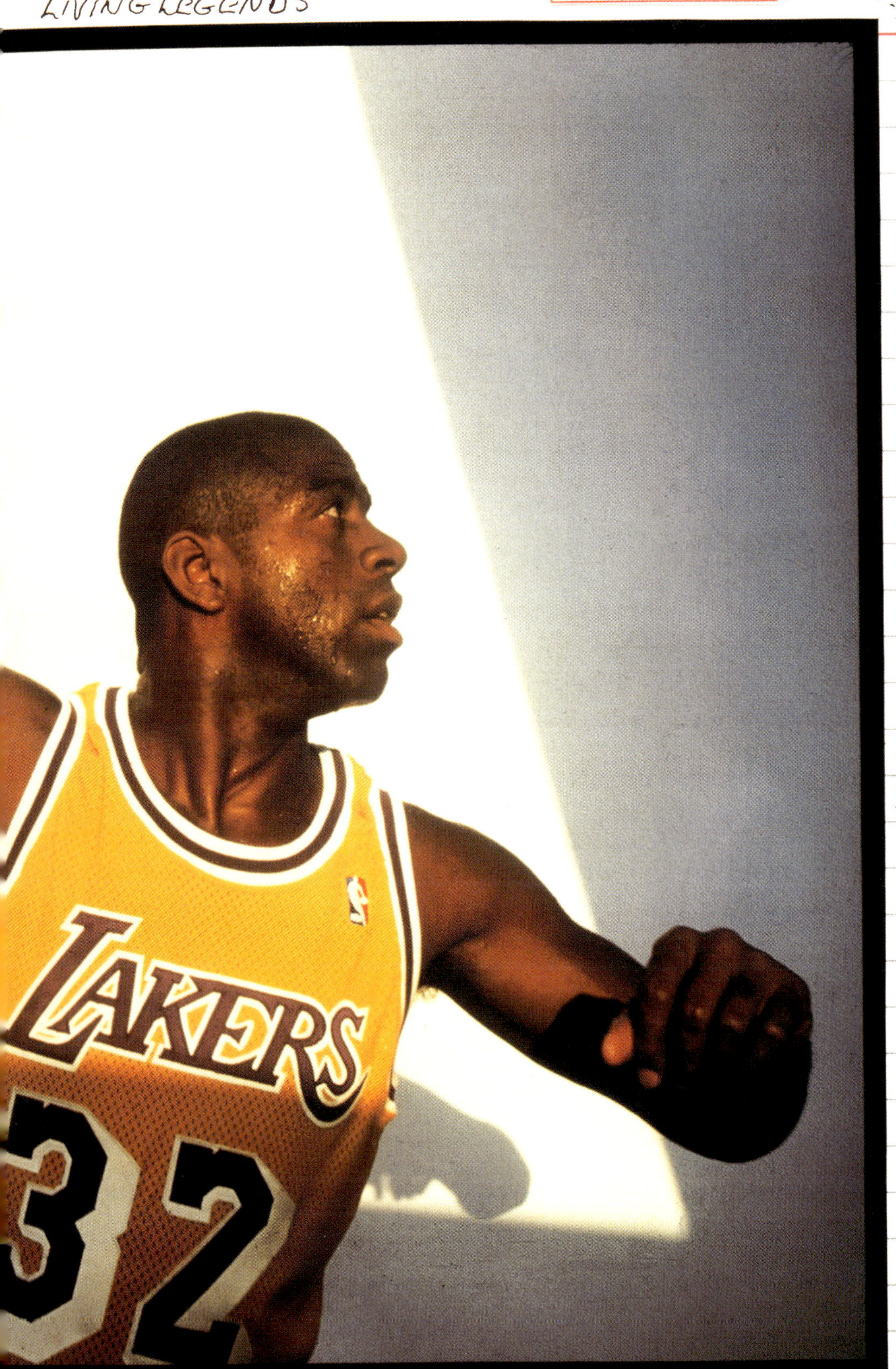

- Lv. L.A. to CHI to ISLIP to MONTAUK -

"THE JUNIOR HOOK"

L.A. MAY

Edwin Moses

1991 142nd day - 223 days follow

Moses runs the hurdles for the first time in a year. Awareness
he's as good as ever. Use huge black velvet backdrop; natural light
with gold fill. Edwin as always gives me as much time as I need.....

..ZANDER & OBA asst.... ~SUSHI~ 35mm LENS (H.S.Camera)
100 Film

...t Wishes to Walter Y
400 47.02 USA Bobsled

THURSDAY 23 MAY

1991 143rd day - 222 days follow ...."LIVING LEGENDS"....

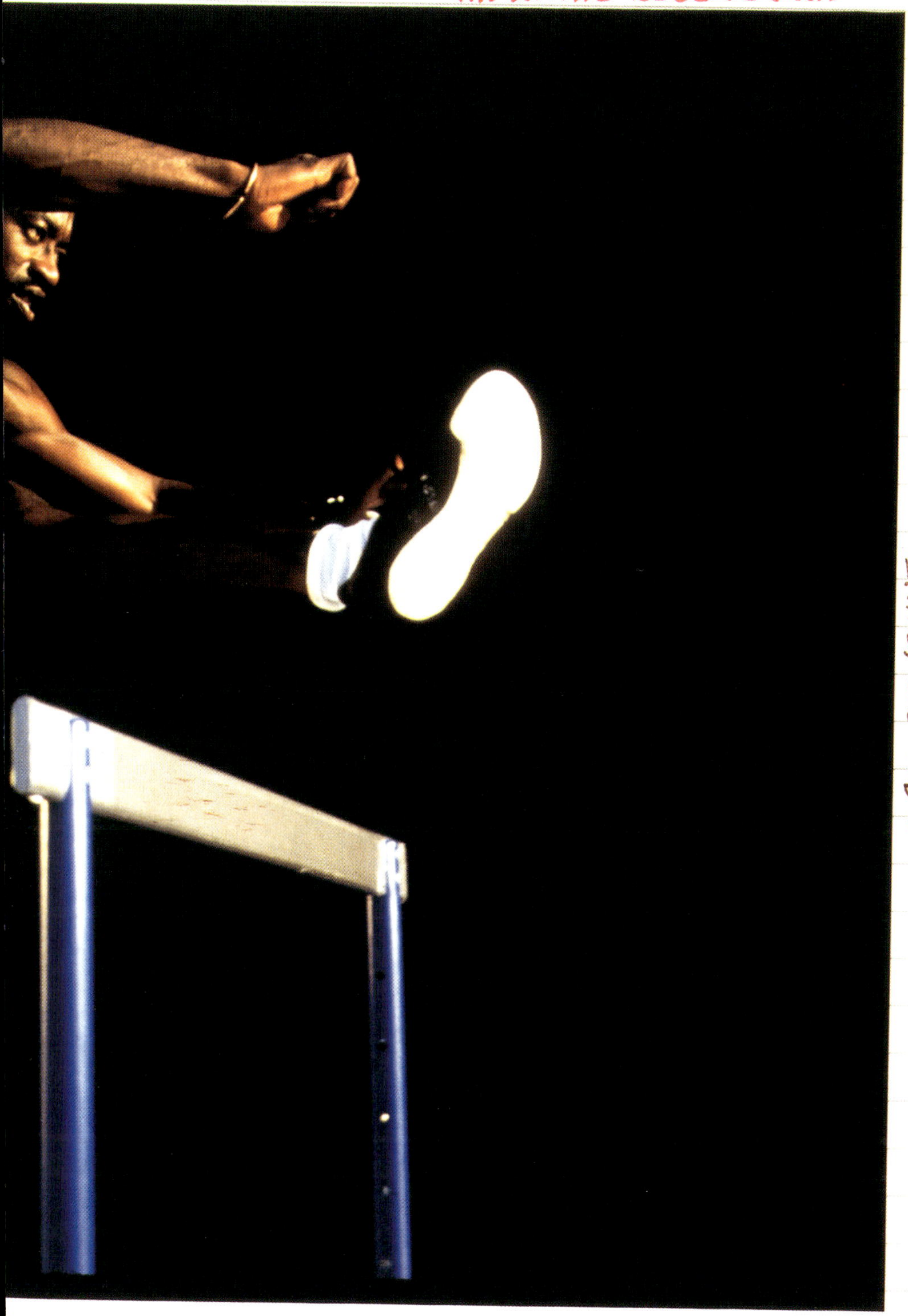

~CAL. ST. IRVINE~

Lv. L.A. FOR N.Y.

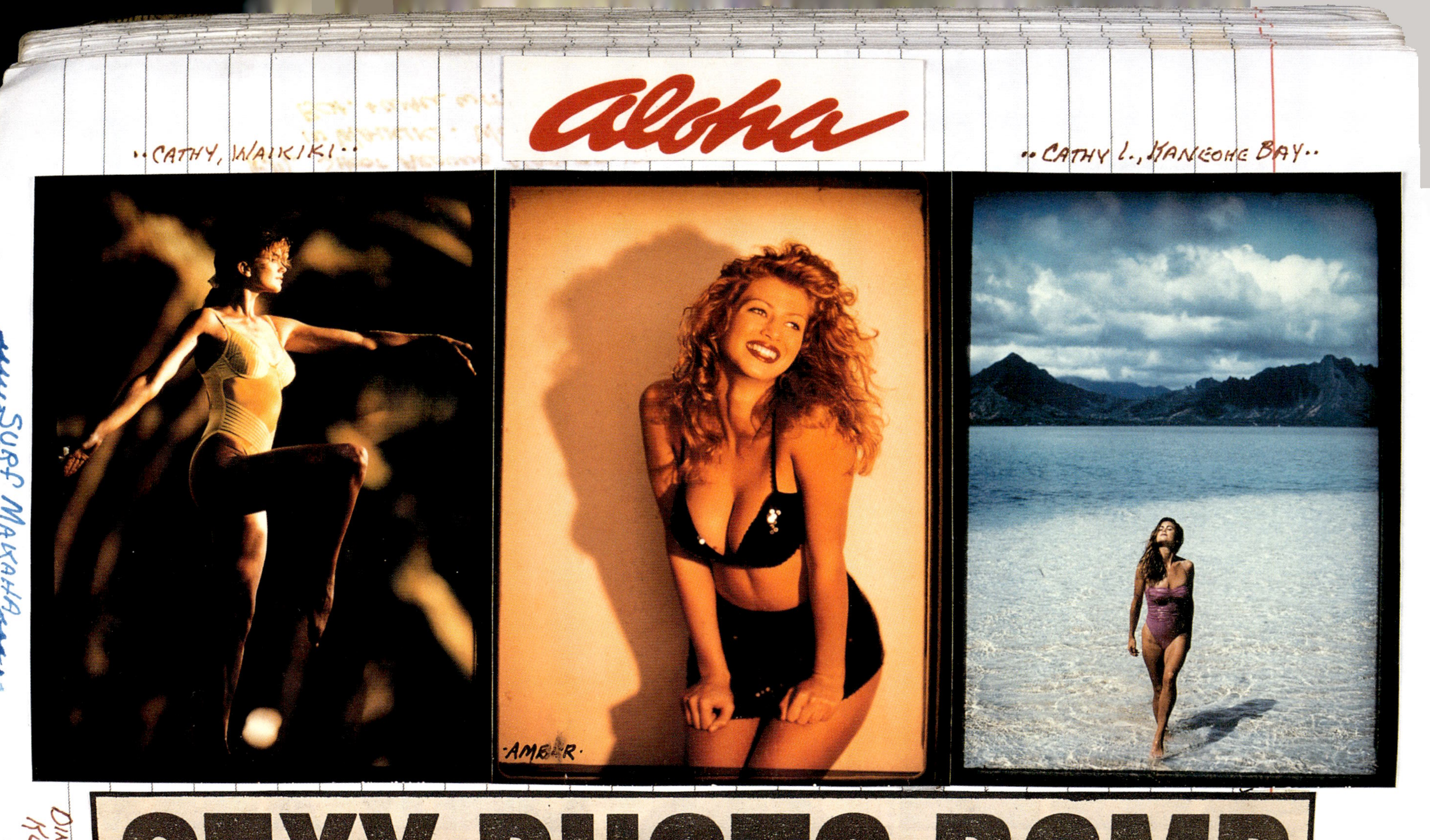
aloha
..CATHY, WAIKIKI..
..CATHY L., KANEOHE BAY..
AMBER
SEXY PHOTO BOMB
SURF MAKAHA
DINNER KEO'S

NAKIYHA AYESHA WATSON

~CATHY, MAKAPUU, DAWN~

Sports Illustrated

HAWAIIAN STYLE

~AMBER, DIAMOND HEAD~

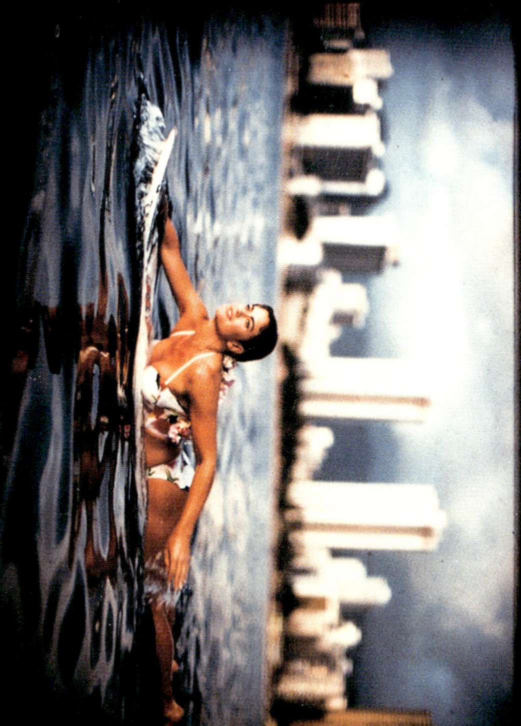

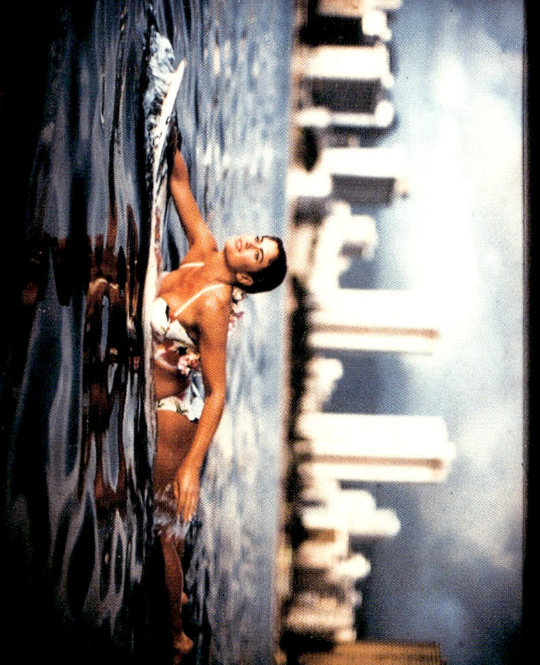

Drive-In Condom Shop Vandalized Before Opening

SURF DIAMOND HEAD

~CATHY, WAIKIKI~

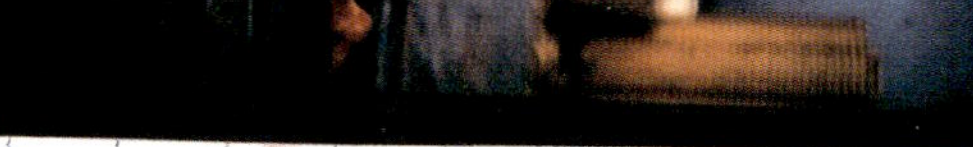

Nude couple fall off lanai, one dies

A.M... Lanai Lookout. H.B.O. + ENT. TONIGHT arr. for shoot. Cameras everywhere. Beautiful dawn......

P.M. Stay around Waikiki... Shoot Cathy at twilight with city as backdrop. Classic HAWAIIAN. LIGHT.

...SUSHI...

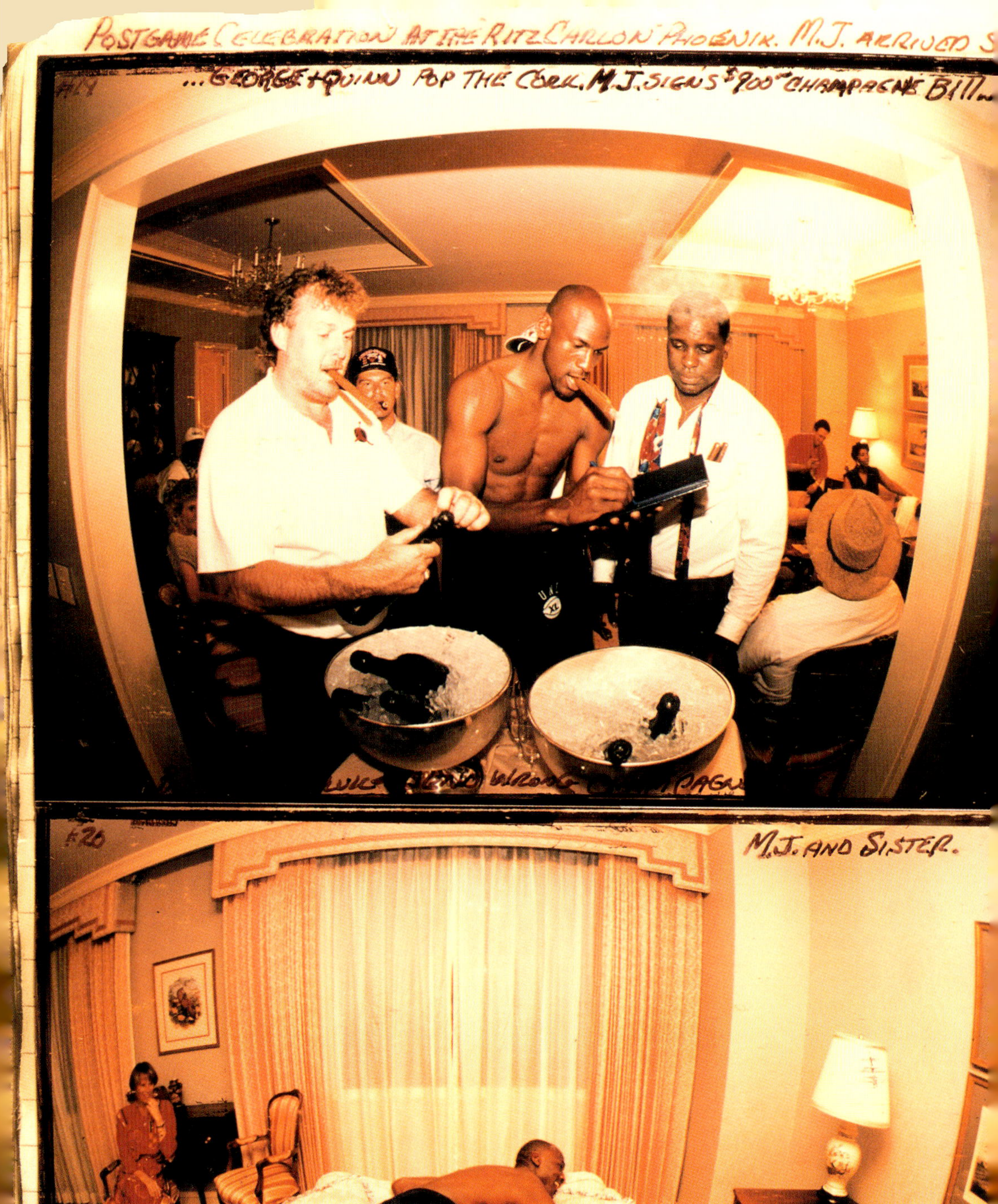

POSTGAME CELEBRATION AT THE RITZ CARLTON PHOENIX. M.J. ARRIVED S
...GEORGE + QUINN POP THE CORK. M.J. SIGNS $900 CHAMPAGNE BILL...
#20
M.J. AND SISTER.
BEFORE BUS LEFT FOR AIRPORT I. MONTAUK-J AND TAKE-OFF CURFEW. TOOK

UNIFORM. HAD to PACK. DRINK, SMOKE, + RELAX WITH FAMILY + FRIENDS IN 40 MINS →

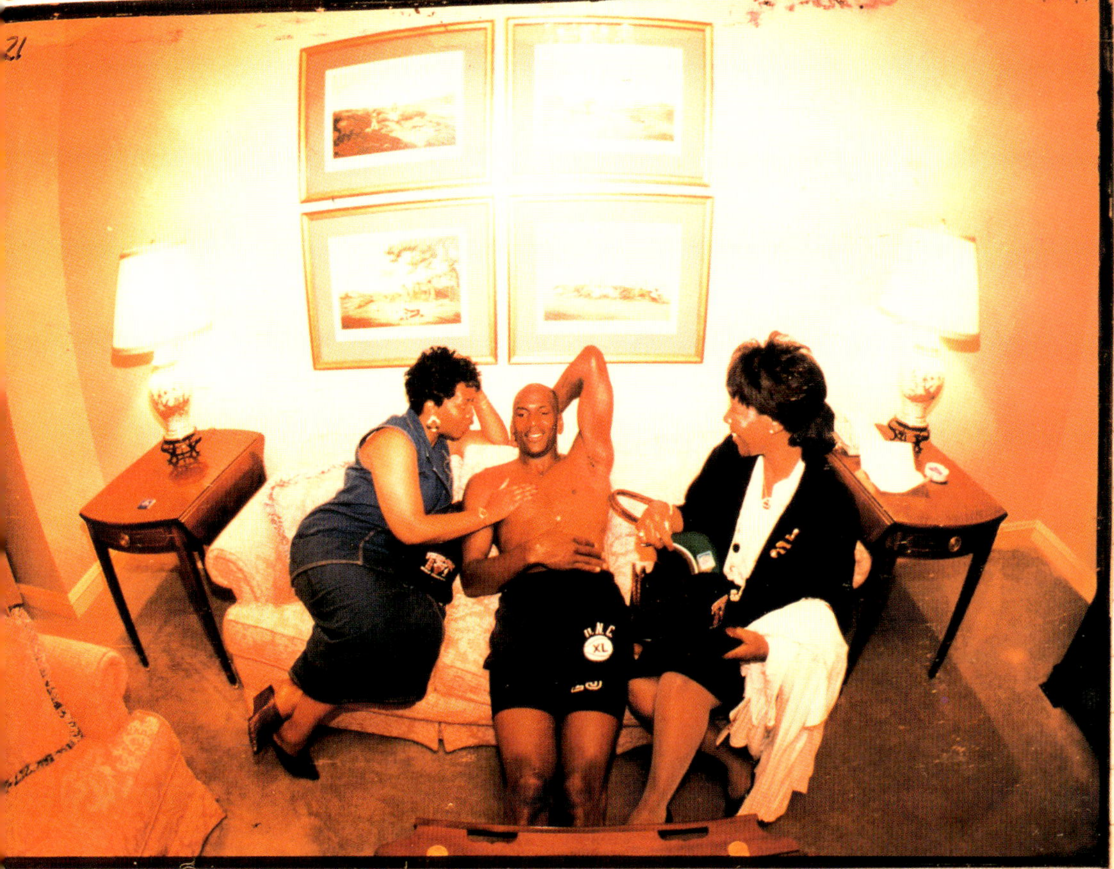

21

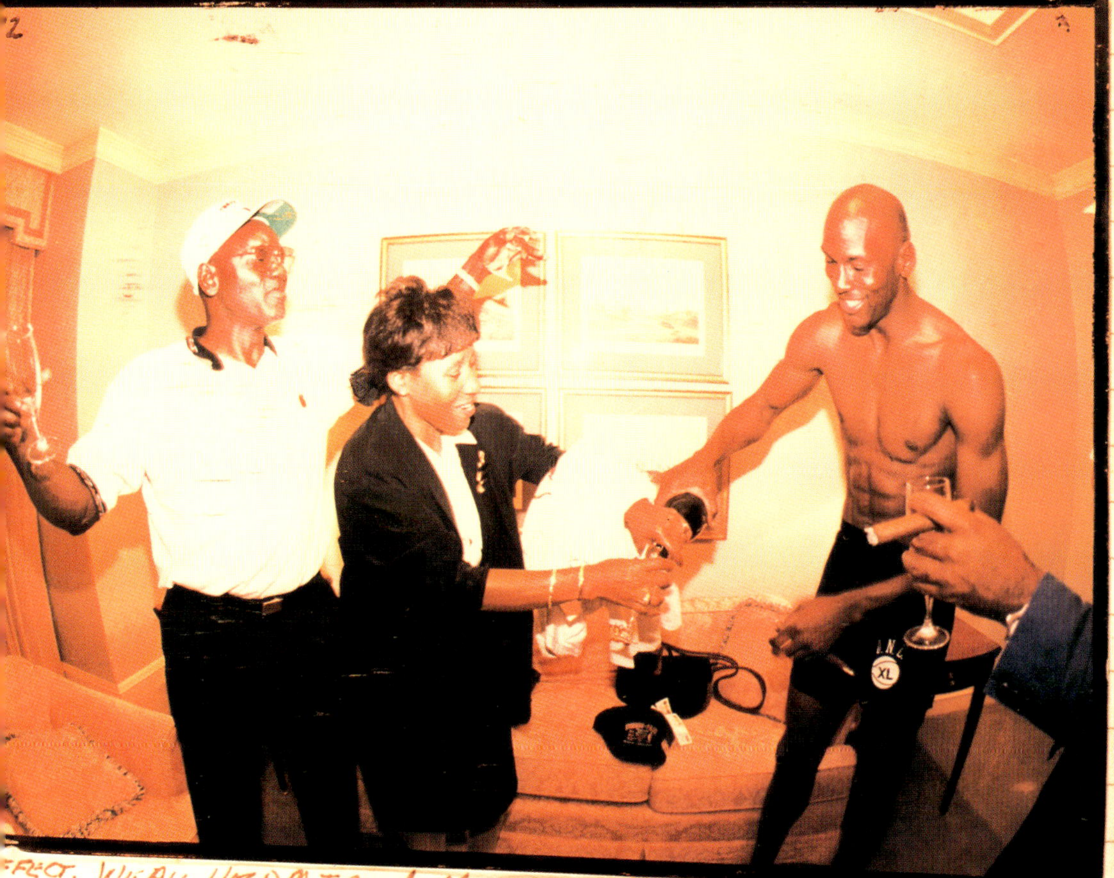

22

FFECT. WE ALL HELP M.J. PACK / MONTAUK / CELEBRATE + SEND HIM to CHICAGO

THE RITZ-CARLTON
CHICAGO
A Four Seasons Hotel

O'MOONEY + 2ND ASST WORK SHOOT

289 days follow

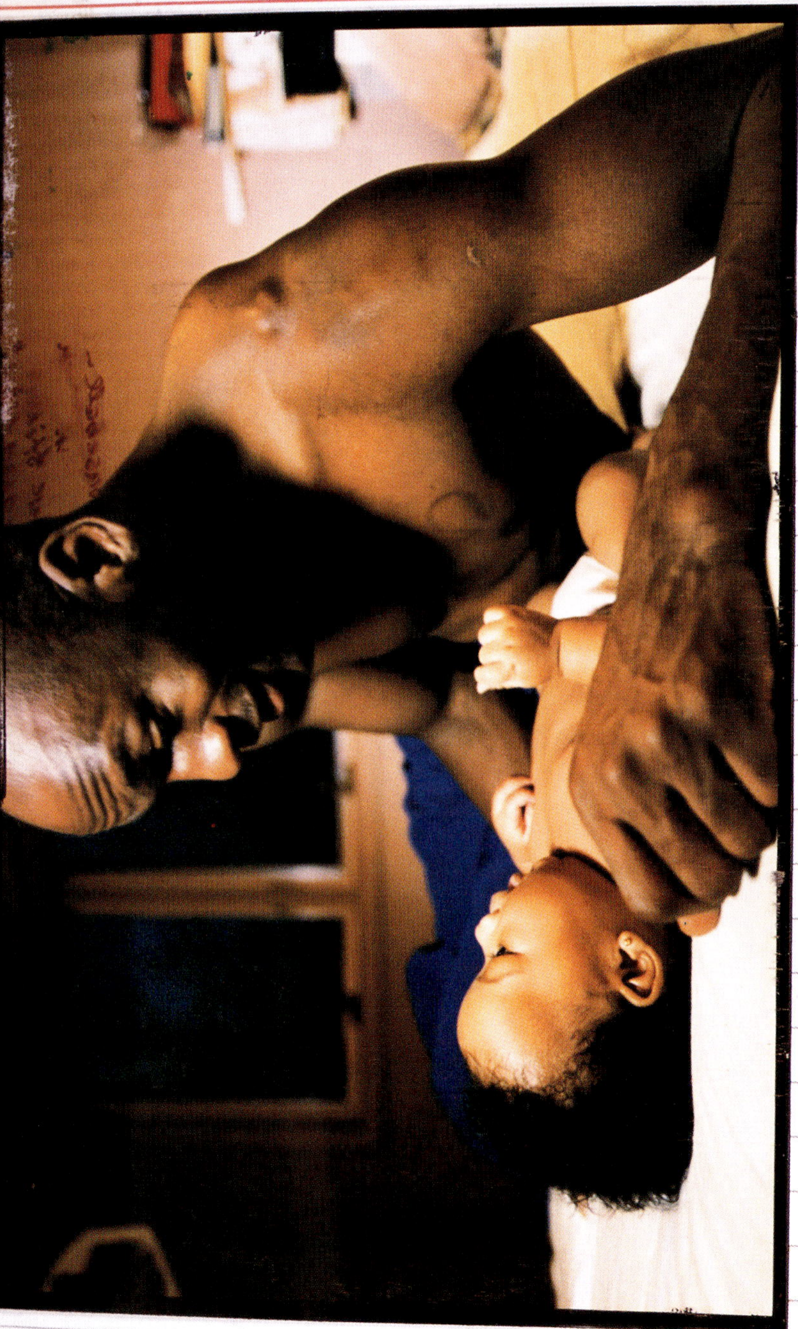

~JASMINE + M.J.~

Bjorn and I meet M.J. after practice. M.J. drives B.J. to his home in his Testarosa. M.J. says B.J. was breaking into a sweat. B.J. claims he hit G force and his face was rippling back like an astronaut. Do one dribbling shot at Berto then do the family portrait, bubble bath, and M.J. with Jasmine. Were with M.J. for 8½ hrs....

Gay soldiers hit city

O'MOONEY + 1
ASST AGAIN

THURSDAY **18** MARCH

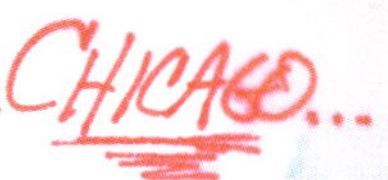
...CHICAGO...

SONIA DADA GROUP

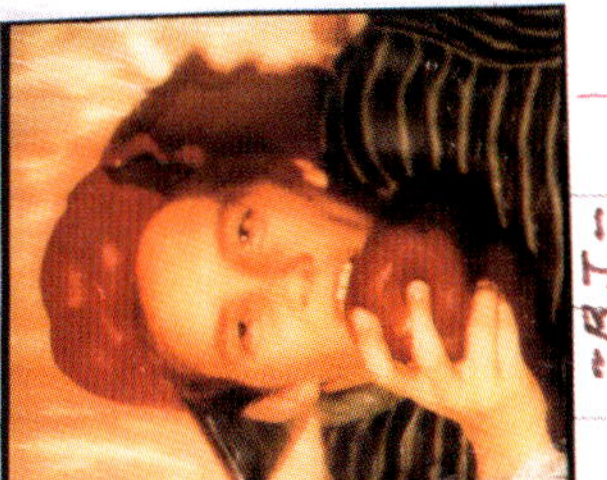

"B.J."

CINDY - 9446655 / K.K. - SLICK WILLIE

TRIPP - OFF / VICKY - S+M

GINO 951-4723 - F.C.+B.

SUE ALTMAN 516 374-6548 - Ass't

MARGIE 8321 POST AVE, M.B., FLA 165-54-1464
33140

SHOOT Blue Dunk shot and play baseball at Bert's, M.J. says "Even if this book stinks I've had a good time"

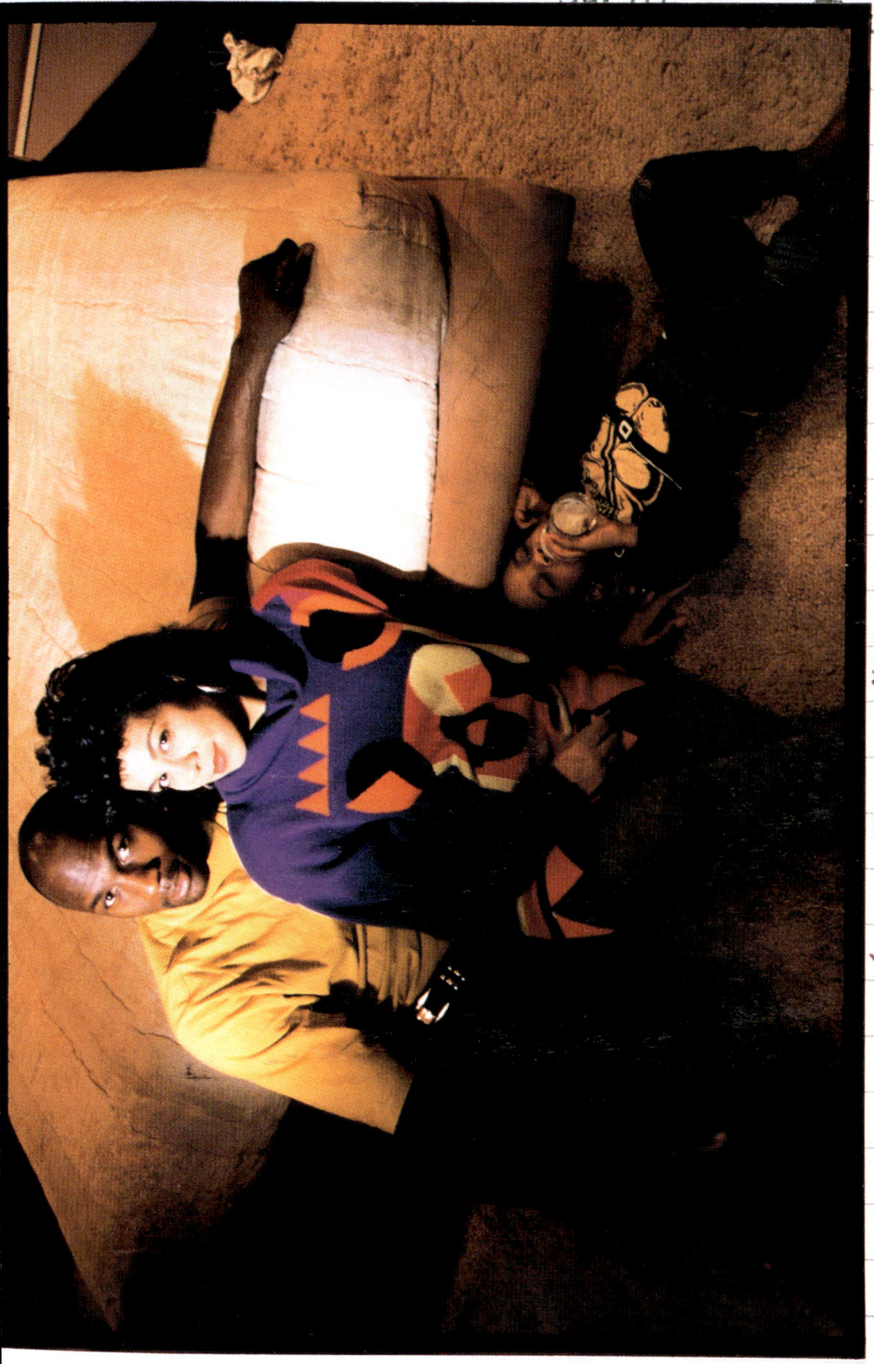

"...MICHAEL, JUANITA, + MARCUS..."

The why of Waco

...BJORN + I Go to "EL MARIACHI"..... SHOOT "FREE THROW"

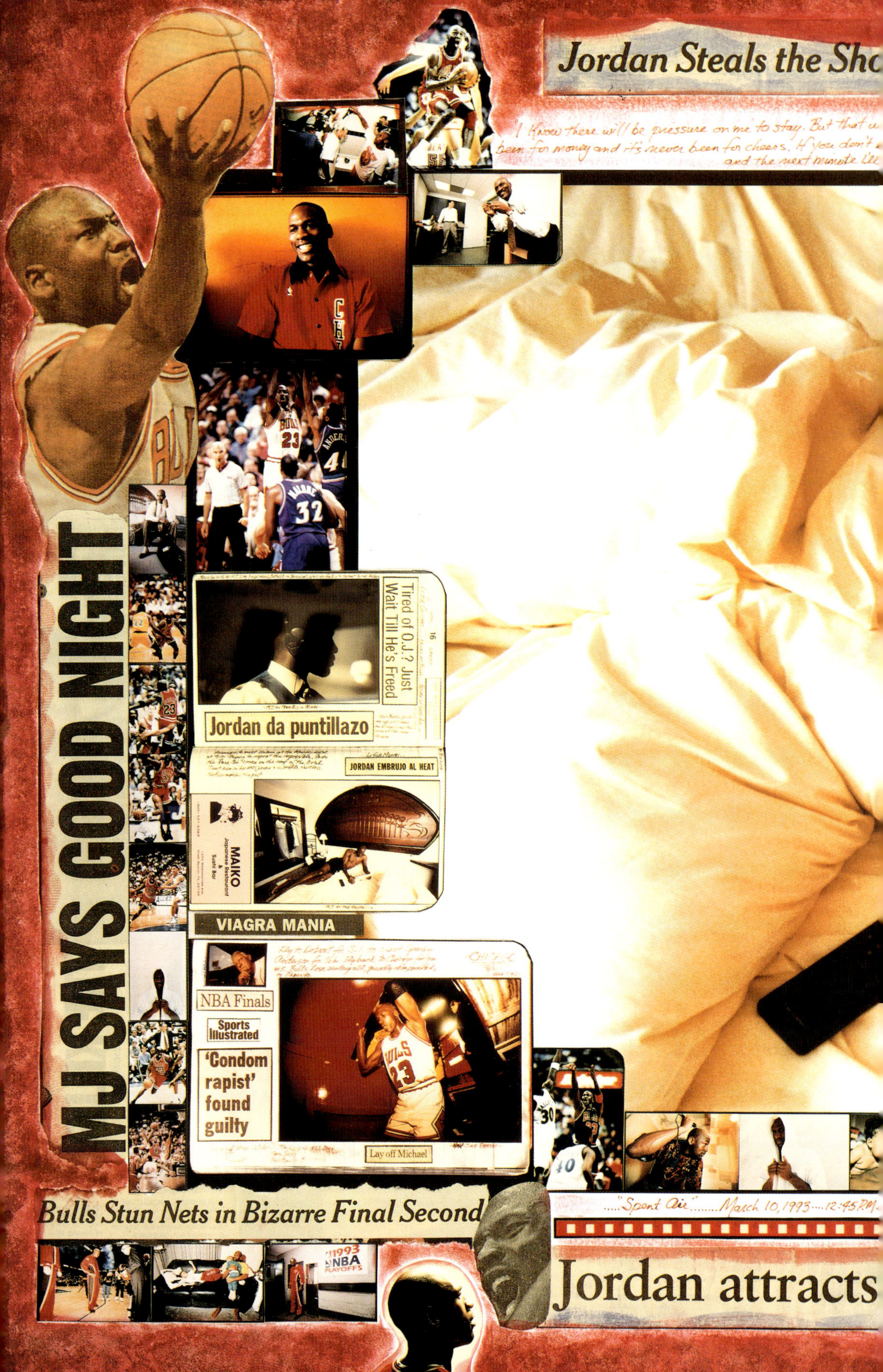
Jordan Steals the Sho
I know there will be pressure on me to stay. But that
been for money and it's never been for cheers. If you don't
and the next minute I'll
MJ SAYS GOOD NIGHT
Tired of O.J.? Just Wait Till He's Freed
Jordan da puntillazo
JORDAN EMBRUJO AL HEAT
MAIKO
VIAGRA MANIA
NBA Finals
Sports Illustrated
'Condom rapist' found guilty
Lay off Michael
Bulls Stun Nets in Bizarre Final Second
"Spent Air".......March 10, 1993....12:45 P.M.
Jordan attracts
1993 NBA PLAYOFFS

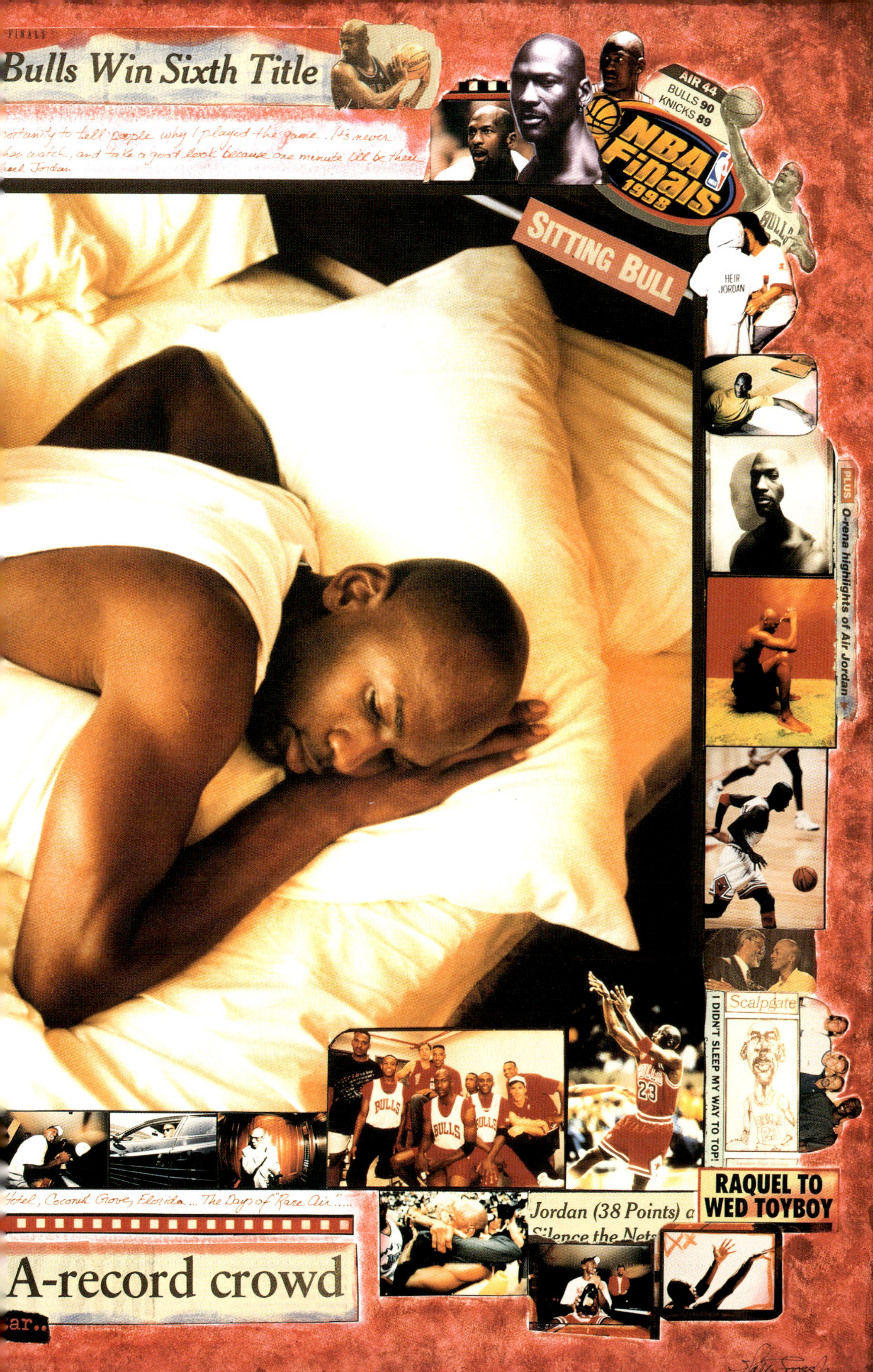

Bulls Win Sixth Title
portunity to tell people why I played the game. It's never
how watch, and take a good look because one minute I'll be there
hael Jordan
AIR 44
BULLS 90
KNICKS 89
NBA Finals 1998
SITTING BULL
HEIR JORDAN
PLUS O-rena highlights of Air Jordan
Scalpgate
I DIDN'T SLEEP MY WAY TO TOP!
RAQUEL TO WED TOYBOY
Jordan (38 Points) a
Silence the Nets
Hotel, Coconut Grove, Florida... The Days of "Rare Air"....
A-record crowd

ANDRETTI
....BOOK....
--MARIO + MIKE, MOTOWN...

→CALLS - Cleo, Maureen, Vanci 708-382-0426, Vicki, Life, Mom, Herb...

JUNE **13** MONDAY ..Lv. DETROIT for ALLENTOWN

Fly on Mario's Jet to Allentown with family. Shoot at his house in Nazareth in afternoon. Meet his beloved pig. Martini.

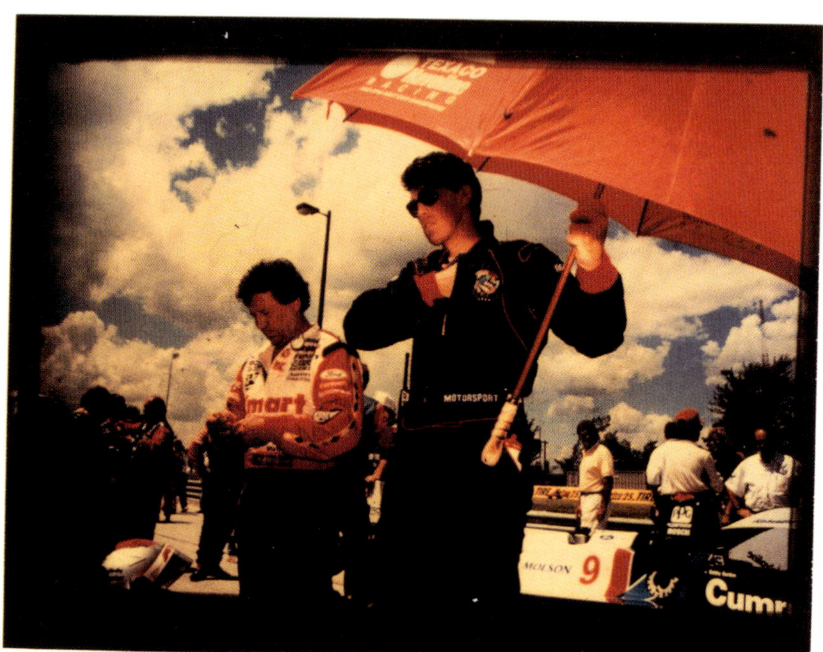

llow

SPEND NIGHT IN ALLENTOWN

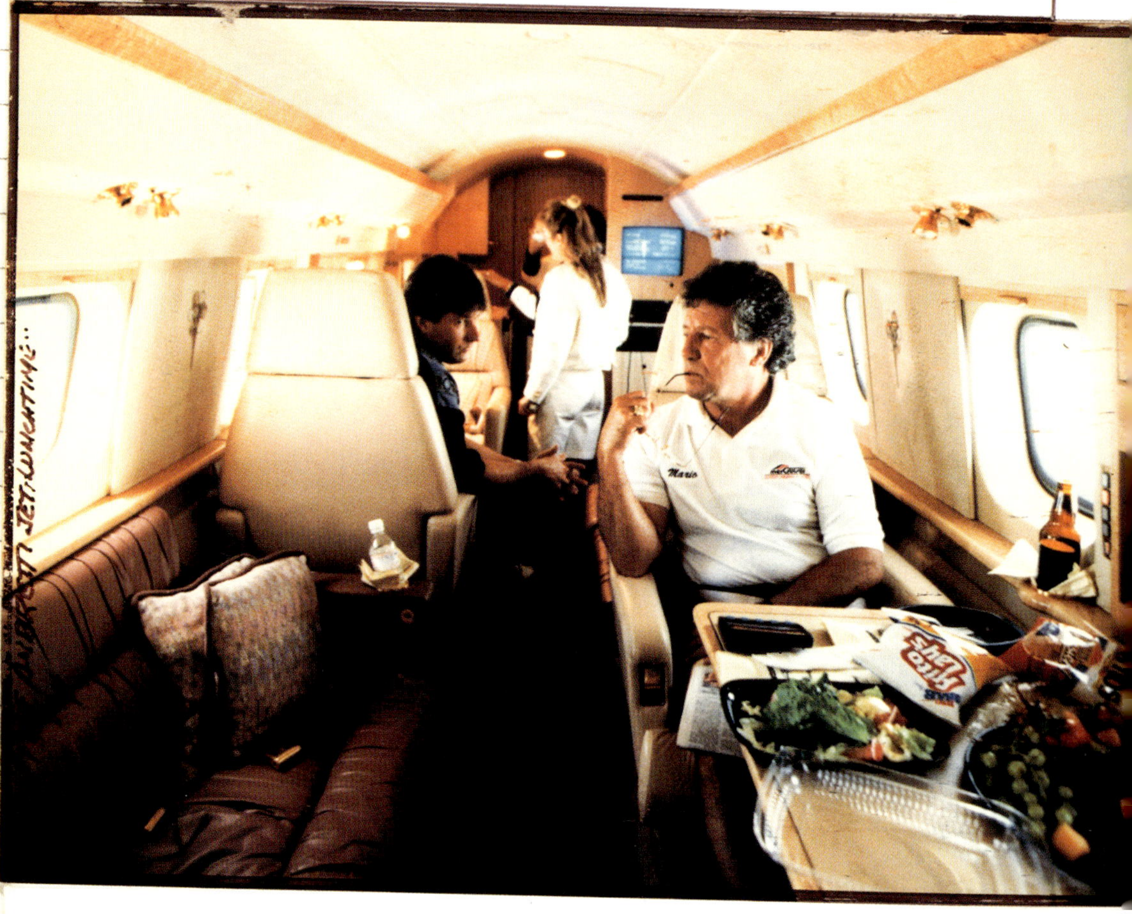

ANDRETTI JET: LUNCHTIME...

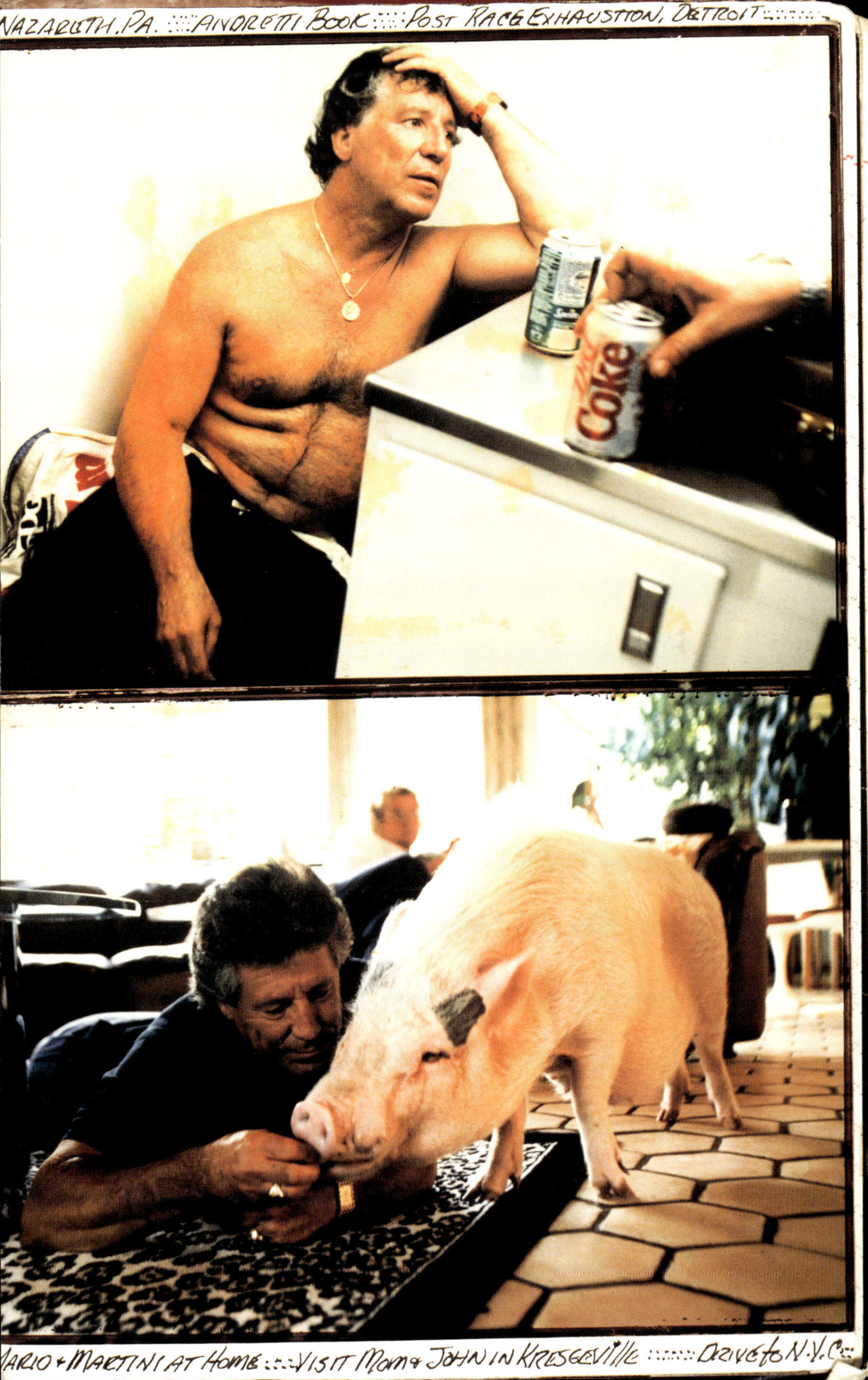
NAZARETH, PA. ANDRETTI BOOK POST RACE EXHAUSTION, DETROIT
Coke
MARIO + MARTINI AT HOME VISIT MOM + JOHN IN KRESGEVILLE DRIVE to N.Y.C.

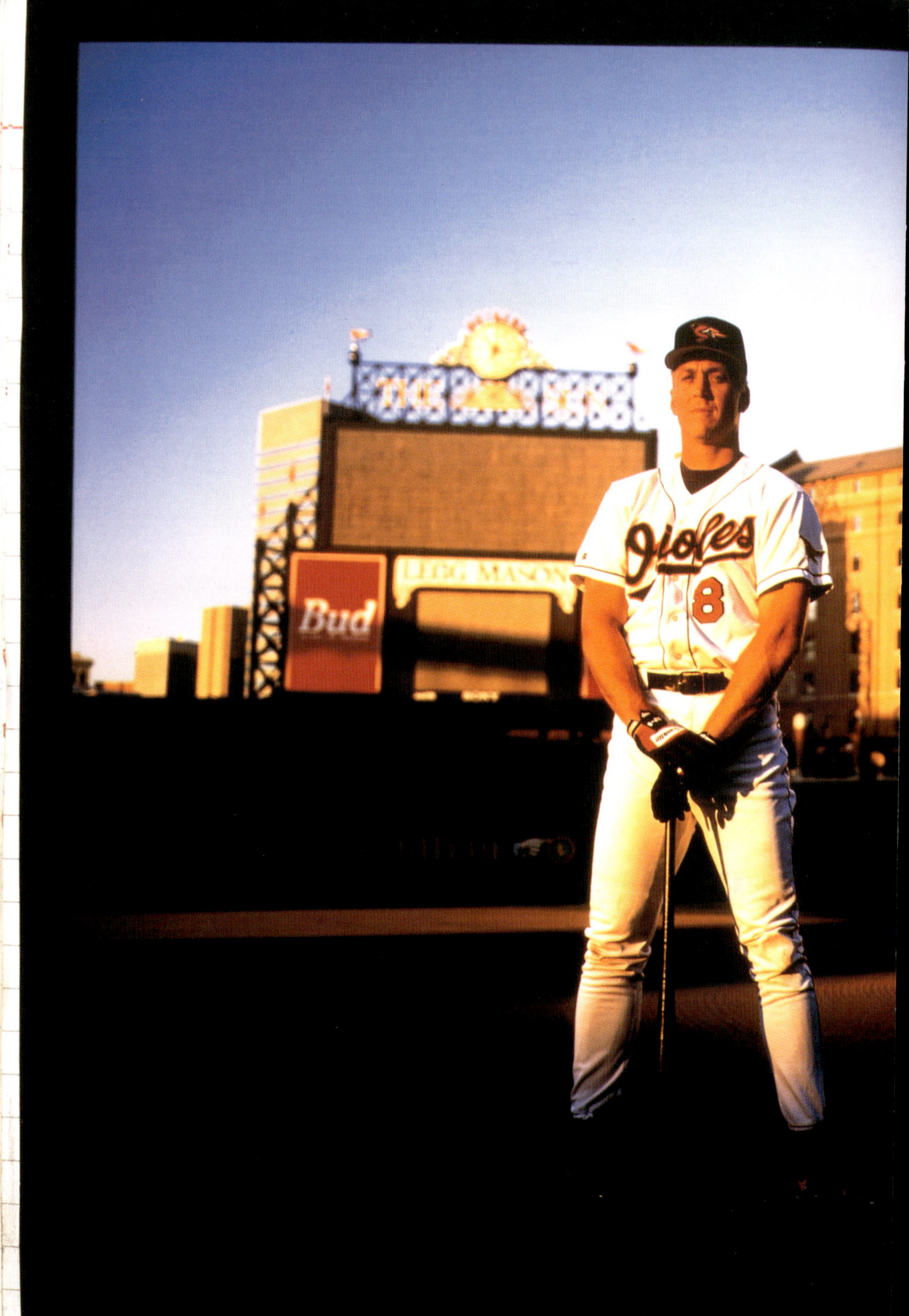

BALTIMORE . . . S.I. . . GAME 2130 . . . . . CAL RIPKIN, JR . . .

Cal stands alone

2,131

INCREDIBLE NIGHT AS RIPKIN BREAKS GEHRIGS RECORD... ..BALTIMORE S.I.

...Lv for Baltimore from Montauk via Groton - Ripkin Exhaust

SEPTEMBER **3** SUNDAY

Meet Cal at 6:15 P.M
After Game for Portrait Sho

"Game 2131"

~S.I. + Ripkin Book Shoot~

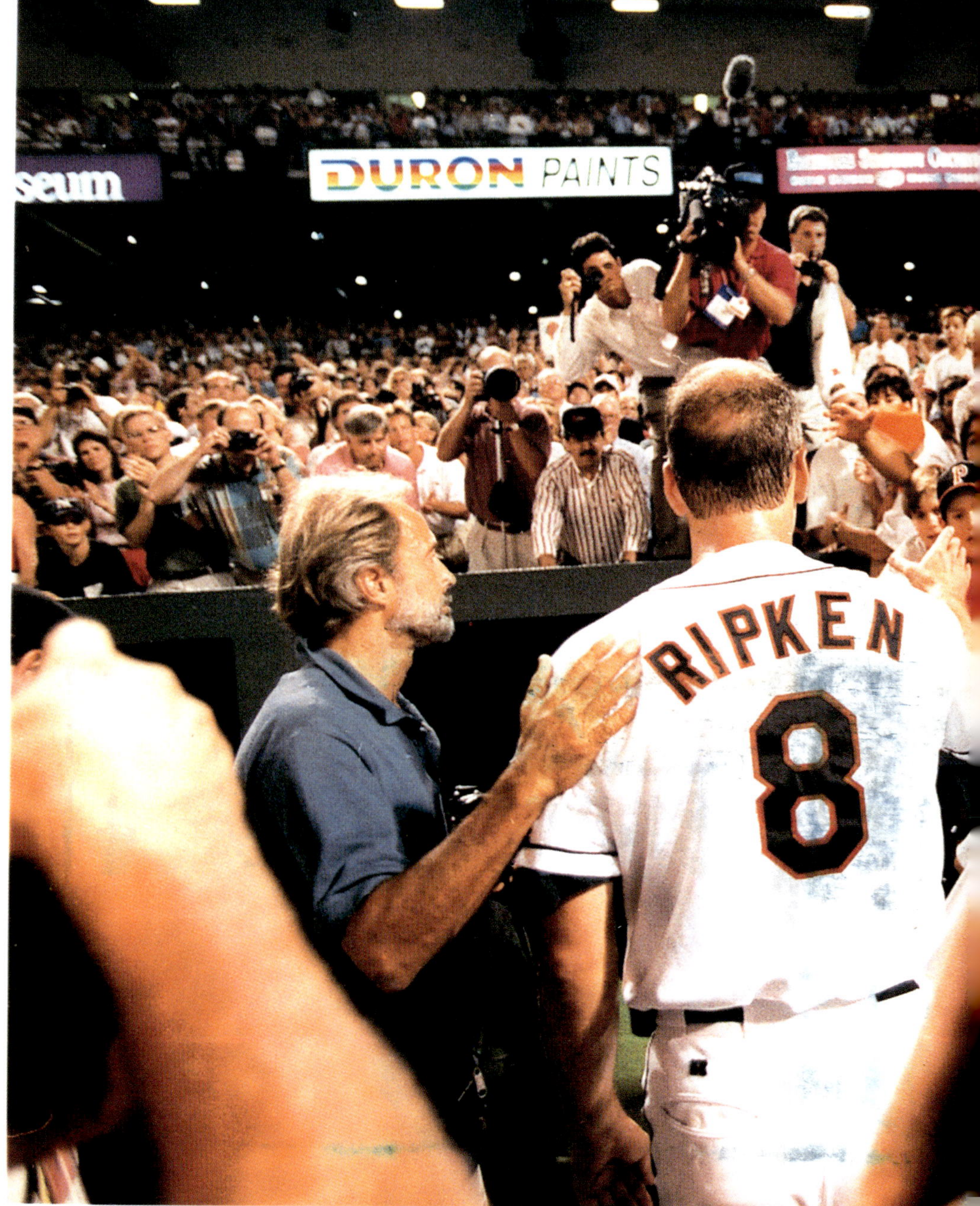

Greg A.
Assists
...Sushi...

1-800-LA
24 Hours

← S.I. + Ripkin Book →

Baltimore...

MONDAY **4** SEPTEMBER

Day Game

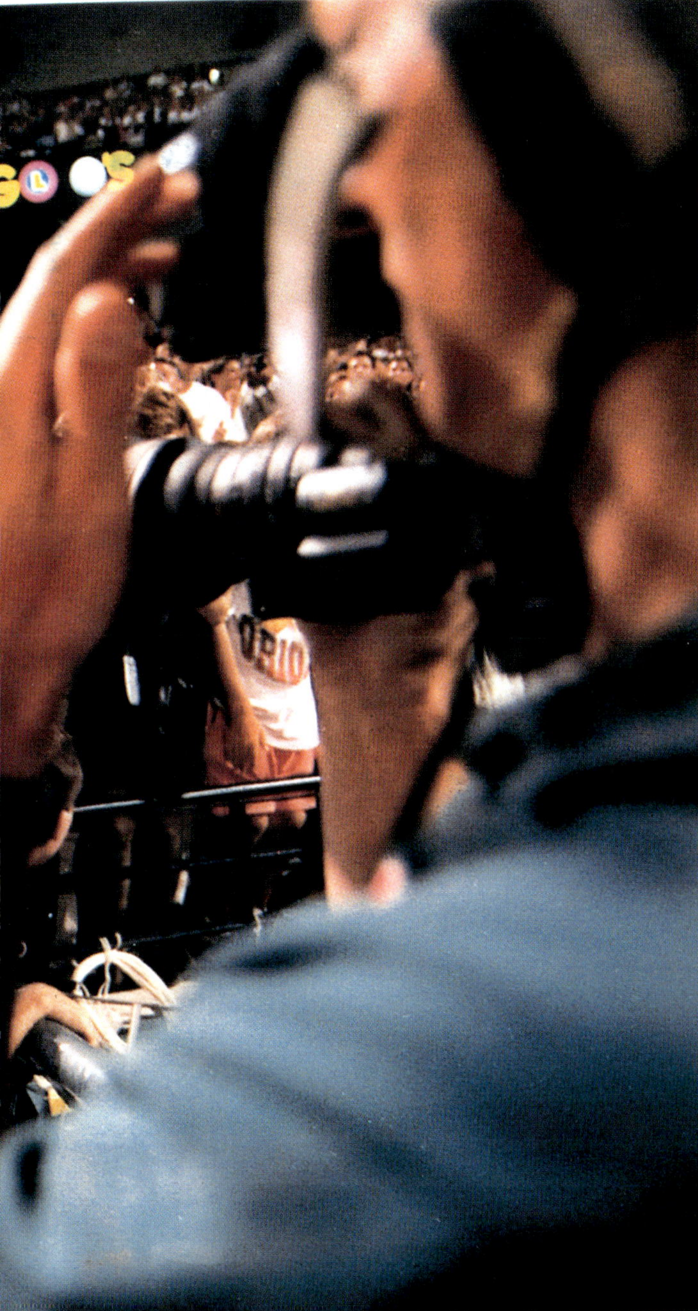

VYERS

ays

Love rage drove dad to blow up his family

Crab-Fest at Jerry's For Dinner.......

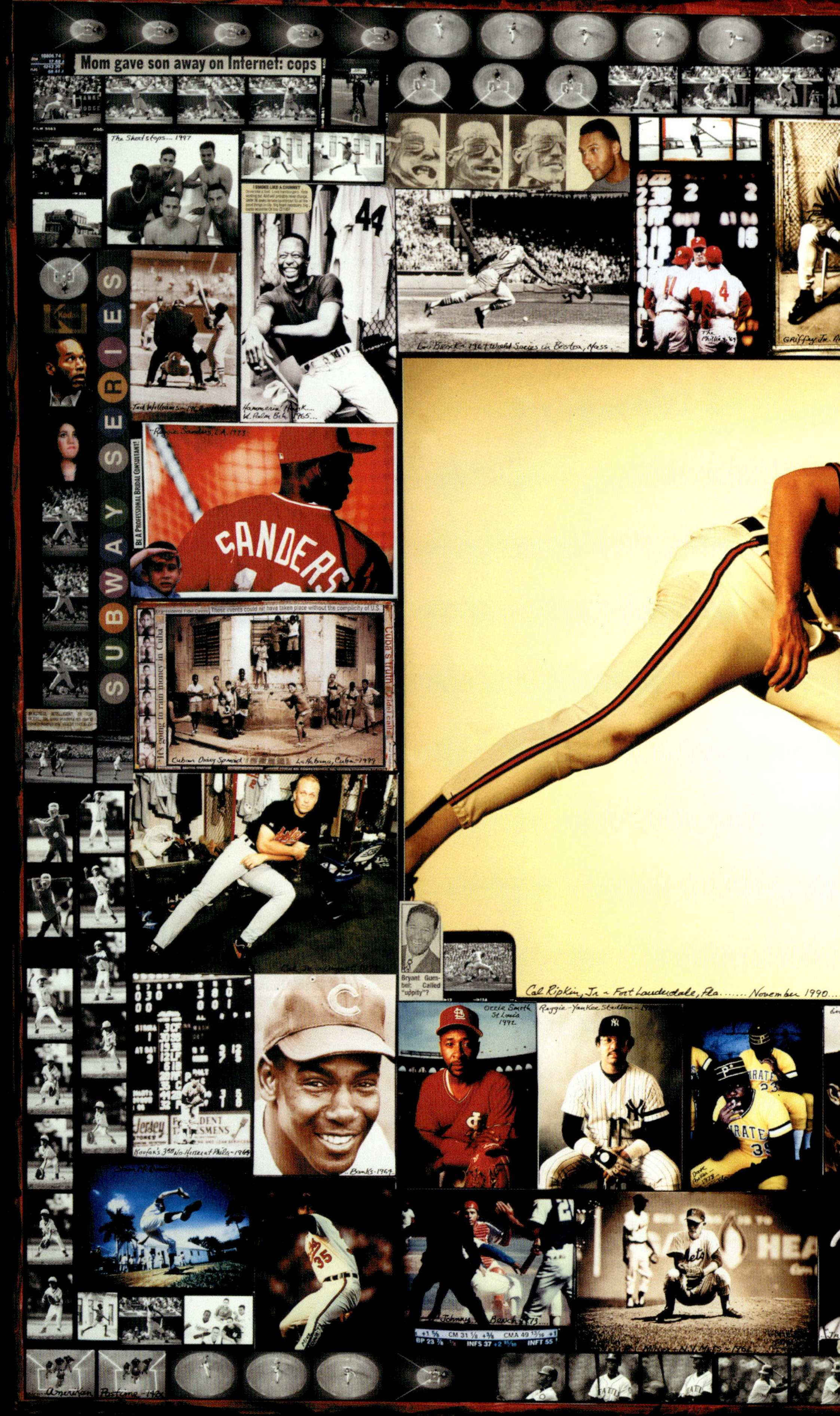

Mom gave son away on Internet: cops
SUBWAY SERIES
SANDERS
Cal Ripkin, Jr. - Fort Lauderdale, Fla. ...... November 1990
Bryant Gumbel: Called "uppity"?

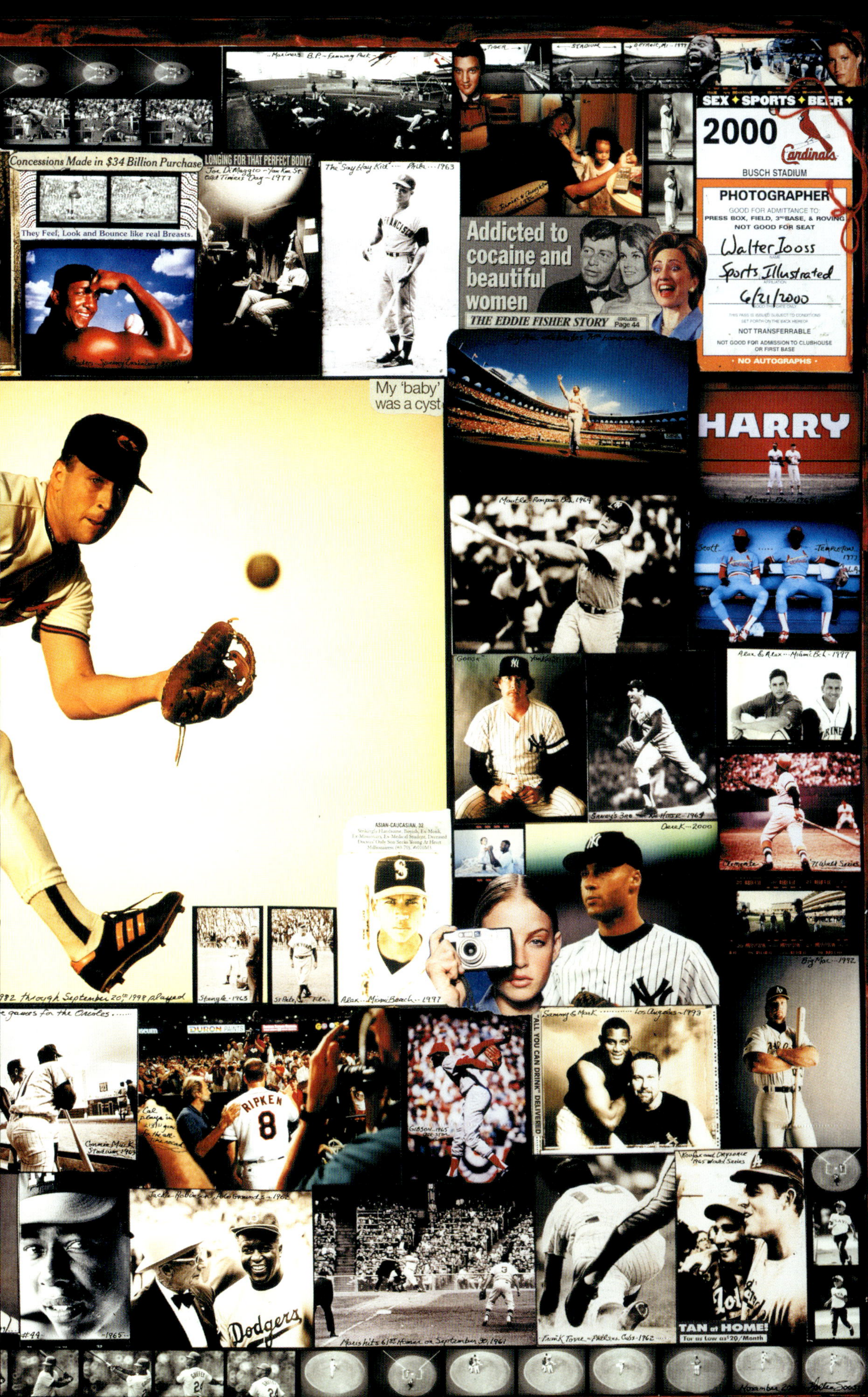
Concessions Made in $34 Billion Purchase
They Feel, Look and Bounce like real Breasts.
LONGING FOR THAT PERFECT BODY?
SEX ✦ SPORTS ✦ BEER
2000
Cardinals
BUSCH STADIUM
PHOTOGRAPHER
GOOD FOR ADMITTANCE TO:
PRESS BOX, FIELD, 3RD BASE, & ROVING
NOT GOOD FOR SEAT
Walter Iooss
Sports Illustrated
6/21/2000
NOT TRANSFERRABLE
NOT GOOD FOR ADMISSION TO CLUBHOUSE OR FIRST BASE
• NO AUTOGRAPHS •
Addicted to cocaine and beautiful women
THE EDDIE FISHER STORY
Page 44
My 'baby' was a cyst
HARRY
ASIAN-CAUCASIAN, 32
DURON PAINTS
RIPKEN
8
"ALL YOU CAN DRINK" DELIVERED
Dodgers
TAN at HOME!
For as low as $20/Month

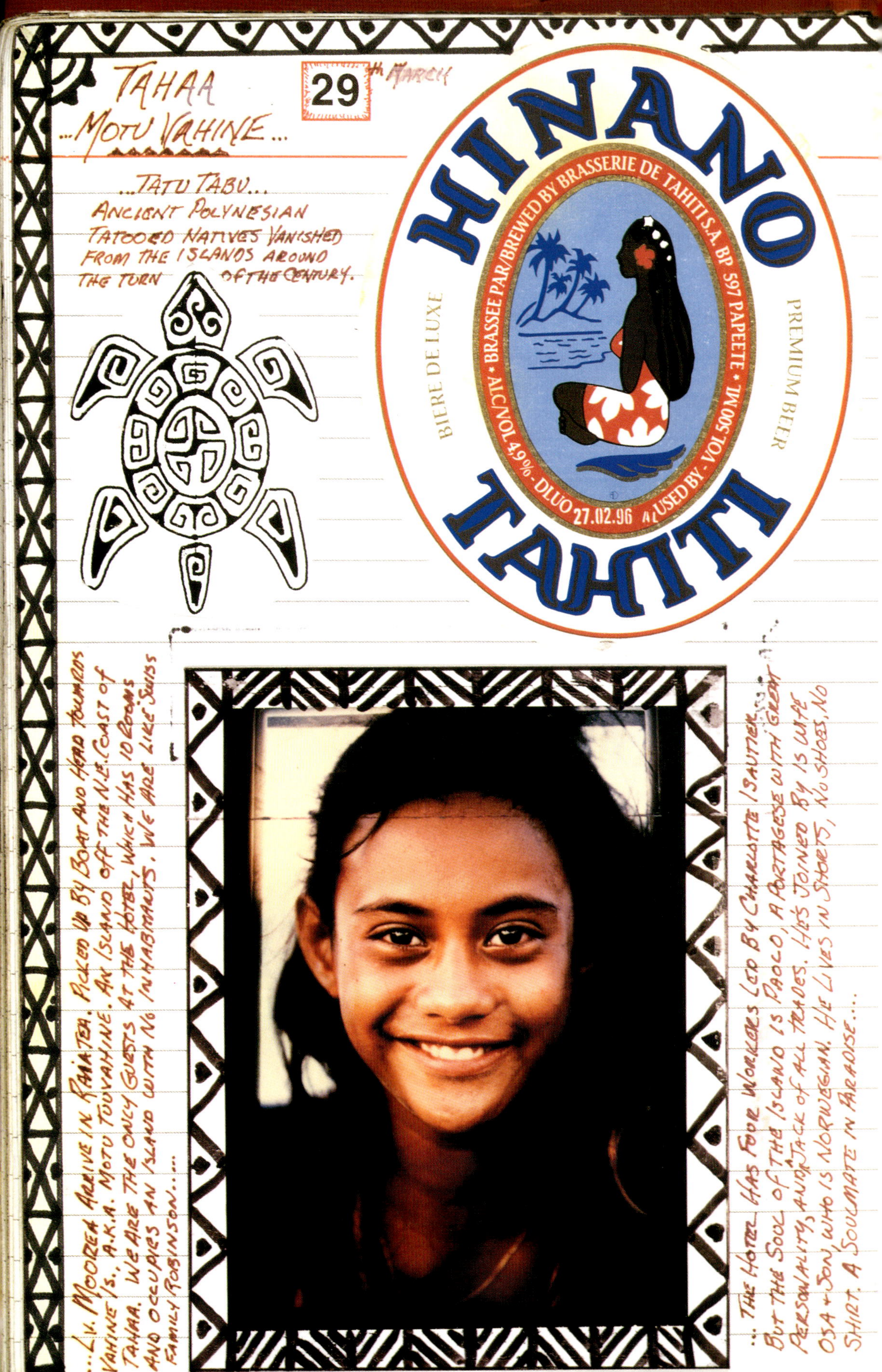
TAHAA
...MOTU VAHINE...
29 th MARCH
...TATU TABU...
ANCIENT POLYNESIAN
TATOOED NATIVES VANISHED
FROM THE ISLANDS AROUND
THE TURN OF THE CENTURY.
HINANO
BRASSEE PAR/BREWED BY BRASSERIE DE TAHITI S.A. BP 597 PAPEETE
ALC/VOL 4,9% · DLUO 27.02.96 A USED BY · VOL 500 ML
BIERE DE LUXE
PREMIUM BEER
TAHITI
...LV. MOOREA ARRIVE IN RAIATEA. PICKED UP BY BOAT AND HEAD TOWARDS
VAHINE IS., A.K.A. MOTU TUUVAHINE. AN ISLAND OFF THE N.E. COAST OF
TAHAA. WE ARE THE ONLY GUESTS AT THE HOTEL, WHICH HAS 10 ROOMS
AND OCCUPIES AN ISLAND WITH NO INHABITANTS. WE ARE LIKE "SWISS
FAMILY ROBINSON"...
...THE HOTEL HAS FOUR WORKERS LED BY CHARLOTTE ISAUTIER...
BUT THE SOUL OF THE ISLAND IS PAOLO, A PORTAGESE WITH GREAT
PERSONALITY, AND A JACK OF ALL TRADES. HE'S JOINED BY IS WIFE
OSA + SON, WHO IS NORWEGIAN. HE LIVES IN SHORTS, NO SHOES, NO
SHIRT. A SOULMATE IN PARADISE...

TAHAA.....
MOTU VAHINE

→ 4/30/95
VACATION

1995 89th

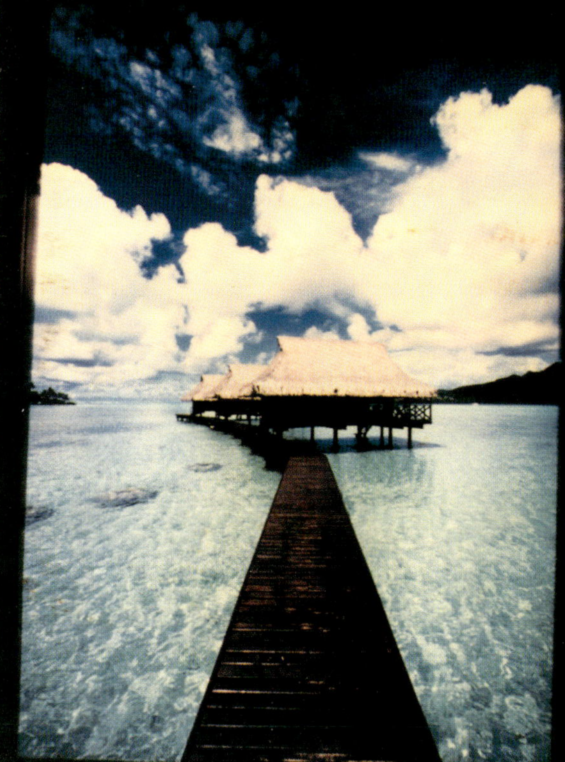

~BUNGALOOS - MOTU TUUVAHINE~

...PAOLO TAKES US ON A 2HR OUTRIGGER BOAT TOUR OF THE LAGOON AROUND TAHAA AND DISCOVER POLYNESIA AS IT MUST HAVE BEEN 100YRS AGO. PRISTINE MOTUS + WATER..

AIR TAHITI

VAHINE ISLAND
Private Island Resort

BP 5_0 - Uturoa - Raiatea - Polynésie Française - Tél : (689) 65 67 38 - Fax : (689) 65 67 70

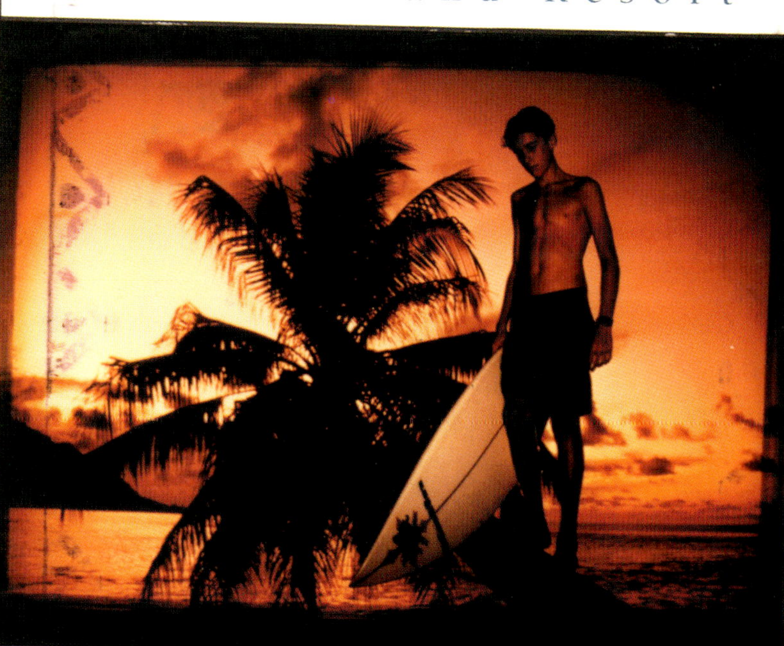

~BJORN. SURF DREAMS~

FRENCH POLYNESIA.

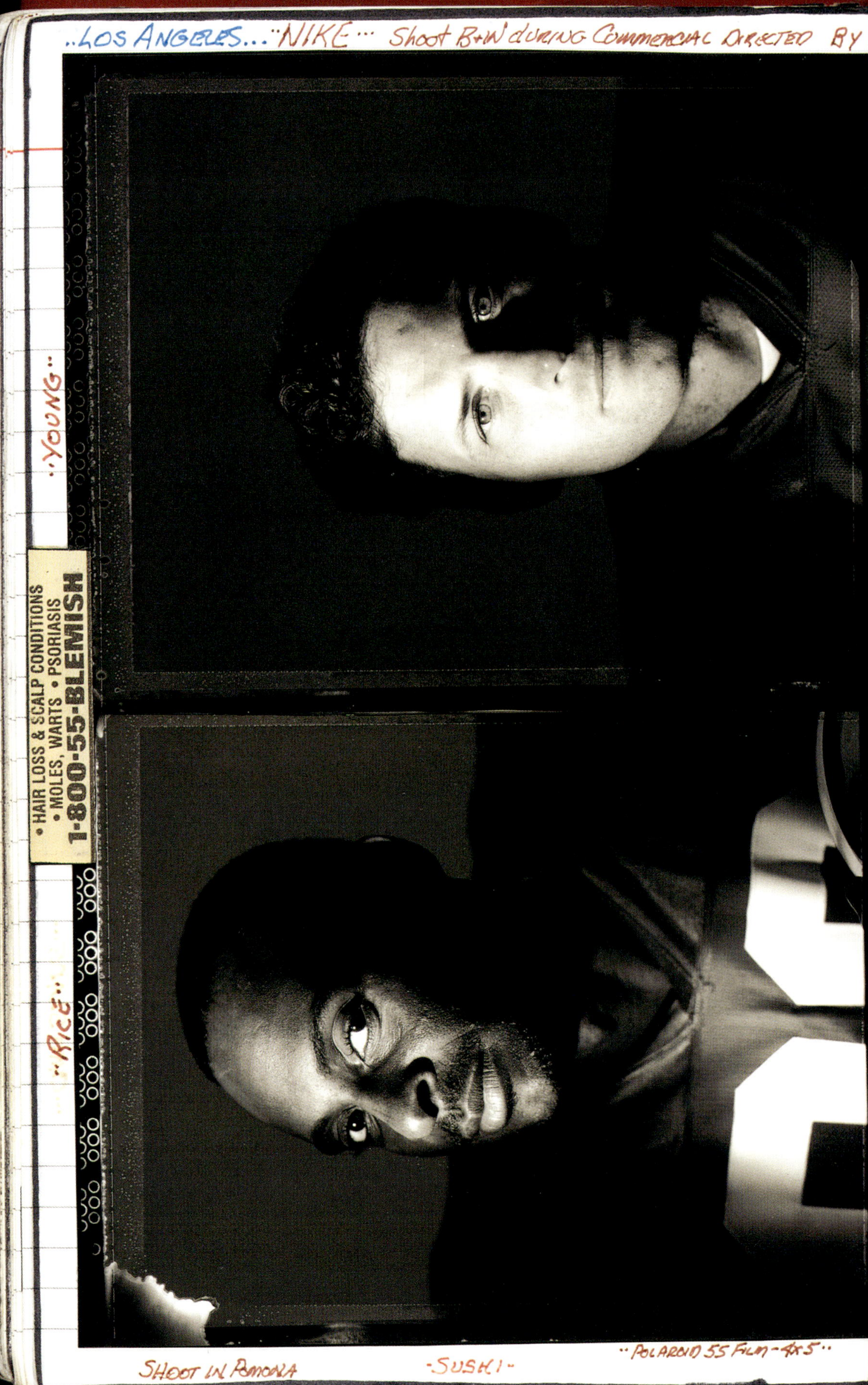
..LOS ANGELES... "NIKE"... Shoot B+W during Commercial Directed By
..YOUNG..
• HAIR LOSS & SCALP CONDITIONS
• MOLES, WARTS • PSORIASIS
1-800-55-BLEMISH
..RICE..
SHOOT IN POMONA
-SUSHI-
..POLAROID 55 FILM - 4x5..

..SUSHI..

..PLIMPTON..

THE RITZ-CARLTON

..BLEDSOE..

…e DITKA, REWRITING PLIMPTON + I for 90's VERSION of "PAPER LION."

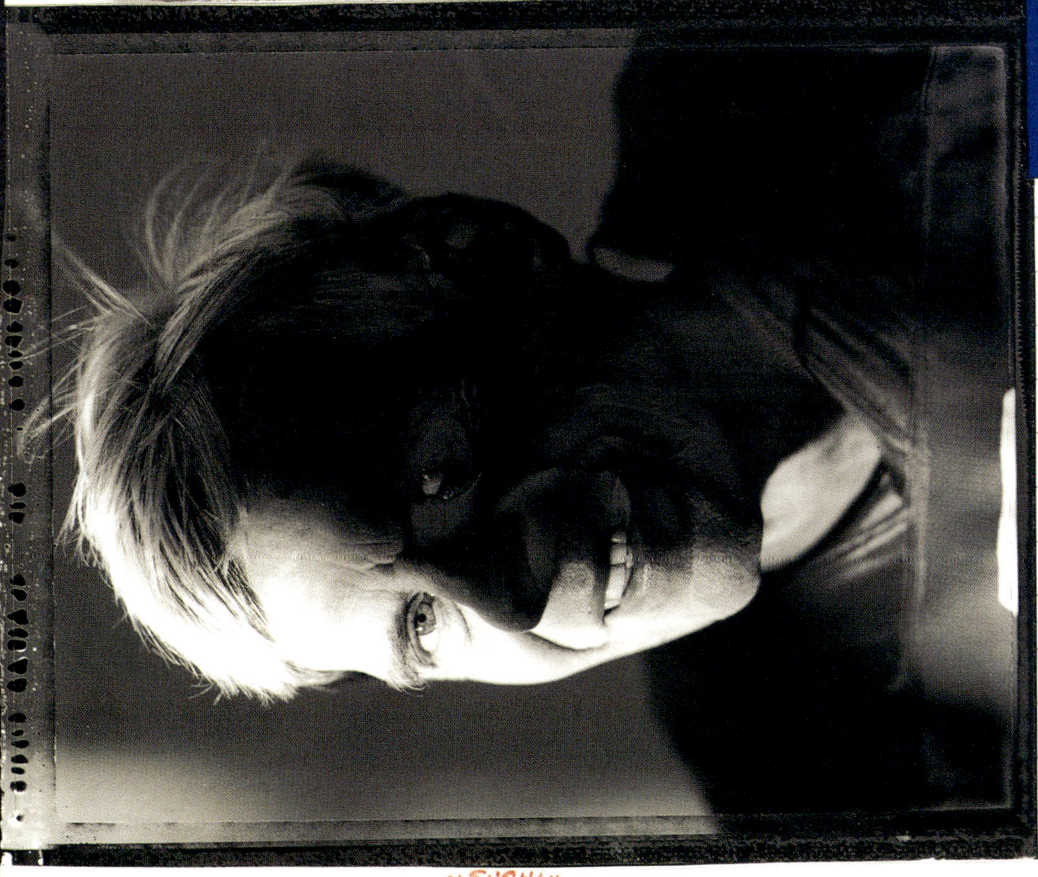

...L.A...

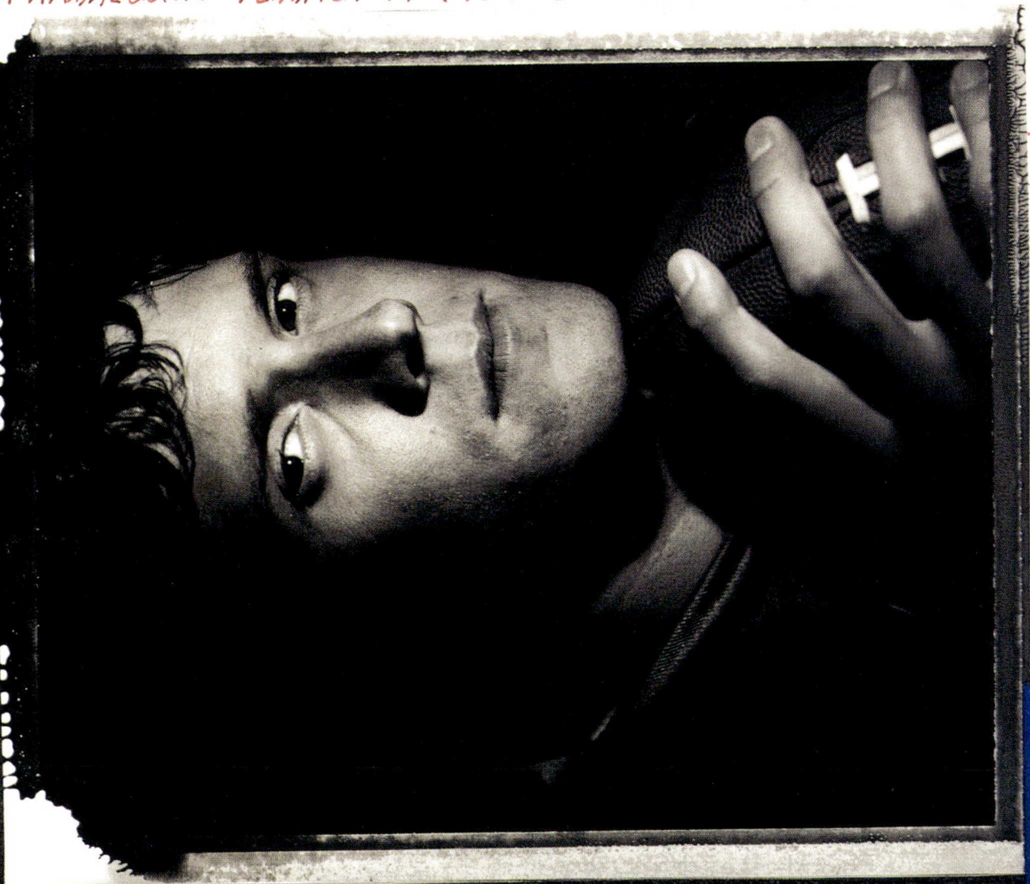

POTENCY PLUS ~SANTA MONICA~

...QUINCY WATTS... NORTHRIDGE, CAL. ST... 85B, BLUE FILTER, VELVIA, + WARMING... 6×7 RZ... OBA ASSISTS... S.I. CALENDER.

SUSHI

2/21/95

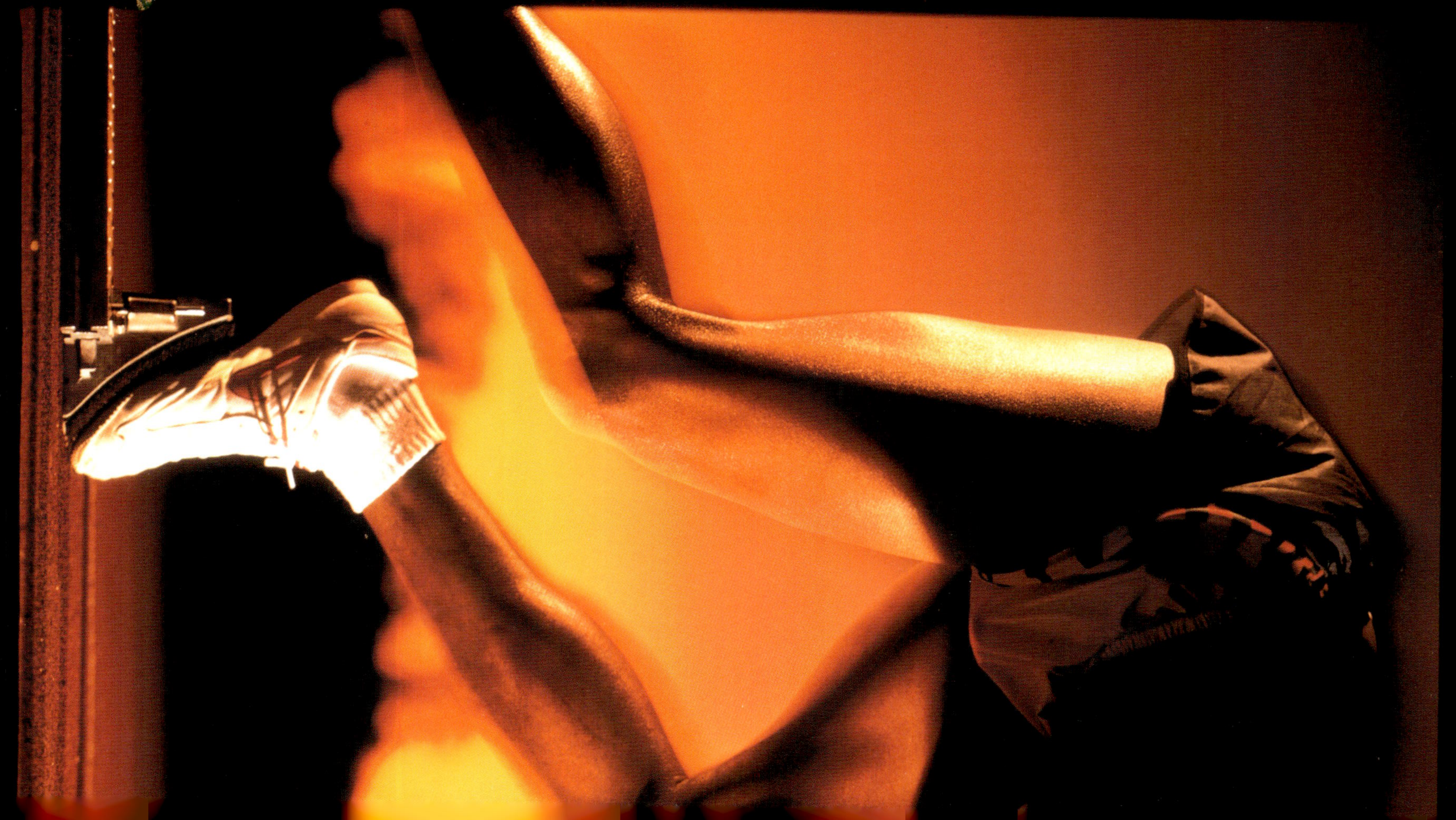

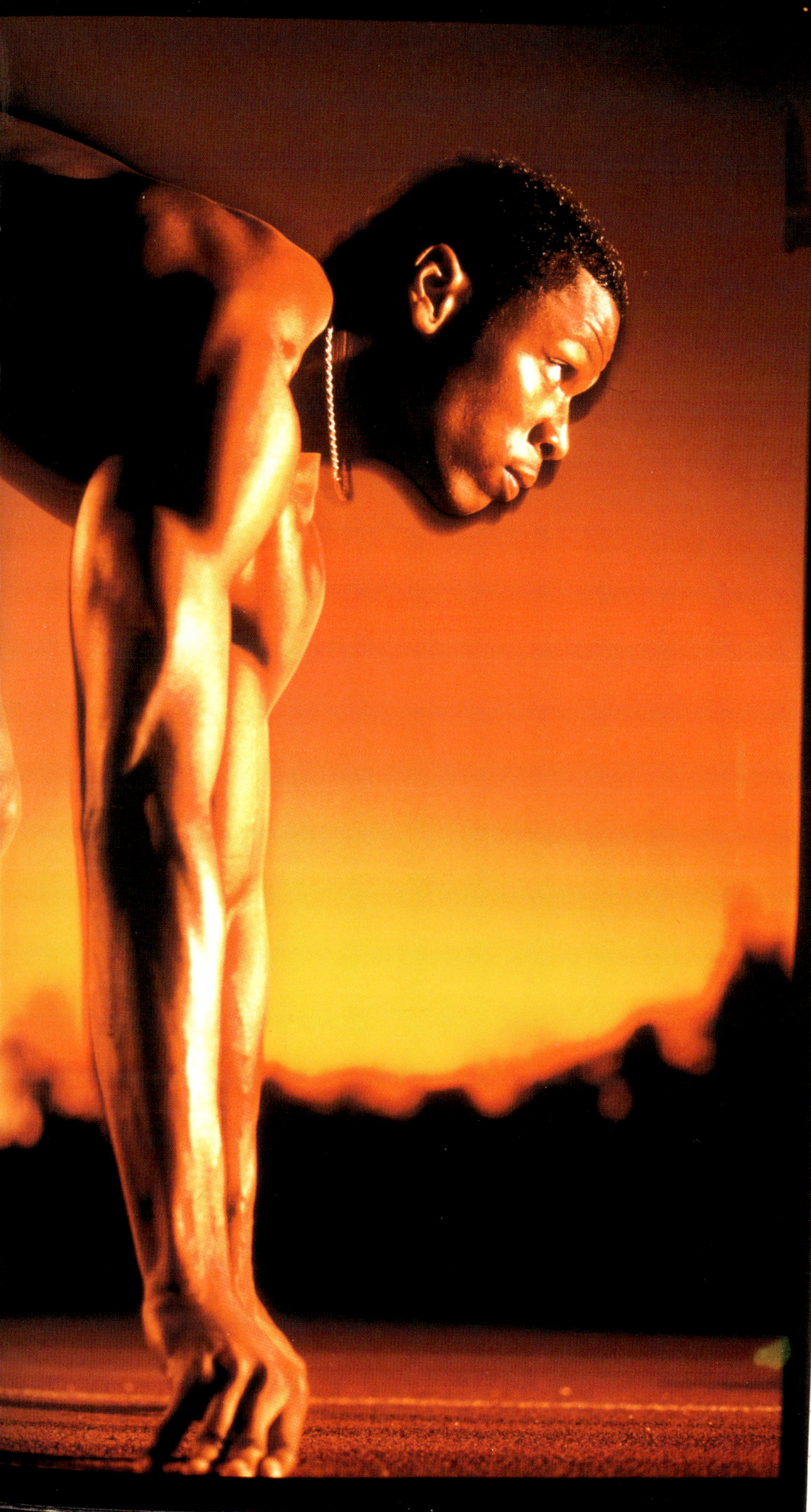

2/22/95

~SANTA MONICA~

BEEPER CITY

..OFF DAY...

:BACKDROP for MR. ROB.

:: INS. CERT ::

:: POLAROID + VELVIA FROM PEL

SUSHI

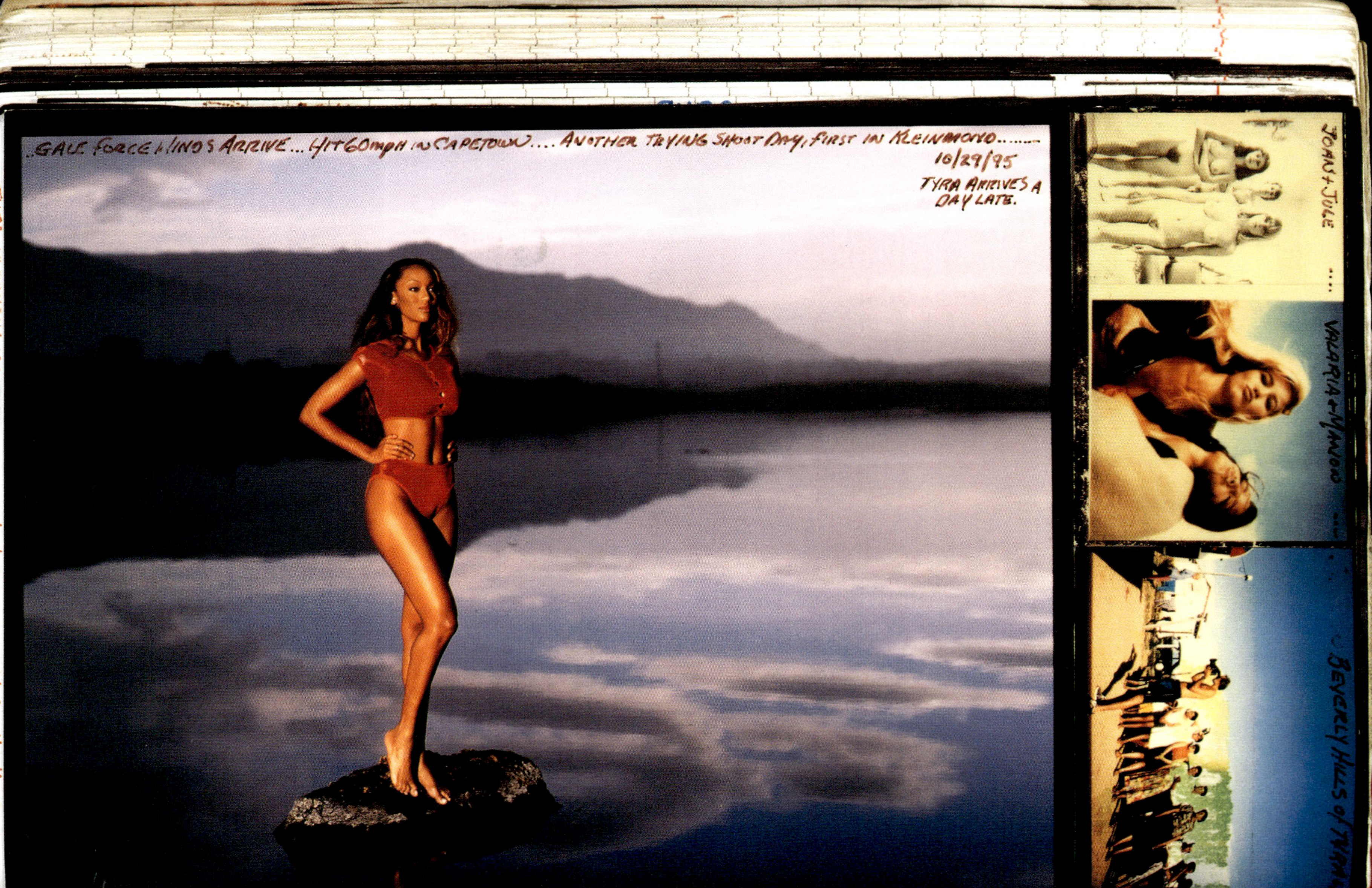

..GALE FORCE WINDS ARRIVE... HIT 60mph IN CAPETOWN.... ANOTHER TRYING SHOOT DAY, FIRST IN KLEINMOND.......
10/29/95
TYRA ARRIVES A DAY LATE.
JOAN + JULE ...
VALARIA + MANON ...
BEVERLY HILLS of TYRA
..TYRA-KLEINMOND LAGOON..
..10/29/95..
..KLEINMOND..S.I. SWIMSU

~S.I. SWIMSUIT-SOUTH AFRKA~ ...10/30/95...

andela to meet accused

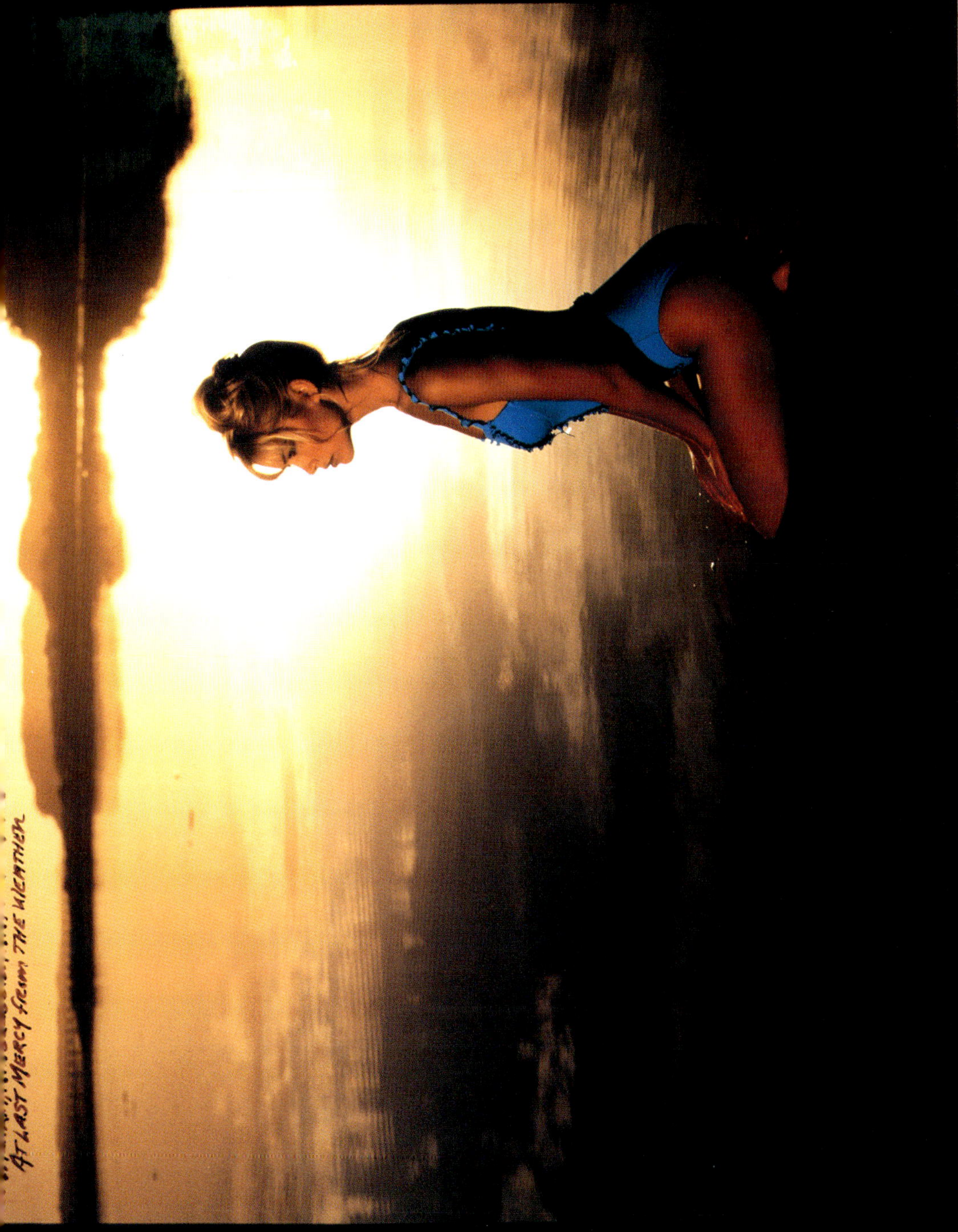

AT LAST MERCY from THE WEATHER

Drunk in a wheelchair'

ONTREAL. — A handicapped man eaving flat out at 5km/h down a street a battery-powered wheelchair has been ned for being in charge of a vehicle hile under the influence of alcohol.

DINNER WITH JOAN IN BAR

DATELINE SOUTH AFRICA......

WINDY 30 mpH +. SHOOT S.A. FLAG RAISING SHOT ON MOUNTAIN DUNES WITH TYRA + VALARIA. FOLLOW WITH TYRA IN REEDS WITH FILL FLASH.

~KLEINMOND~

the BEACH HOUSE

EDIT.. WITH TOM

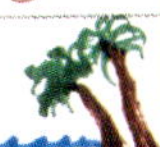

HUNTERS - PLETTENBURG
S.I.
OCTOBER **19**

Bothasig bloodba

MANON ARRIVES

1995 292nd day — 73 days follow

..VALARIA MASSA - KLEINMOND LAGOON AT DAWN.....

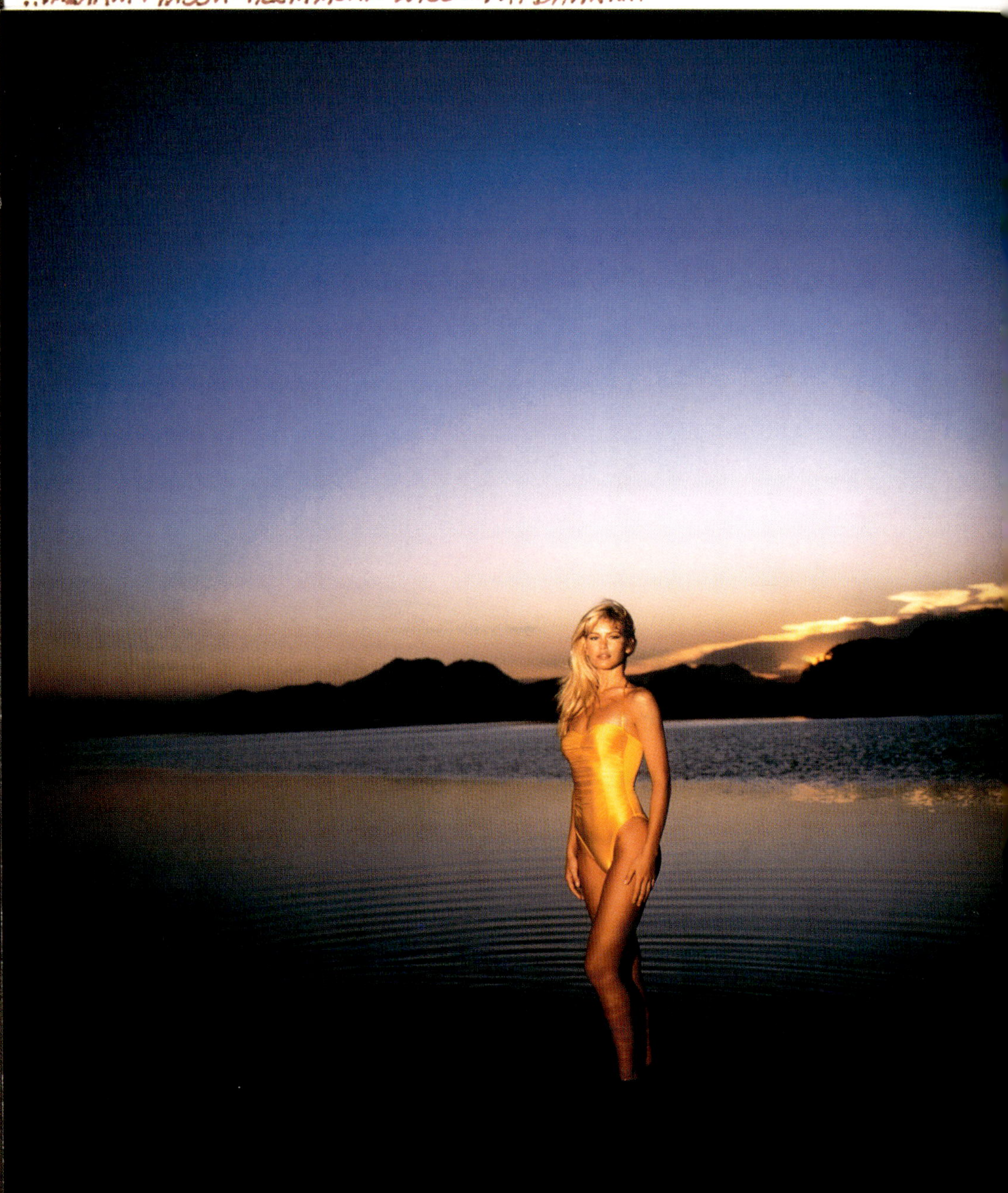

DAMP, COLD A.M. AT DREADFUL HUNTERS. SUN SHINES DO 2 OF STACY.... JULE SICK.....

Sexwale

P.M. FINALLY A CHANCE TO SHO ANOTHER GIRL. PUT MANON ON TRAMP AND THEN LIGHT FAILS.

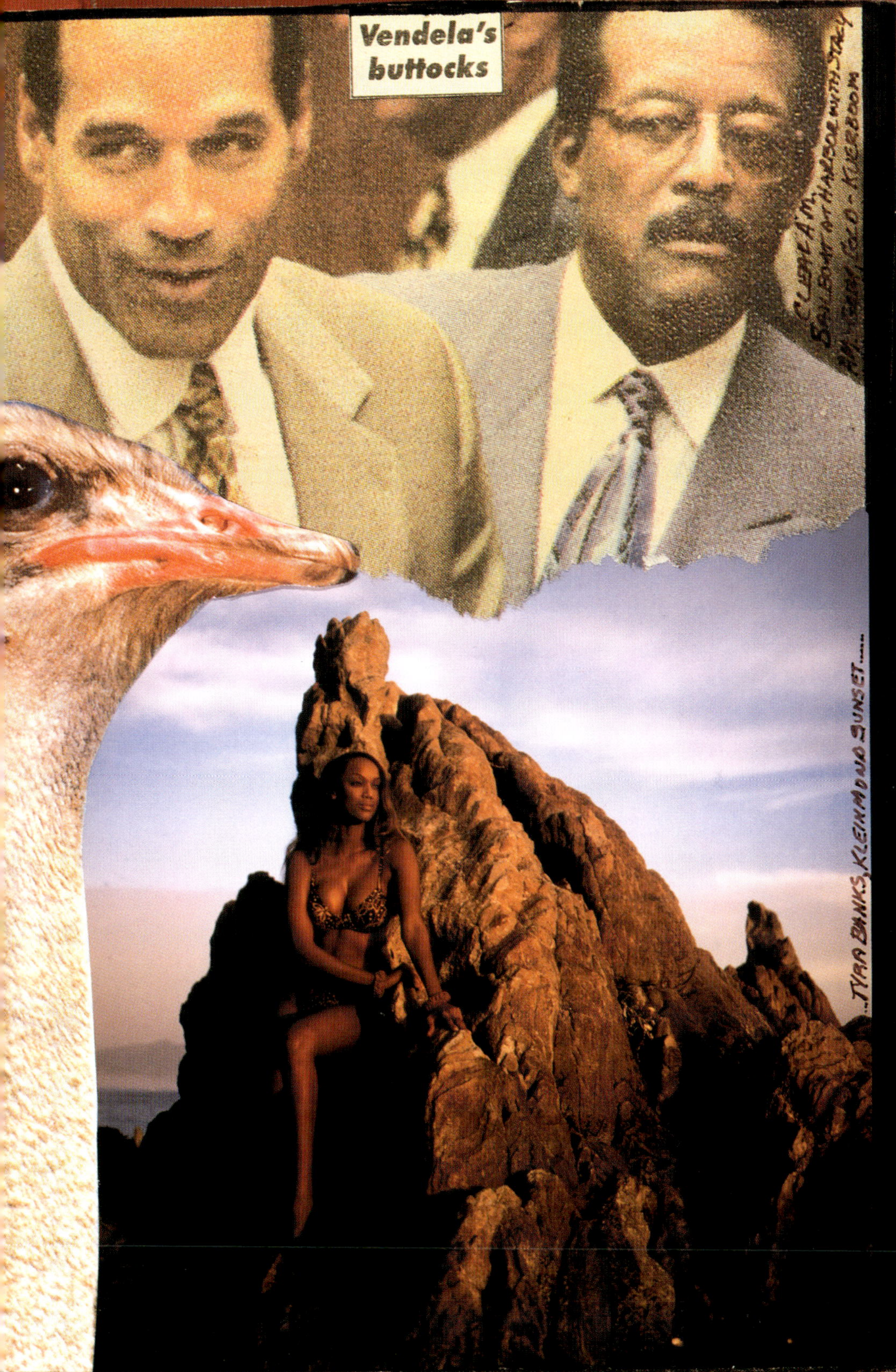

J's outcast

SANTA MONICA JULY 25 FRIDAY ADIDAS

ASTIA + 85B FILTER - 70-200 ZOOM

FRIDAY-ADOLPHE ... NAME OF THE DAY ... NUNSOCKNOY YOOTASANGUMTORN ... DINNER SEAFOOD MARKET

DRU-OBA-ADIDAS TEAM ... SUSHI-KATSU ...

Shutters

SATURDAY **26** JULY SANTA MONICA

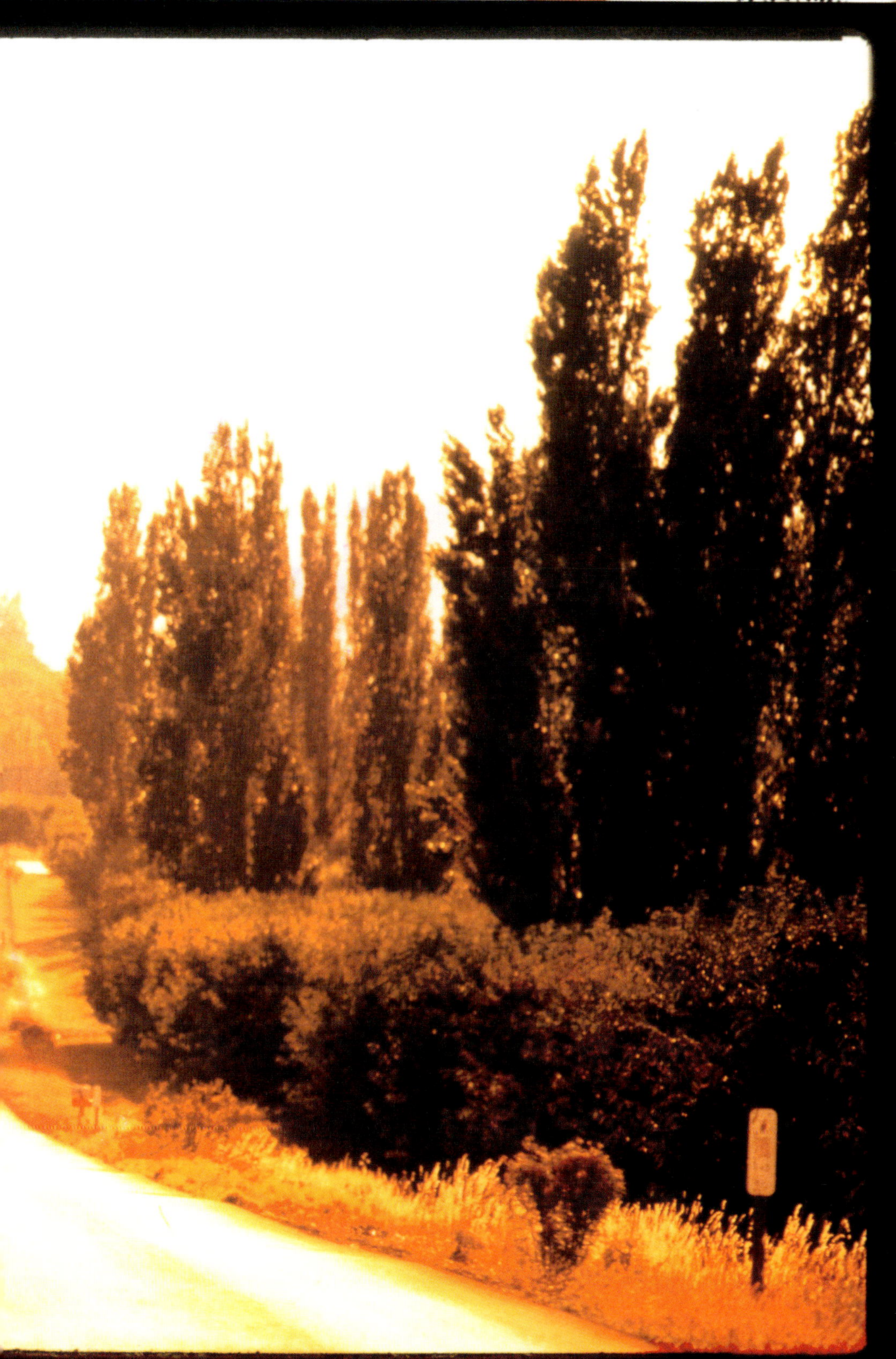

.....SHOOT AT U.S.C. POOL---MEXICAN AT THE "BORDER GRILL.....

"THE GORGE" HOOD RIVER, OREGON, 1 HR. OUTSIDE PORTLAND - RUNNER WAS I

S.I. SWIMSUIT _ISSUE OCTOBER **25** WEDNESDAY SOUTH AFRICA....

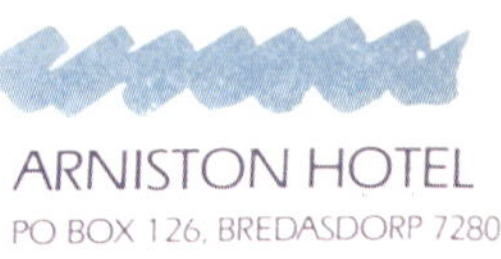

ARNISTON HOTEL
PO BOX 126, BREDASDORP 7280

A.M... POSTPONED, Rain, highwinds, +freezing. Tom Sick, STACY leaves VALARIA ARR.

1995 298th day — 67 days follow

P.M. Start at 5:00 because of cold + wind shoot Valaria 1st.

then Manon on street with beautiful light coming through fence, Shot bel

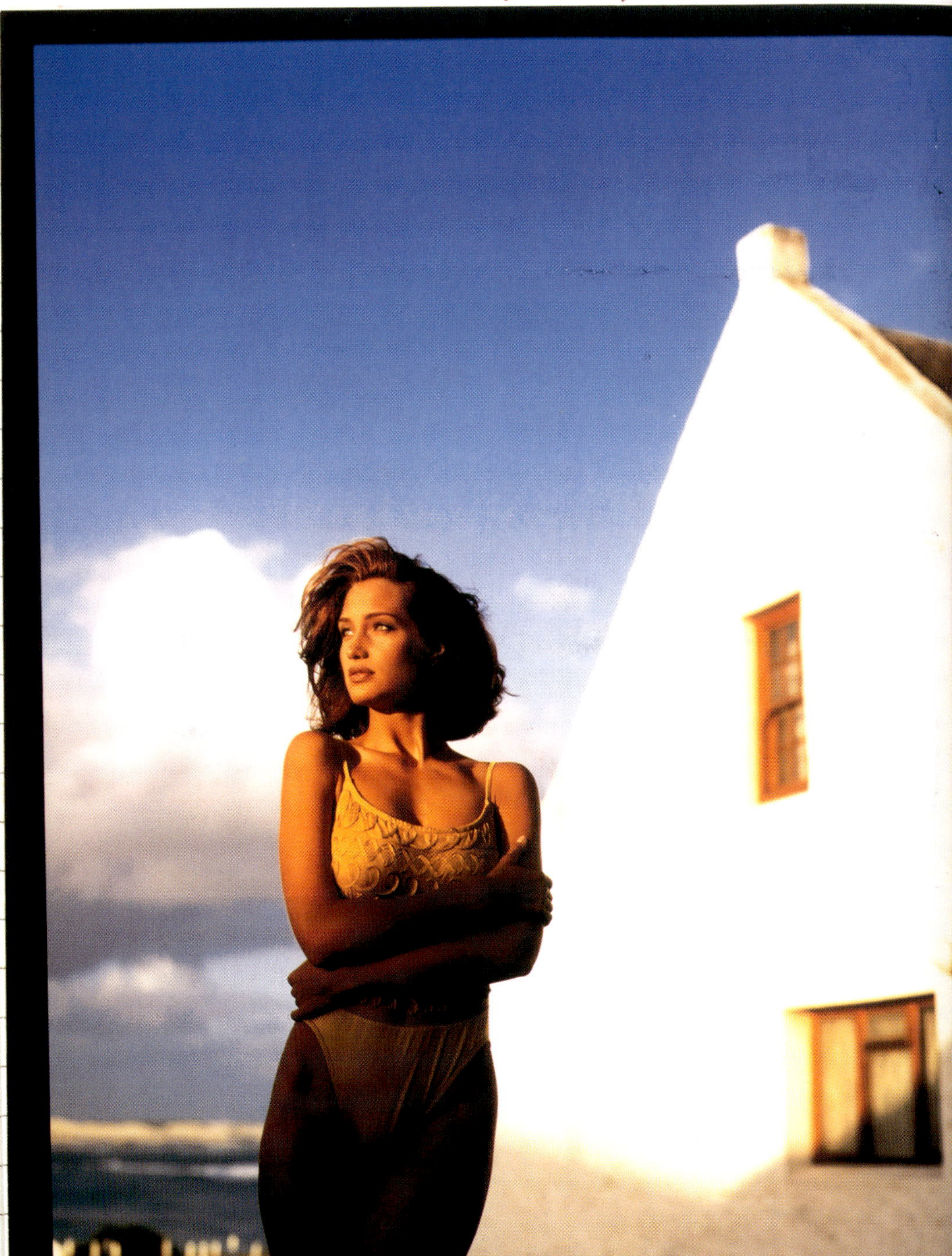

...MANON ON THE "STREETS OF ARNISTON"...

'I have 11 drinks a day!'

BRYANT GUMBEL BATTLING BOOZE

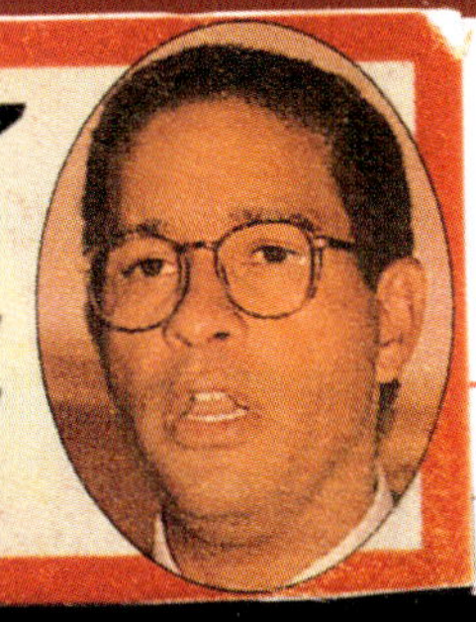

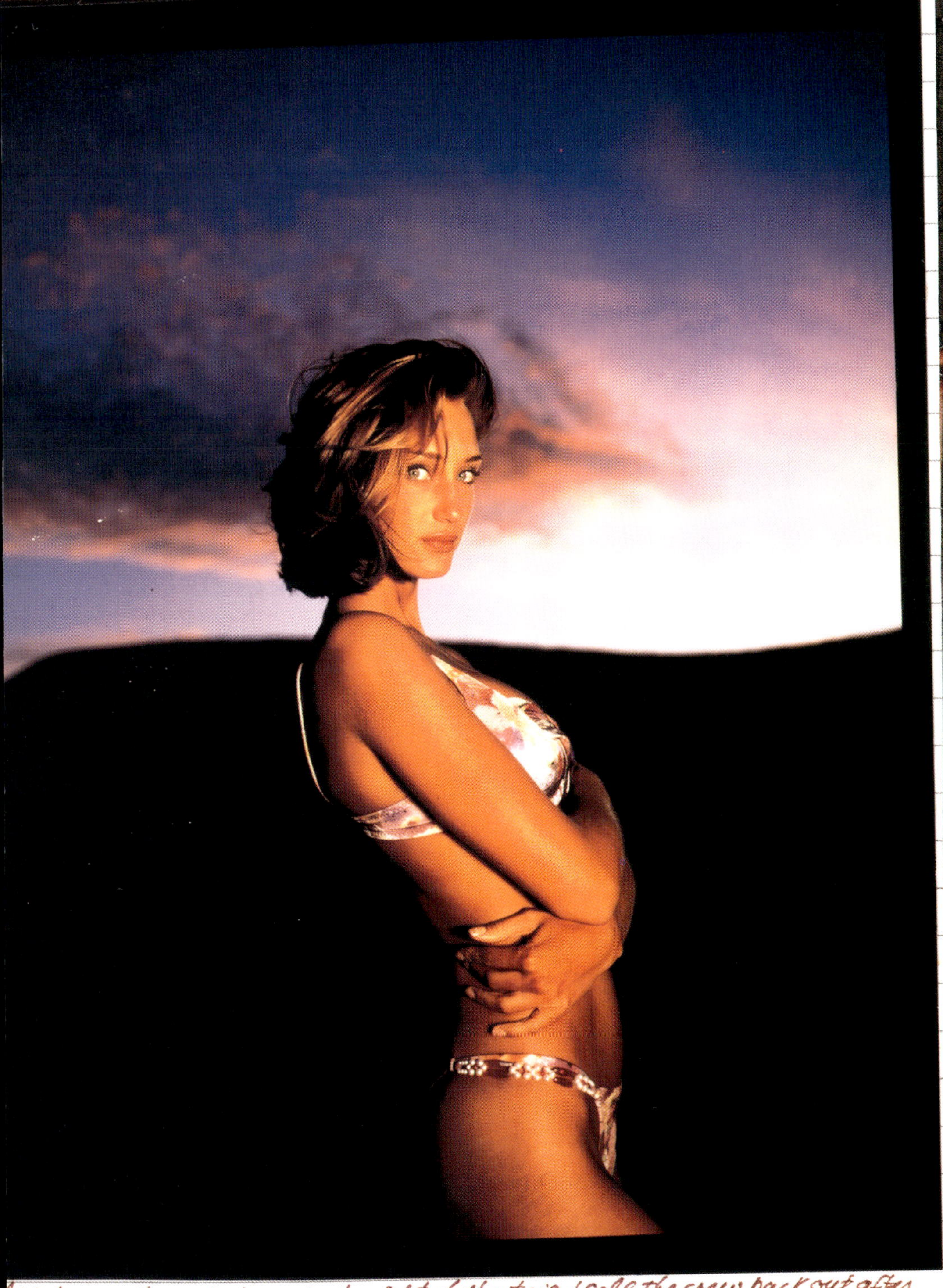

SURF

ANON... On the coldest, windiest night of the trip I call the crew back out after
e quit to do this shot. Shoot 6 frames on the '7.' Conditions unbearable, but beautiful.

S.I. SWIMSUIT STORY — OCTOBER **15** SUNDAY — PLETTENBURG BAY S.I.

1995 288th day —

A.M. - EXTREAMLY WINDY. START PRE-DAWN AT HOTEL POOL WITH STACY. THEN to NOETZIE BCH WITH IT'S CASTLES.

Man bitten by prostitute contracts Aids

~VALARIA + TYRA - KLEINMOND~

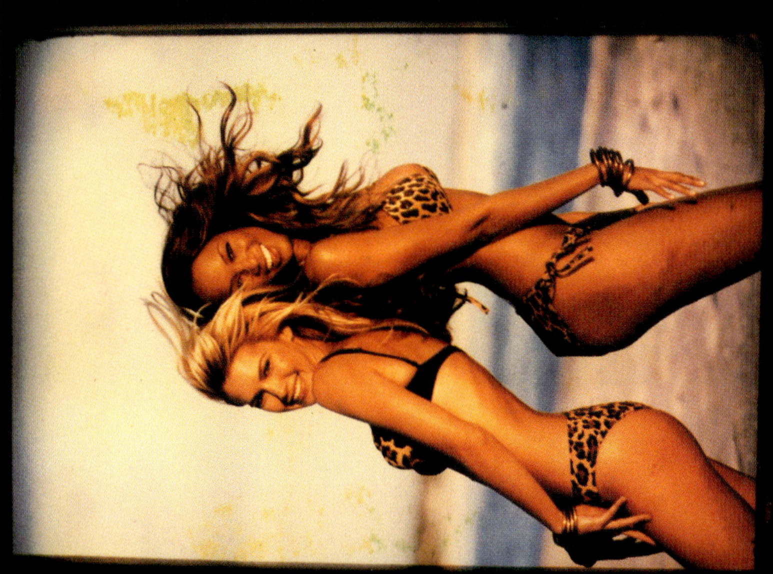

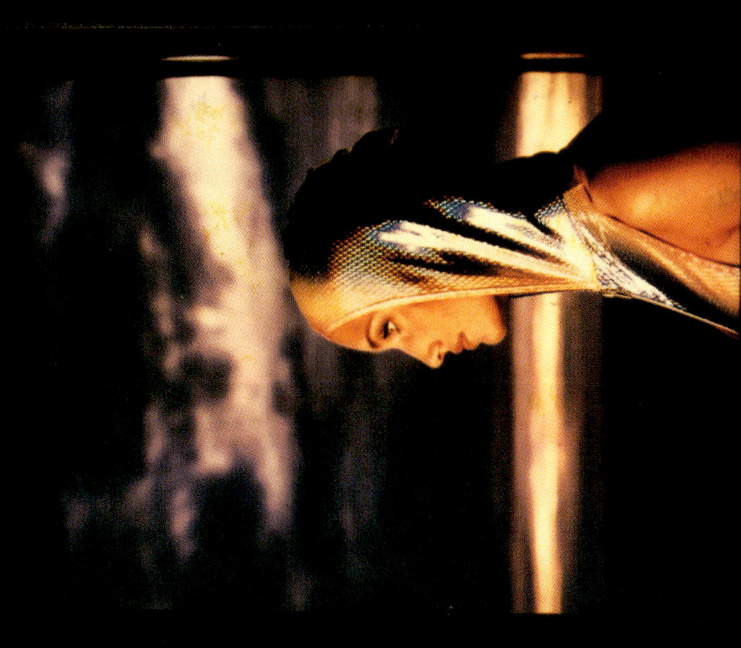

~MANON - ARNISTON DUNES~

The Asylum Street Spankers

P.M. HIGH WINDS PERSIST. GO to WHITE MENS ROOM (PAINTED WHITE) + DO STACY AGAINST ITS CURVED WALLS. THEN DO DOG SHOT ON PLETT. BCH. WITH NO DOGS ALLOWED SIGN UNTIL WE ARE ALL SANDBLASTED WITHIN 5 MINS. SHOOT CALLED FOR THE DAY..

The Plettenberg
★ ★ ★ ★ ★

S.I. SWIMSUIT

MONDAY **16** OCTOBER

PLETTENBERG BAY, S. AFRICA

VALARIA - KLEINMOND

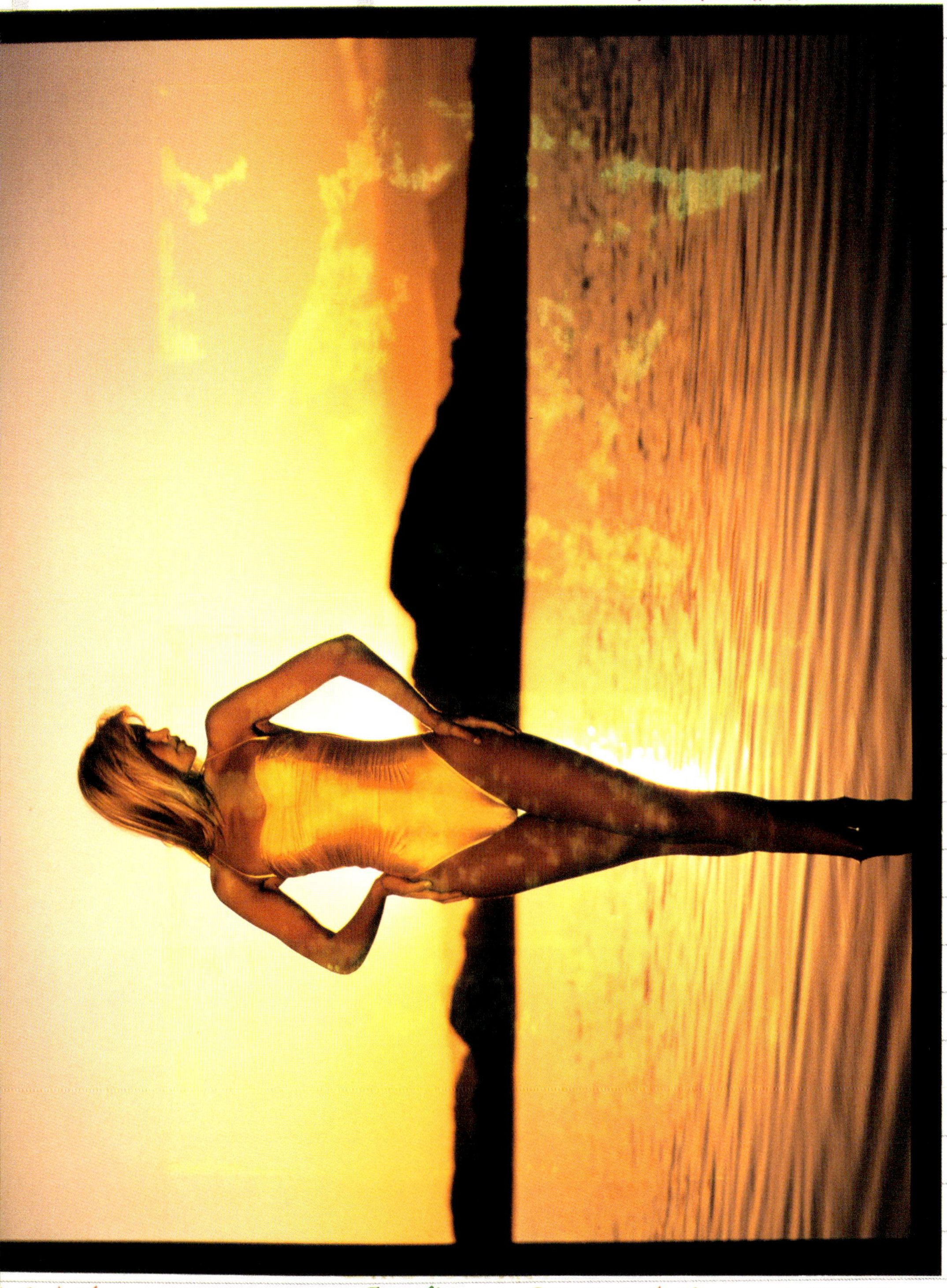

Go to KUERBOOM BCH. GOOD
ZY LIGHT FOR STACY. TRAMP.
FINISHES MORNING.

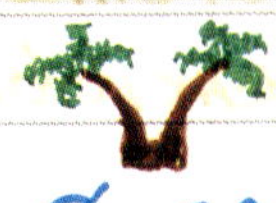

SURF

P.M BACK to KUERBOOM STRAND.
STARTS OFF GOOD BUT SUN DISAPPEARS,
DO STACY DANCING to 'SEX MACHINE'

...SANTA MONICA ......
JULY 23 WEDNESDAY
..ADIDAS....

9-Year-Old Accus
Of Stalking a Girl

Bad Breath & Bitter Taste Cured!

...U.S.C. Pool - Swimming + Dining....

.... SUSHI

1-800-55-MOUTH
Dr. Gary Herskovits

KATSU....

Newborn found alive in gym bag

..ADIDAS..

THURSDAY

SHOOT AEROBICS IN STUDIO

24

SANTA MONICA

Shutters

ON THE BEACH

...2000 lbs of WEIGHTS + MACHINES

I will end your Pain!

MOVED INTO STUDIO FOR SHOOT - 4 MODELS...

Cheating NY WIVES #'S

1-900-737-1122 Ext 131

~ATLANTA~ 8/28/96 ~TRIPLE JUMP~

Olympic Snapshot

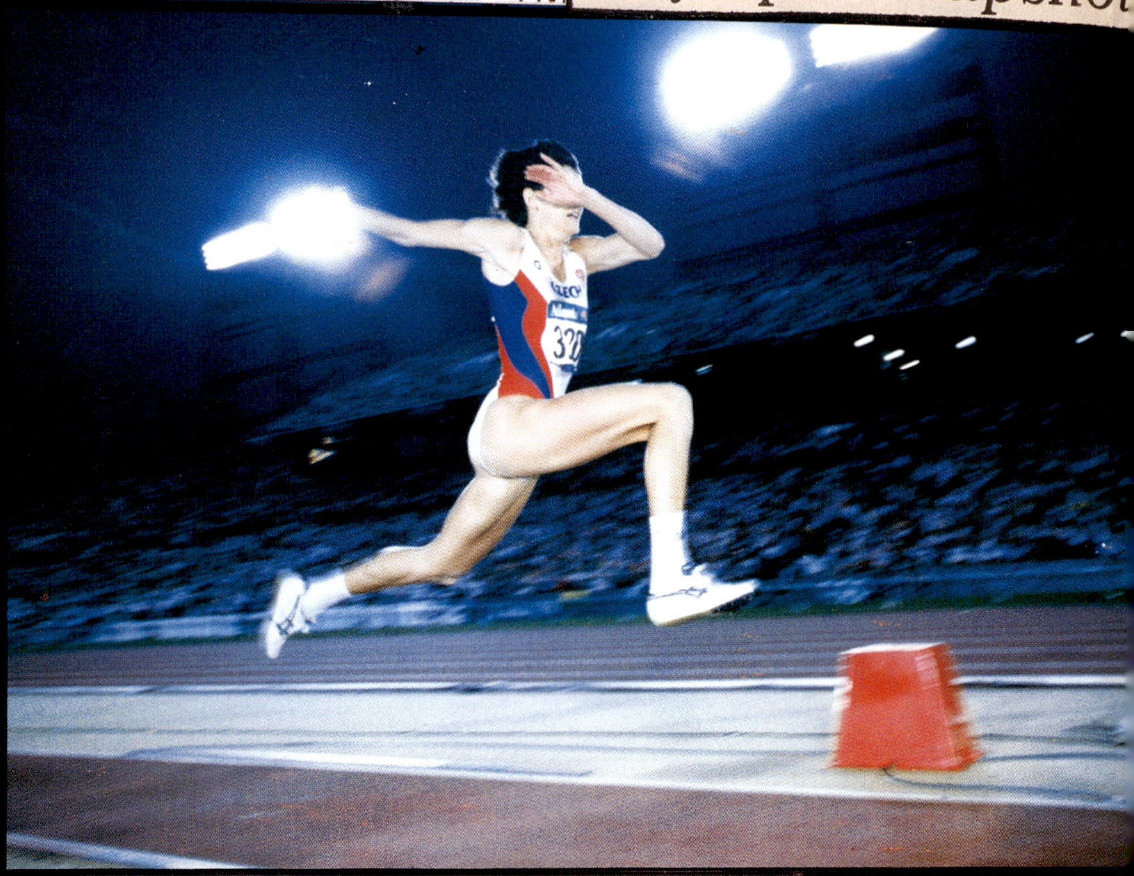

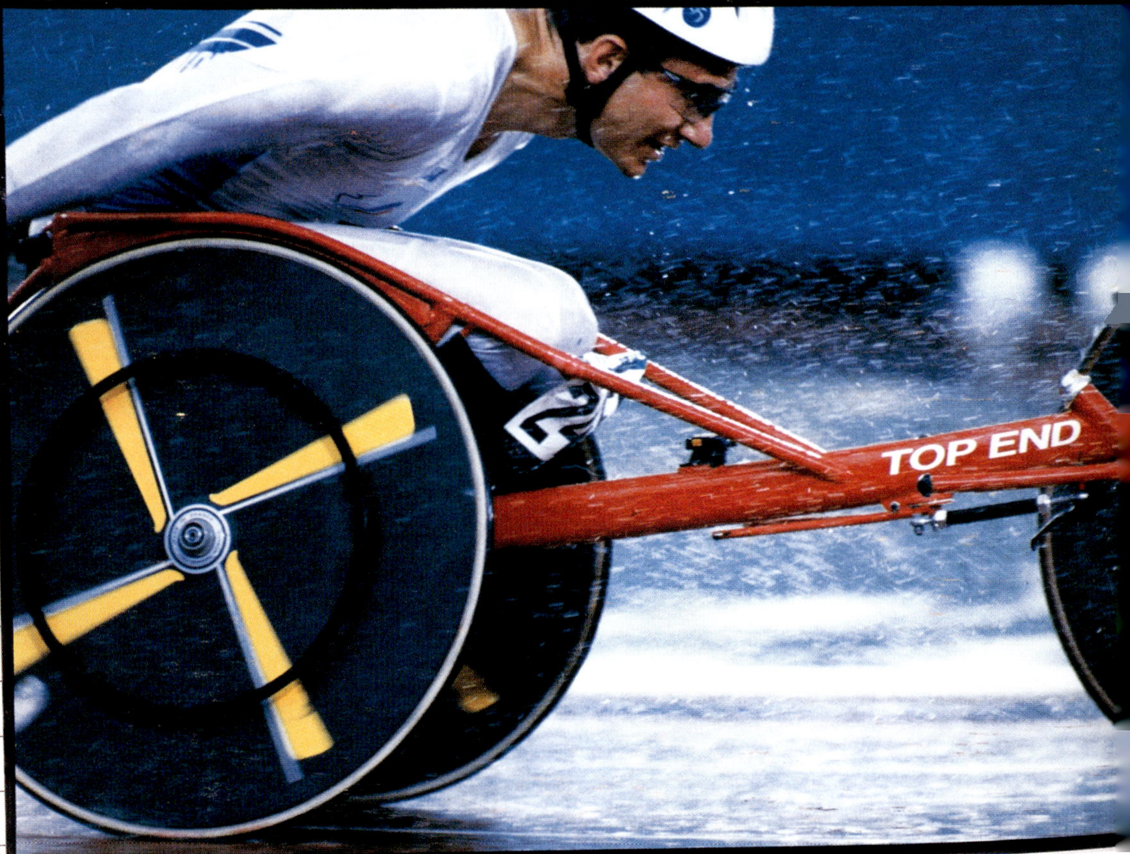

_COVER TRACK + FIELD - A.M. + P.M. — 1500m WHEELCHAIR FINAL - DINNER WITH Bill EPPRIDGE .. SUSH

at Will Never Fade

8/29/96 ...STAY AT THE DIS-COMFORT INN-

~THE MEDIA~ ...ATLANTA...

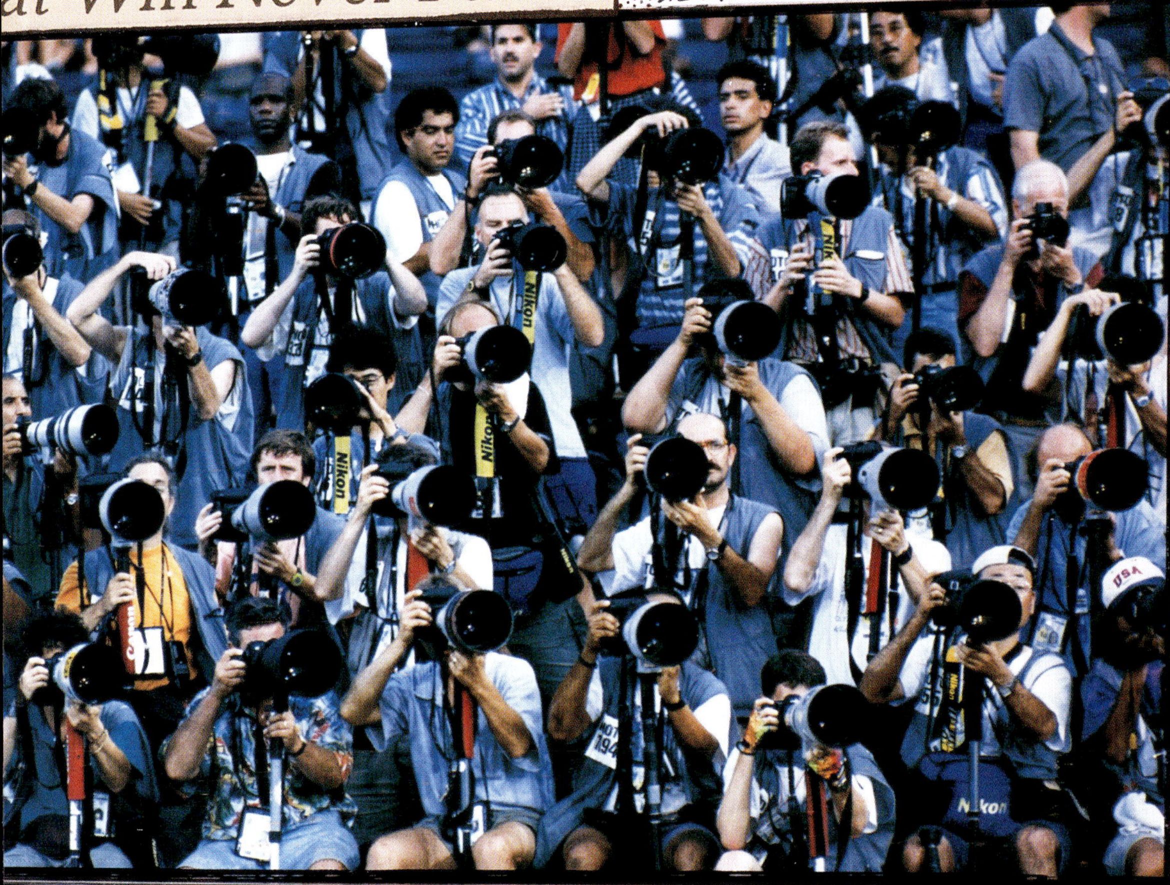

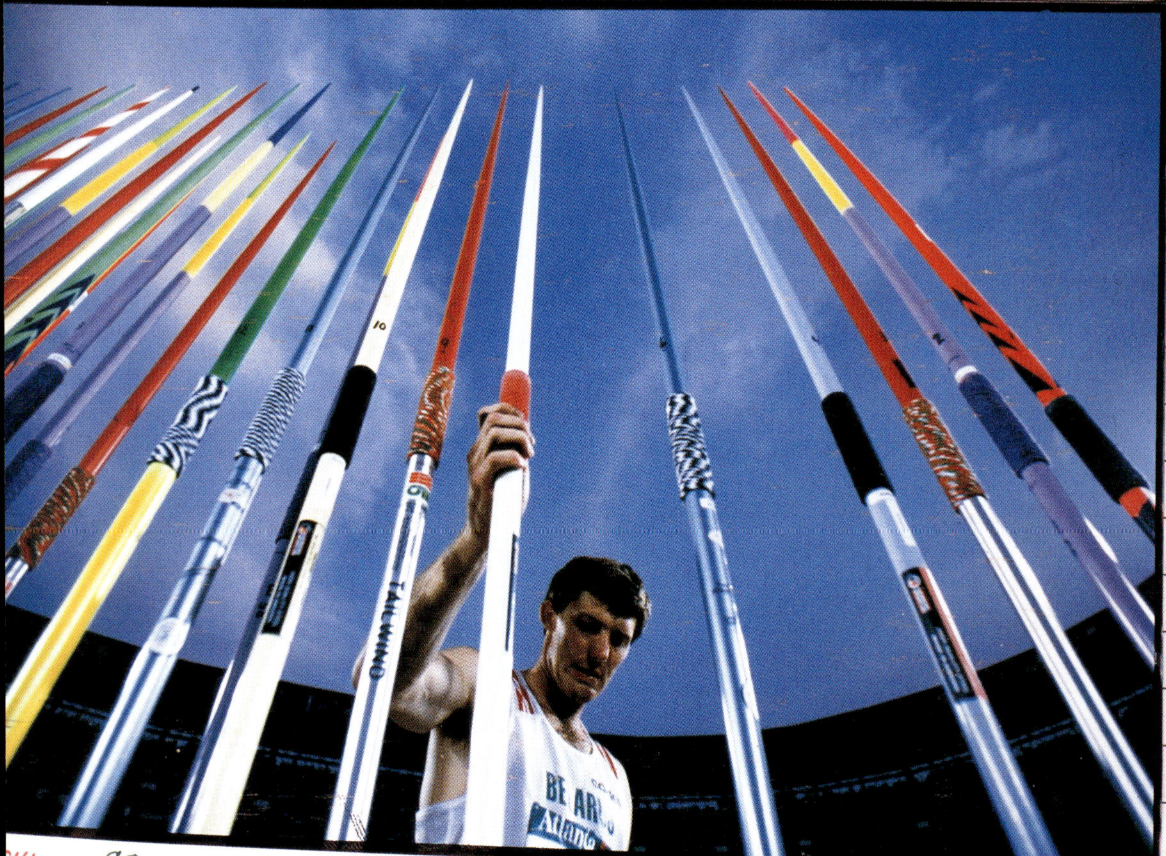

SHI.. ...SPORTS ILLUSTRATED.. ~FISHEYE JAVALINS~ ..96 OLYMPICS.. DAY #11.....

"....It's All About Heide." Elaine.....

//

Stacey-Poolhall

..Todos Santos Sunrise......

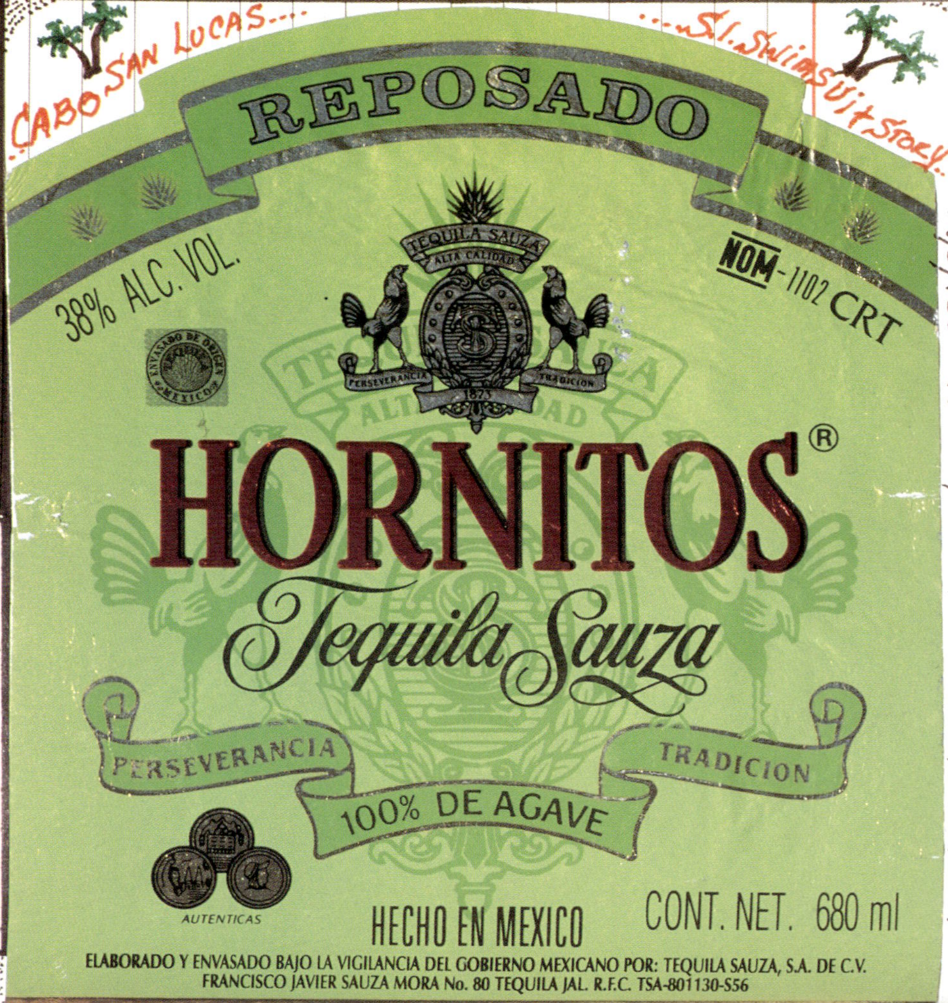

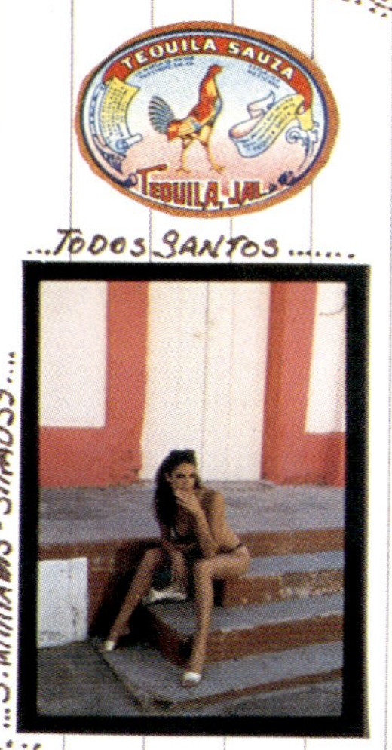

..Todos Santos......

..S. Williams-Strauss...

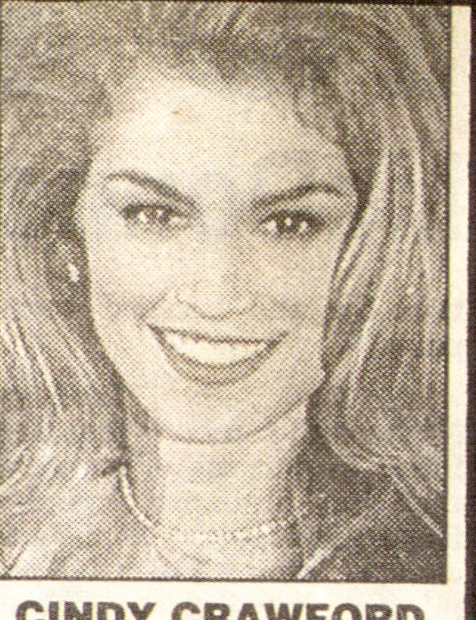

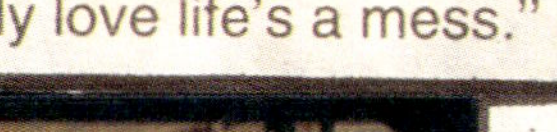

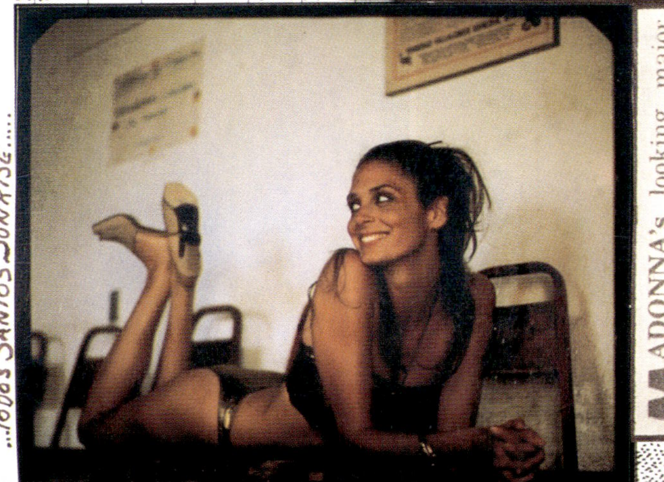

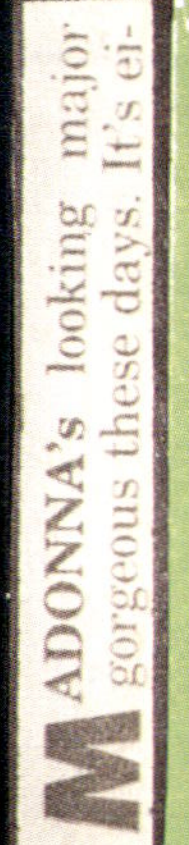

Cabo San Lucas....

....S.I. Swimsuit Story...

...12/5/96 – Terrasol Hotel. Shoot Steff & Graf A.M. + P.M.

REPOSADO

38% ALC. VOL.

NOM-1102 CRT

TEQUILA SAUZA
ALTA CALIDAD
PERSEVERANCIA
TRADICION
1873

ENVASADO DE ORIGEN MEXICO

HORNITOS®

Tequila Sauza

PERSEVERANCIA

100% DE AGAVE

TRADICION

AUTENTICAS

HECHO EN MEXICO

CONT. NET. 680 ml

ELABORADO Y ENVASADO BAJO LA VIGILANCIA DEL GOBIERNO MEXICANO POR: TEQUILA SAUZA, S.A. DE C.V.
FRANCISCO JAVIER SAUZA MORA No. 80 TEQUILA JAL. R.F.C. TSA-801130-S56

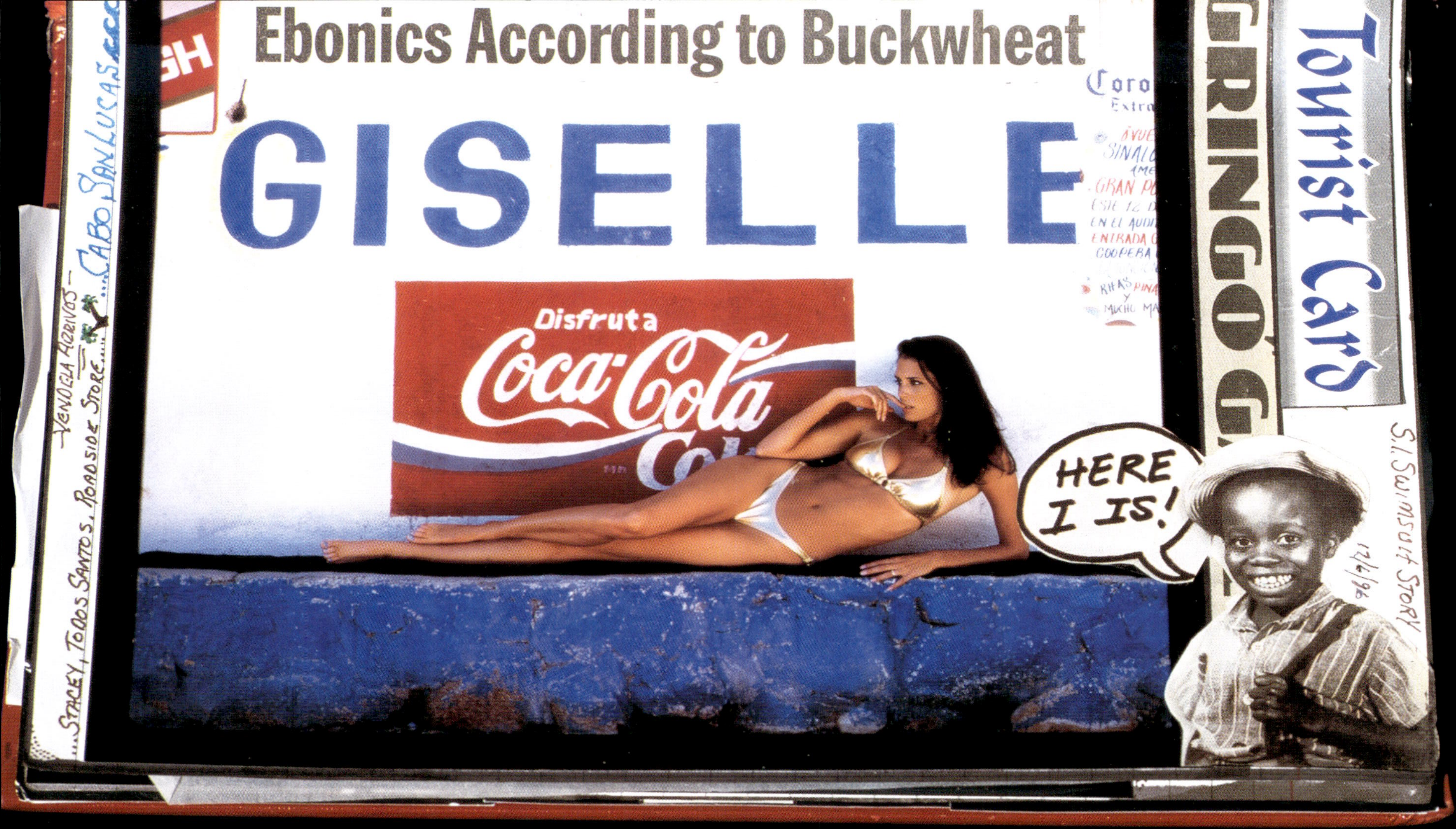

Ebonics According to Buckwheat

GISELLE

Disfruta
Coca-Cola

HERE I IS!

Tourist Card

S.I. Swimsuit Story
12/6/96

Stacey, Todos Santos, Roadside Store ... Cabo San Lucas

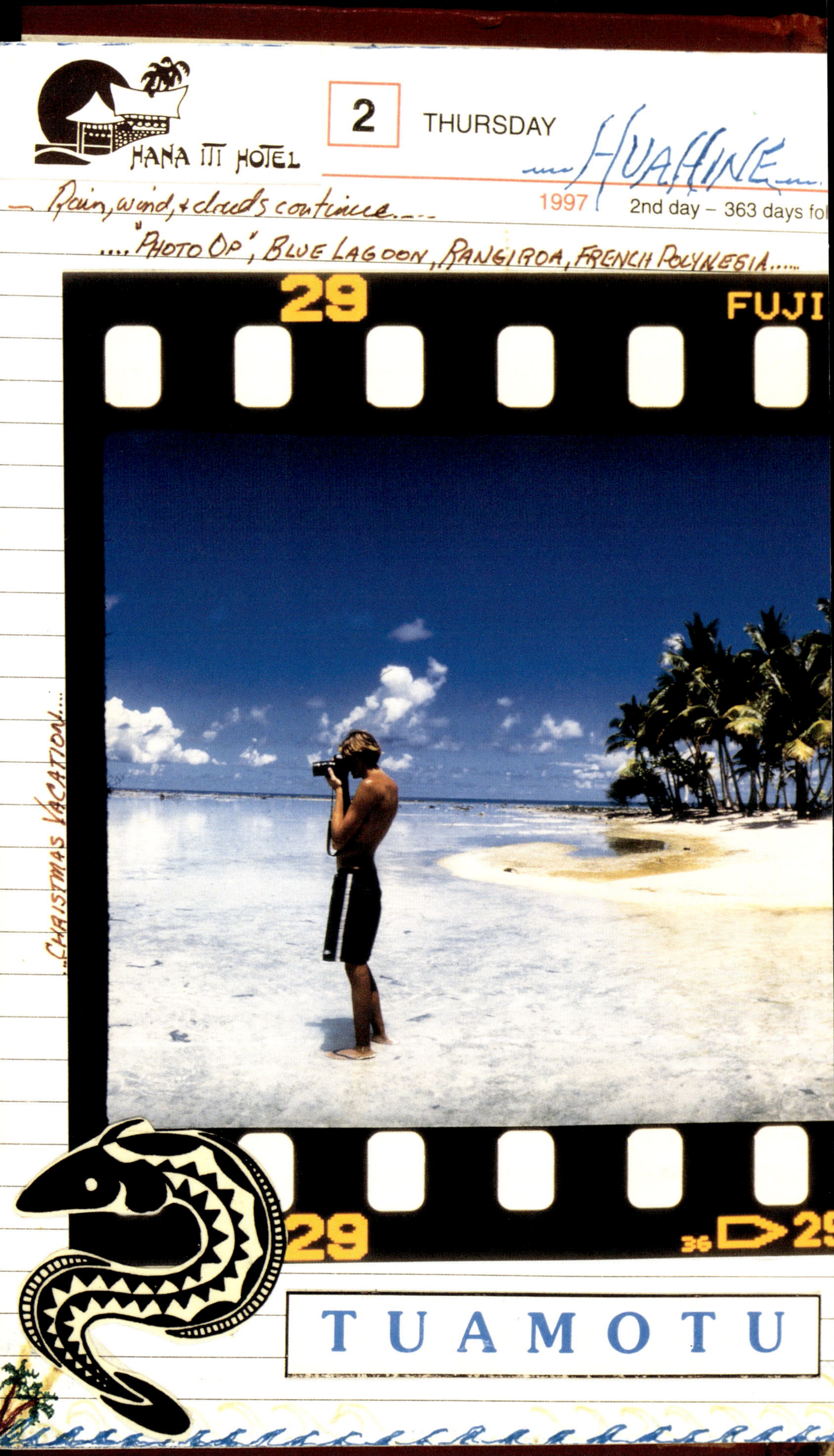
HANA ITI HOTEL
2
THURSDAY
...HUAHINE...
1997
2nd day – 363 days fol
– Rain, wind, & clouds continue...
...."PHOTO OP", BLUE LAGOON, RANGIROA, FRENCH POLYNESIA.....
29
FUJI
...CHRISTMAS VACATION...
29
36 29
TUAMOTU

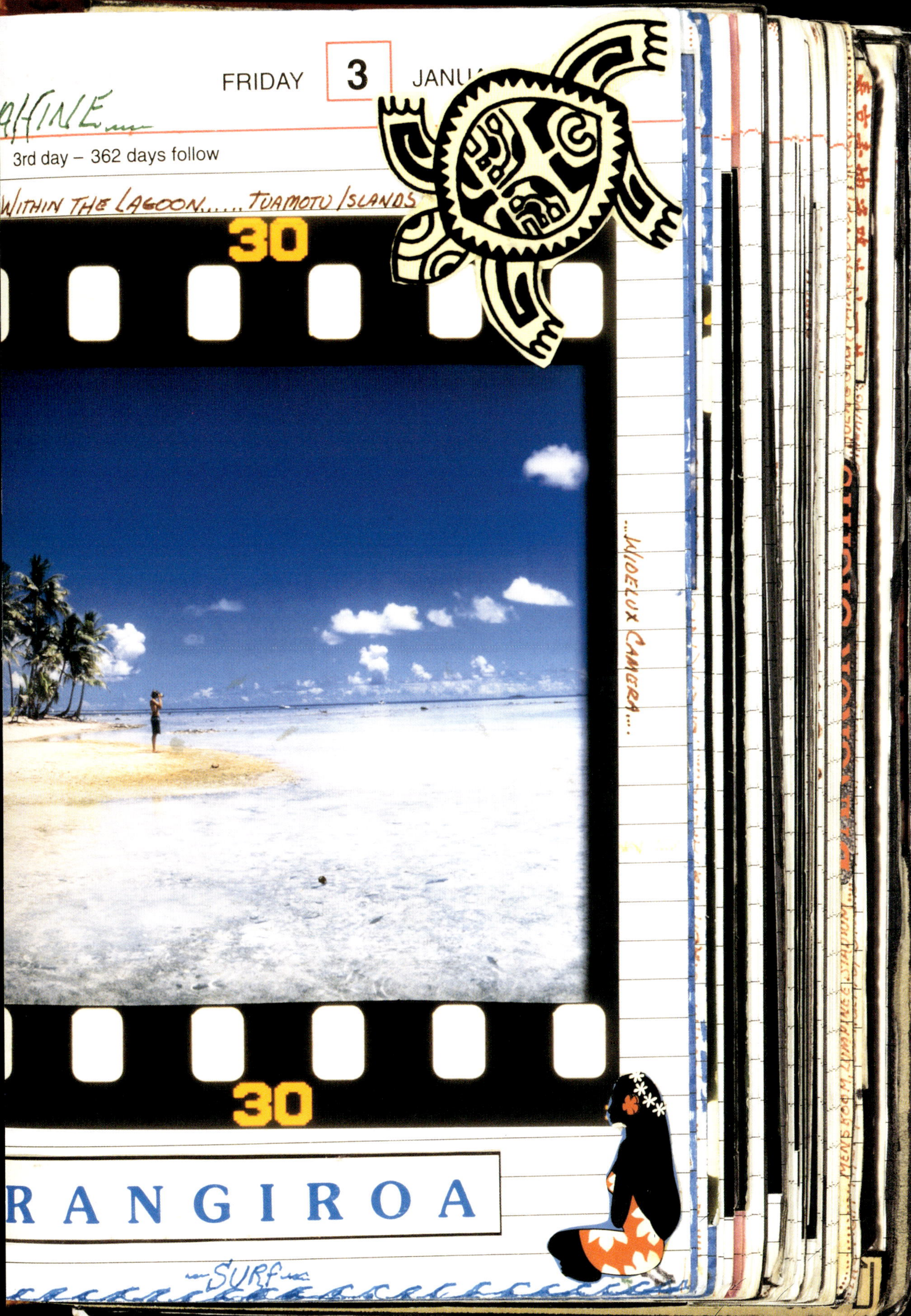
FRIDAY
3
JANU
AHINE
3rd day – 362 days follow
WITHIN THE LAGOON..... TUAMOTU ISLANDS
30
...WIDELUX CAMERA...
30
RANGIROA
SURF

KIA ORA SAUVAGE

~CHRISTIAN-BLUE LAGOON, RANGIROA~

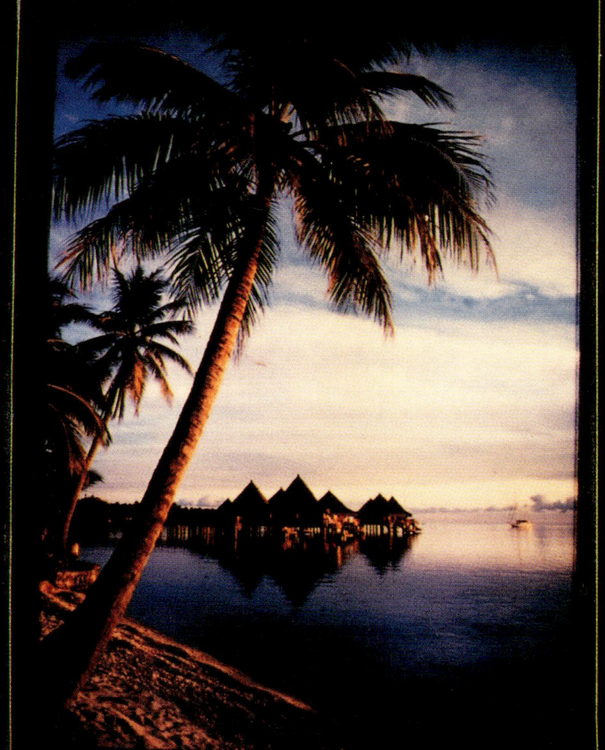

~KIA ORA VILLAGE~

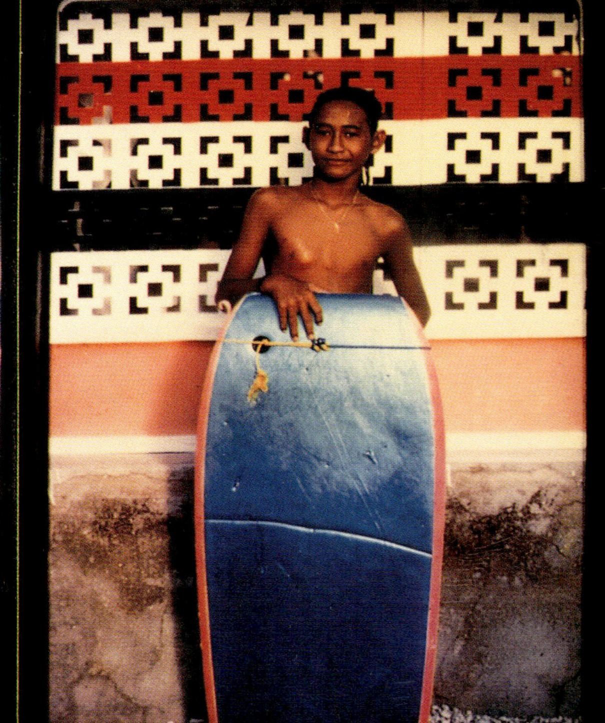

~YOUNG BODYBOARDER-TIPUTA VILLAGE~

Tobacco Chiefs Say Cigarettes Aren't Addictive

IGIROA, TUAMOTU ISLANDS - KIA ORA VILLAGE HOTEL ~ VISIT BLUE LAGOON ~

~ TEFARERII VILLAGE, HUAHINE, FRENCH POLYNESIA ~ INFARED FILM - 17mm LENS ~ CHRISTMAS VACATION '96+'97 ~

~ SANDWICH ISLANDS - OCEANIA ~

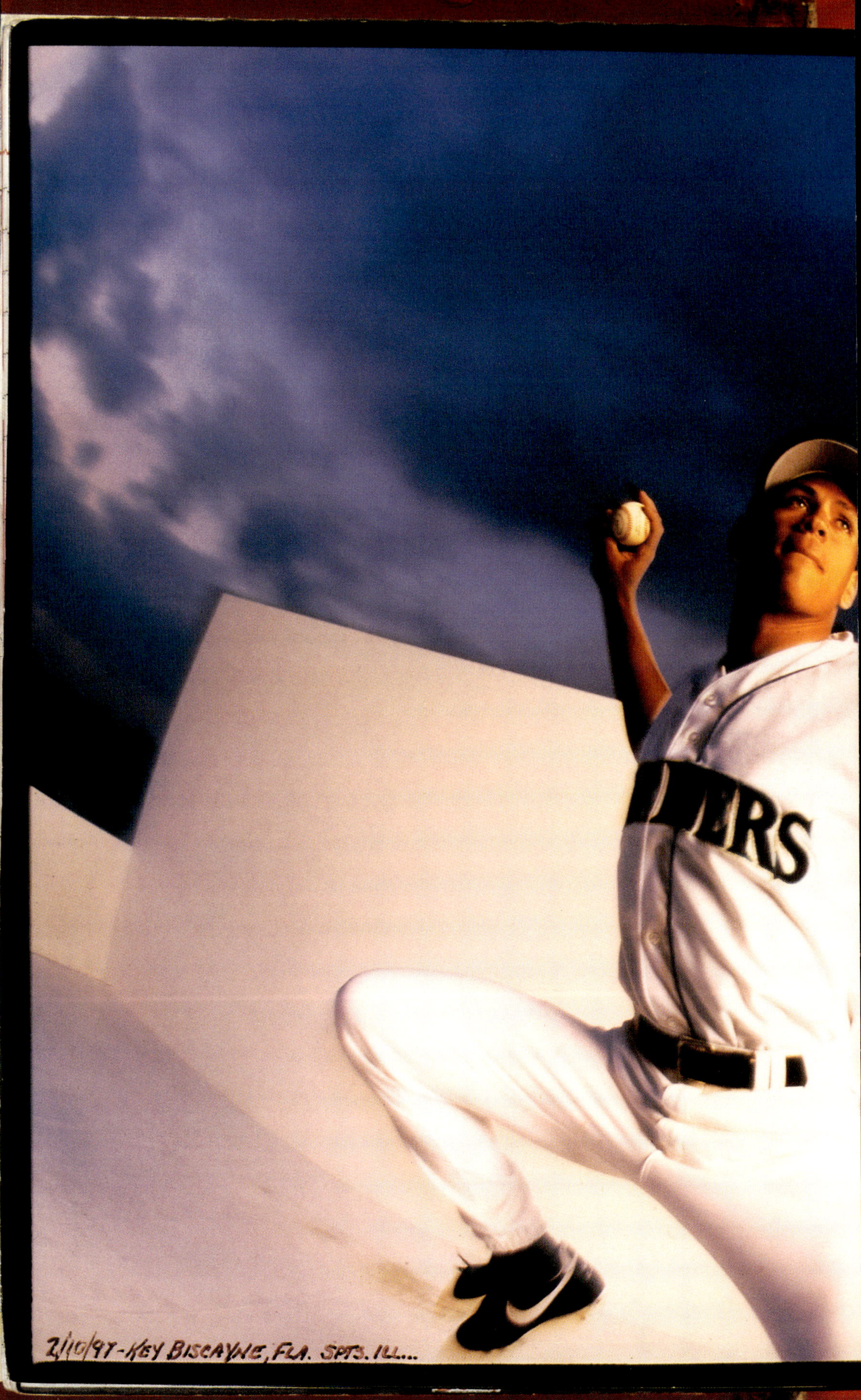
2/10/97-KEY BISCAYNE, FLA. SPTS. ILL...

FEB. 10, 1997

TRAVEL DAY
LV. MIAMI FOR
ST. PETE. BCH.

WE HAVE YOUR STOOL

...S.I. AND ADIDAS DAY OF TRAVEL...

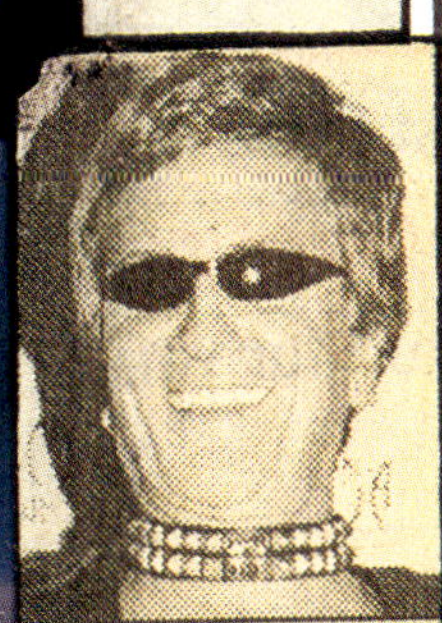

By Fred Prouser, Reuters

Boone: Booted out.

SUSHI...

MIAMI BCH.

.... ALEX RODRIGUEZ - BIG TIME STUDIOS....

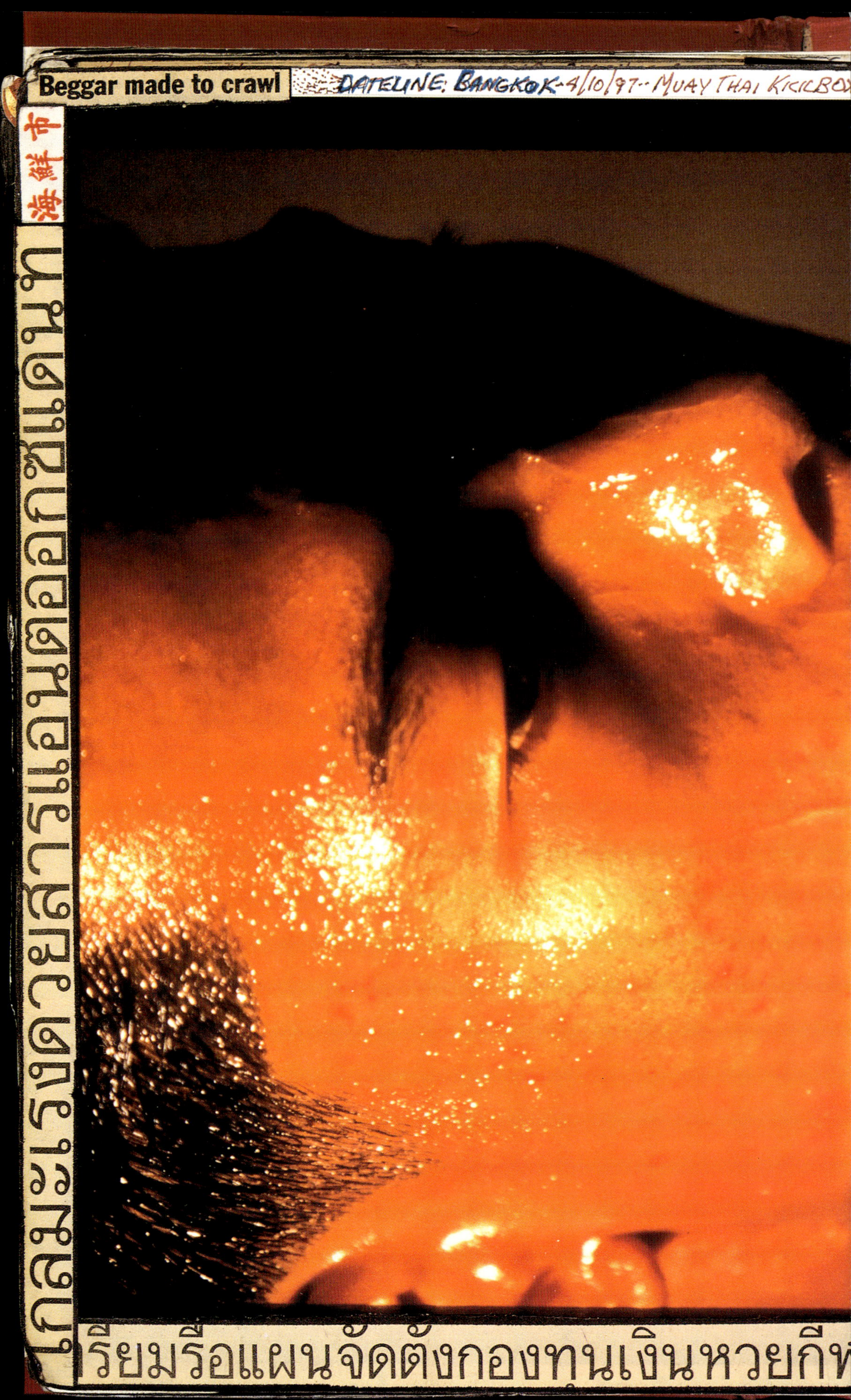

Beggar made to crawl

DATELINE: BANGKOK-4/10/97-- MUAY THAI KICKBOX

海鮮市

เกลมะเรงดวยสารแอนตออกซแดนท

รียมรือแผนจัดตังกองทุนเงินหวยกี

PTS. ILL. THE BOXER, GREASED WITH LINIMENT, IN PRE-FIGHT BUDDIST TRANCE.

THE ORIENT
BANGKOK

ได้ลงทุนในปีเดียว/โยงช่วยพยุงอีสเทิร์นซีบอร์

PHOTO
TAKEN AT
LUMPINEE
FRIDAY NITE
9/10/97
BANGK

Sea Food
MARKET &
RESTAURANT
IF IT SWIMS WE HAVE IT

ทมมี'ขึ้นจากเดิมเอ็นดับอยู่ที่54ขอ

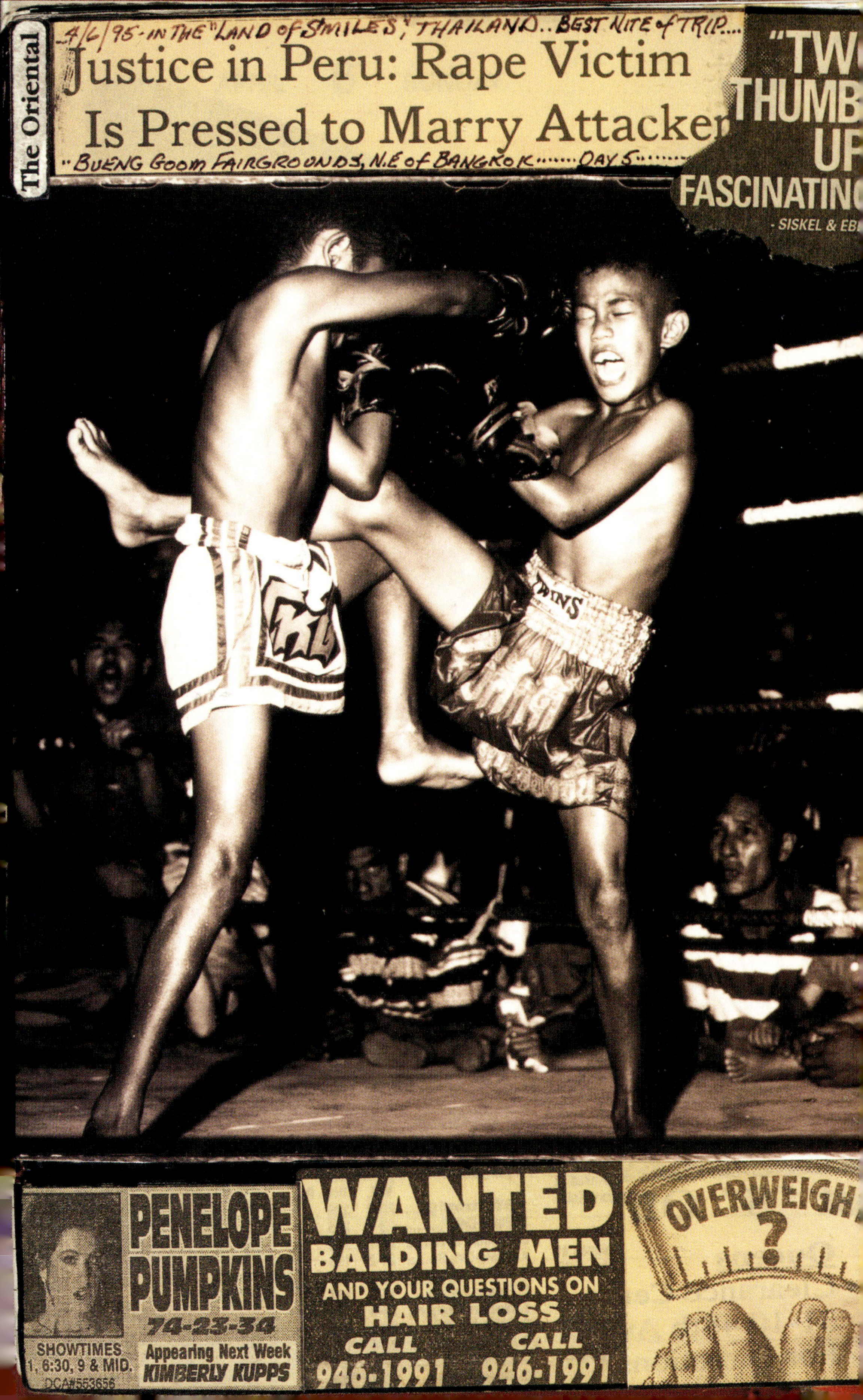

The Oriental

4/6/95 - IN THE "LAND of SMILES," THAILAND.. BEST NITE of TRIP...

Justice in Peru: Rape Victim Is Pressed to Marry Attacker

..BUENG GOOM FAIRGROUNDS, N.E of BANGKOK...... DAY 5 ......

"TW
THUMB
UF
FASCINATING
- SISKEL & EB

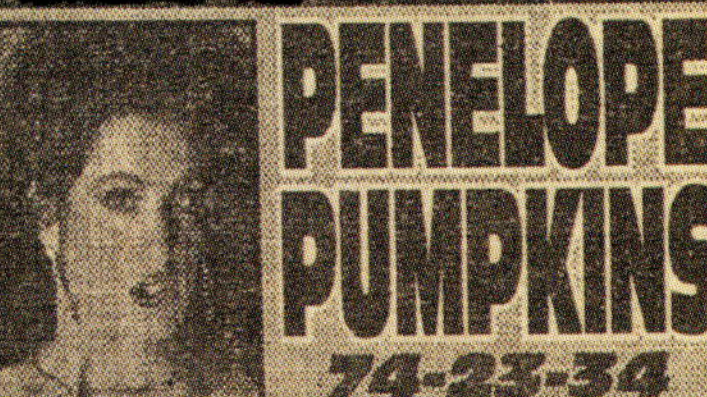

WANTED
BALDING MEN
AND YOUR QUESTIONS ON
HAIR LOSS
CALL 946-1991 CALL 946-1991

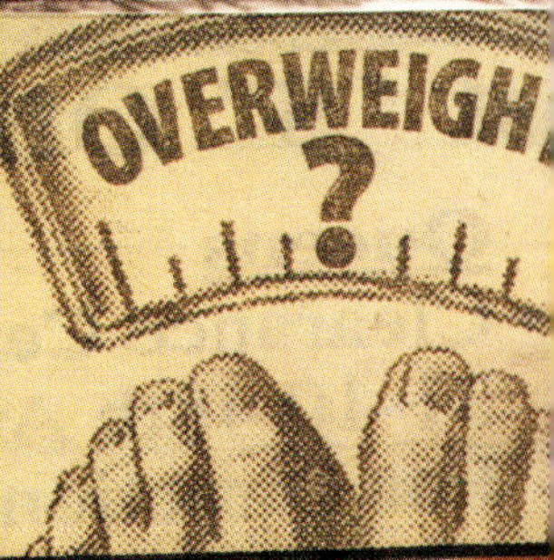

..SPORTS ILL. MAG.. ..APRIL 7, 1995.. ..MUAY THAI STORY..

KICKBOXER - BANGKOK, THAILAND - PRASIT FACKTY

ธีเปิด–ปิด‘บางกอกเกมส์’180ล้าน/เปิ

BANGKOK, THAILAND .... ORIENTAL HOTEL .... KICKBOXING STORY - S.I. 4/14

OFF DAY - POOLTIME ... NAME OF THE DAY ..... NUMSOCKNOY YOOTGANGUMTORN ... DINNER SEAFOOD MARKET ......

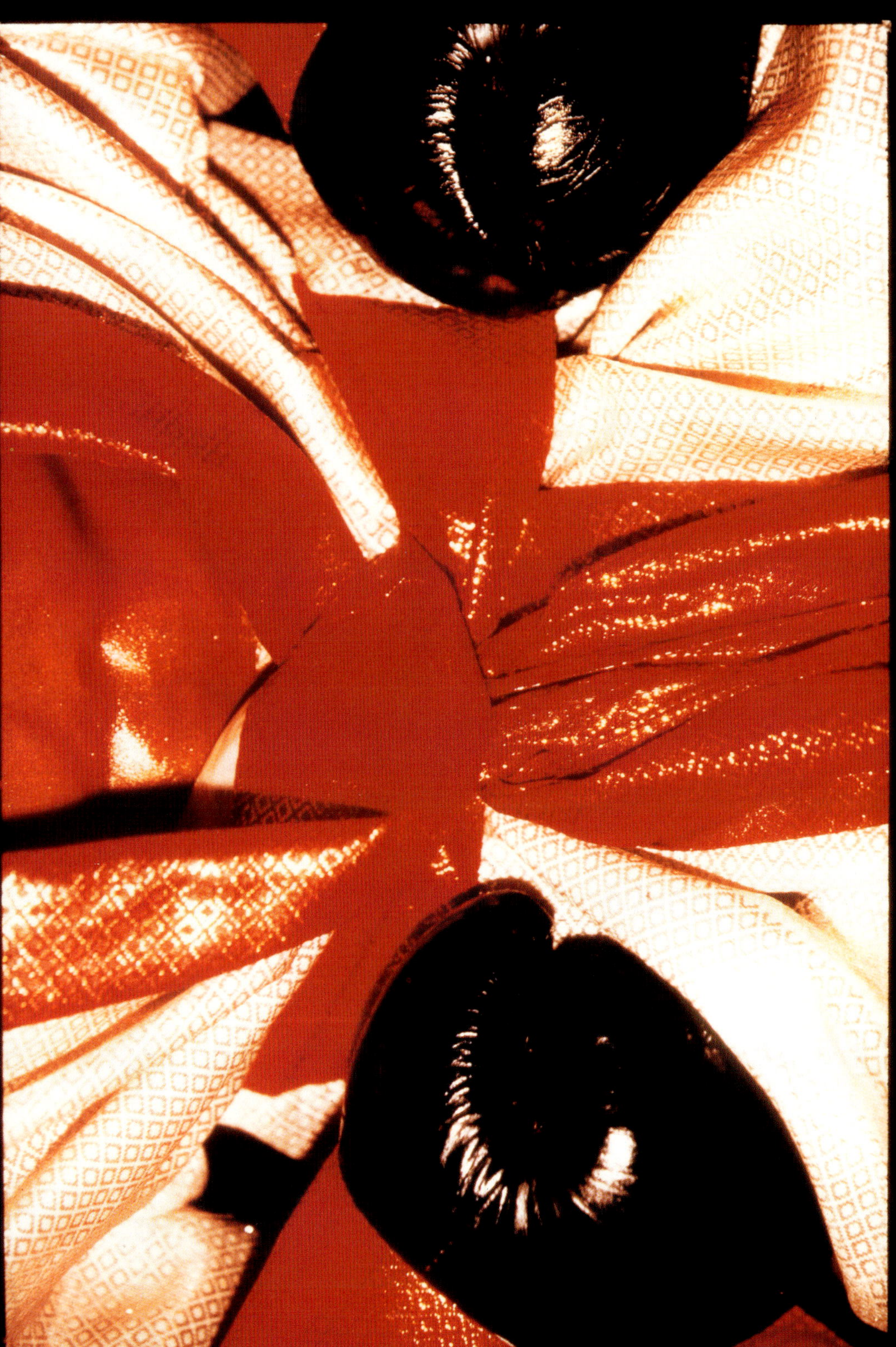

ROBED MUAY THAI BOXER WITH SIX PACK, RATCHADUMNEN STADIUM

ANGKOK for N.Y. VIA TOKYO..... ARRIVE HOME BEFORE I LEFT to PEACEFUL+CLEAN N.Y...

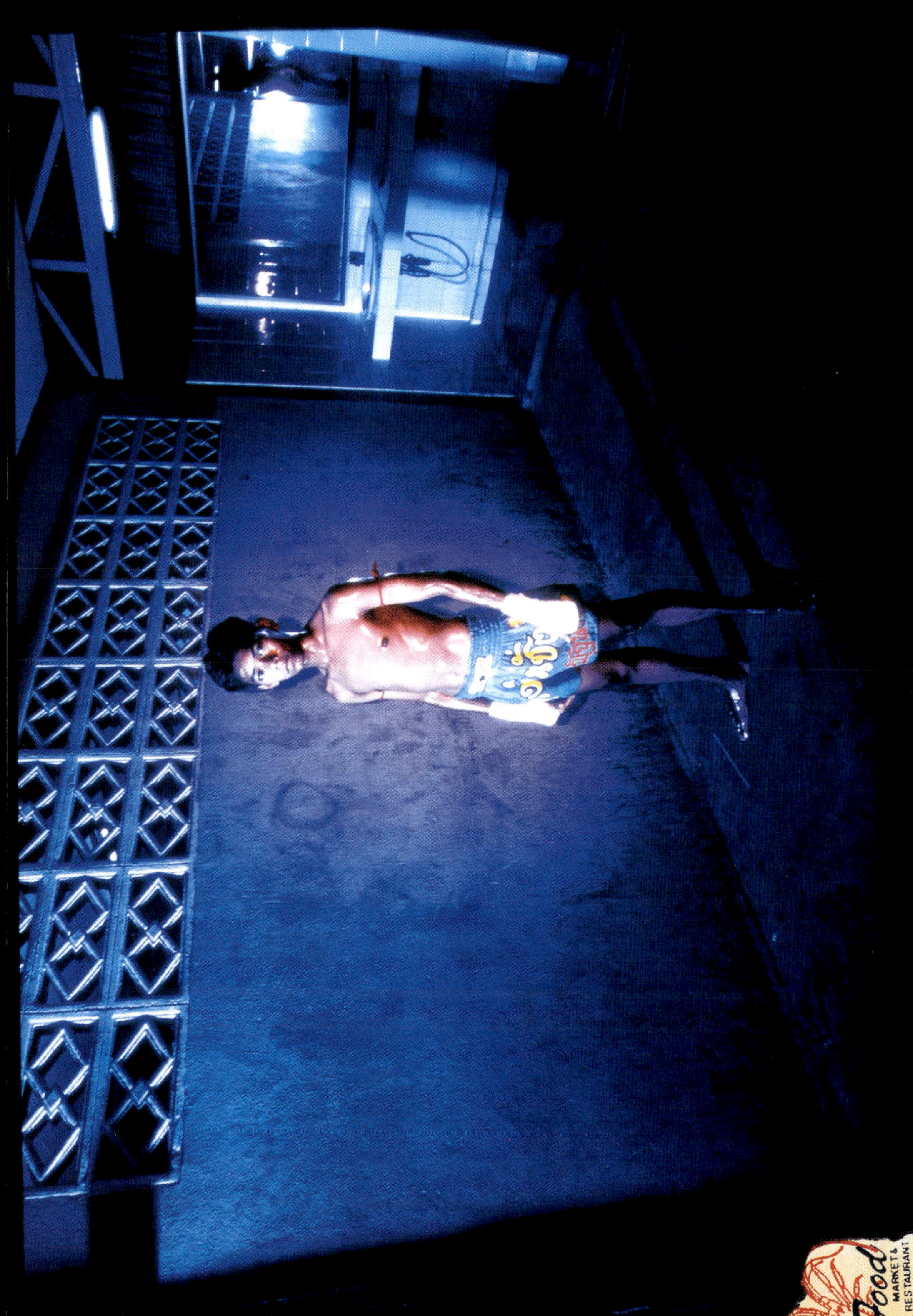

MENS ROOM, LUMPINEE STADIUM, PRE-FIGHT SHADOW BOXING.... BLUE MOOD.......

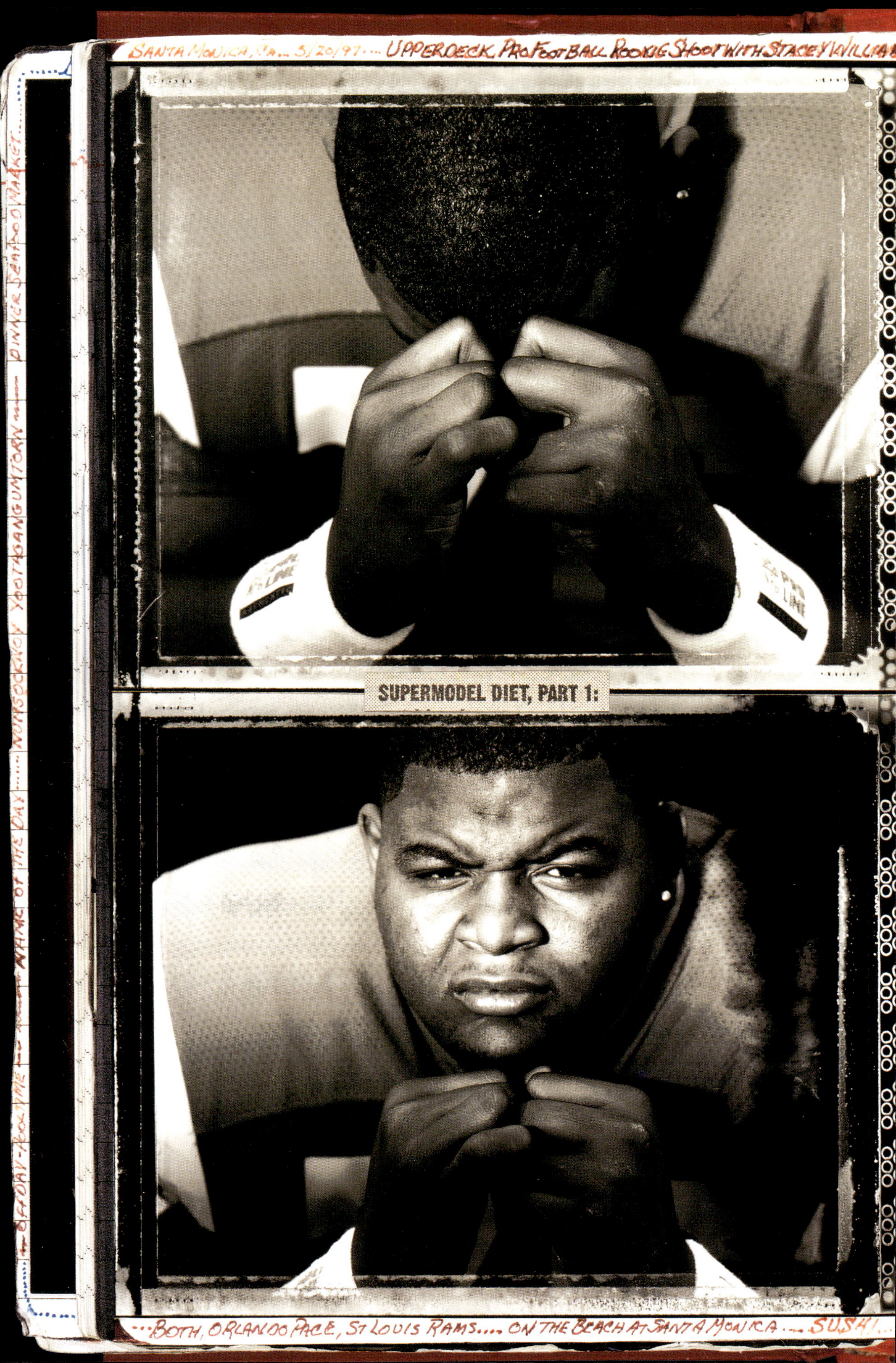

SANTA MONICA, CA... 5/20/97.... UPPERDECK PRO FOOTBALL ROOKIE SHOOT WITH STACEY WILLIAM

SUPERMODEL DIET, PART 1:

...BOTH, ORLANDO PACE, ST LOUIS RAMS.... ON THE BEACH AT SANTA MONICA.... SUSHI...

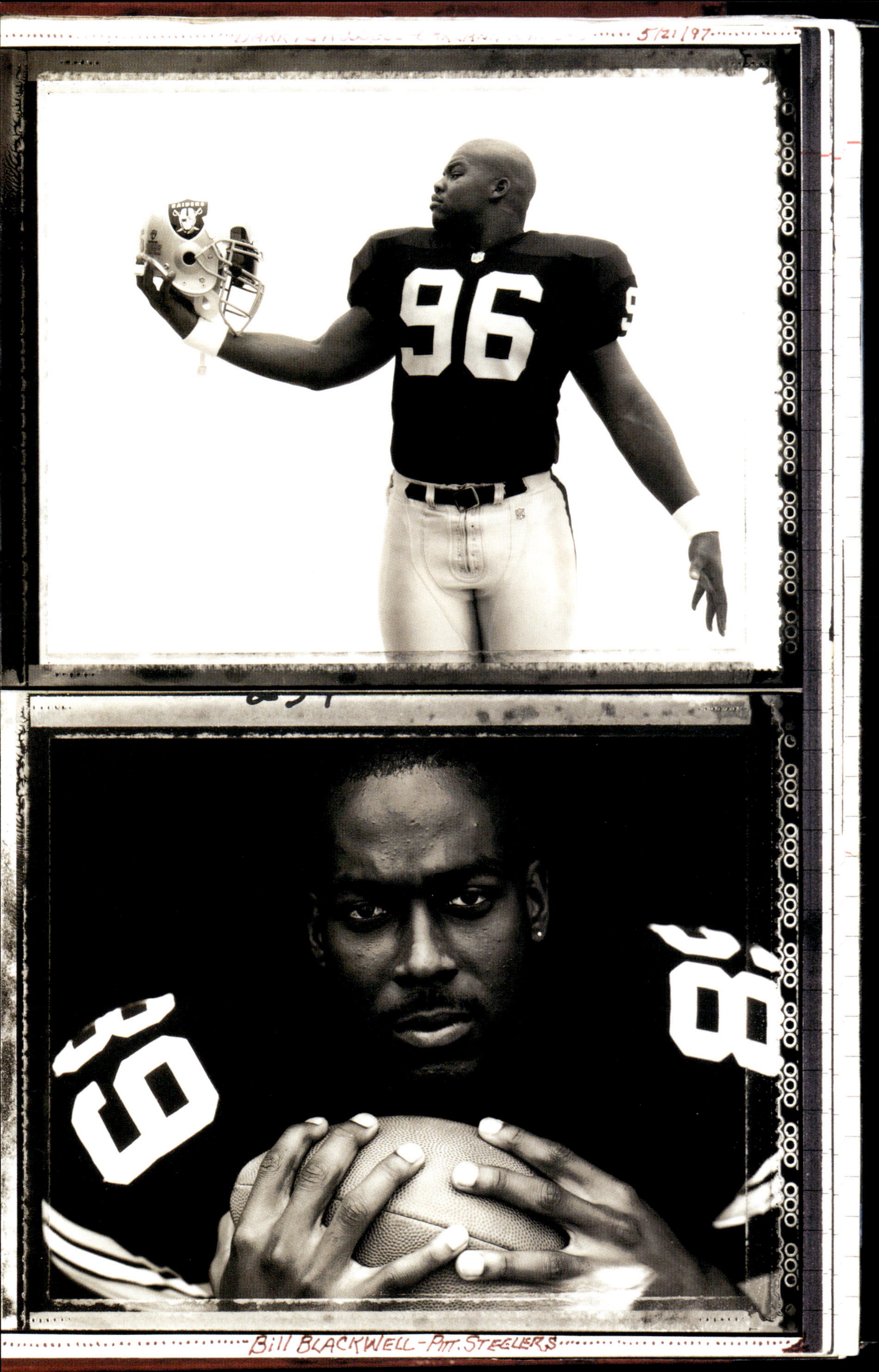

5/21/97

Bill Blackwell-Pitt. Steelers

OPRAH'S

Halitosis Treatment Center

PROSTATE ENLARGEMENT

1-800-MD-HAIRS

11/25/97 .. Dateline Tampa Bay, Fla; Minnesota Vikings lose to Tampa Bay Bucs., on a splendid day, at "the Sombrero." Coach Tony Dungy (Below), Robert Smith (right). Stay in Clearwater, Ramon asst's. Shoot for S.I. and Canon, using new Stabilizer lens.

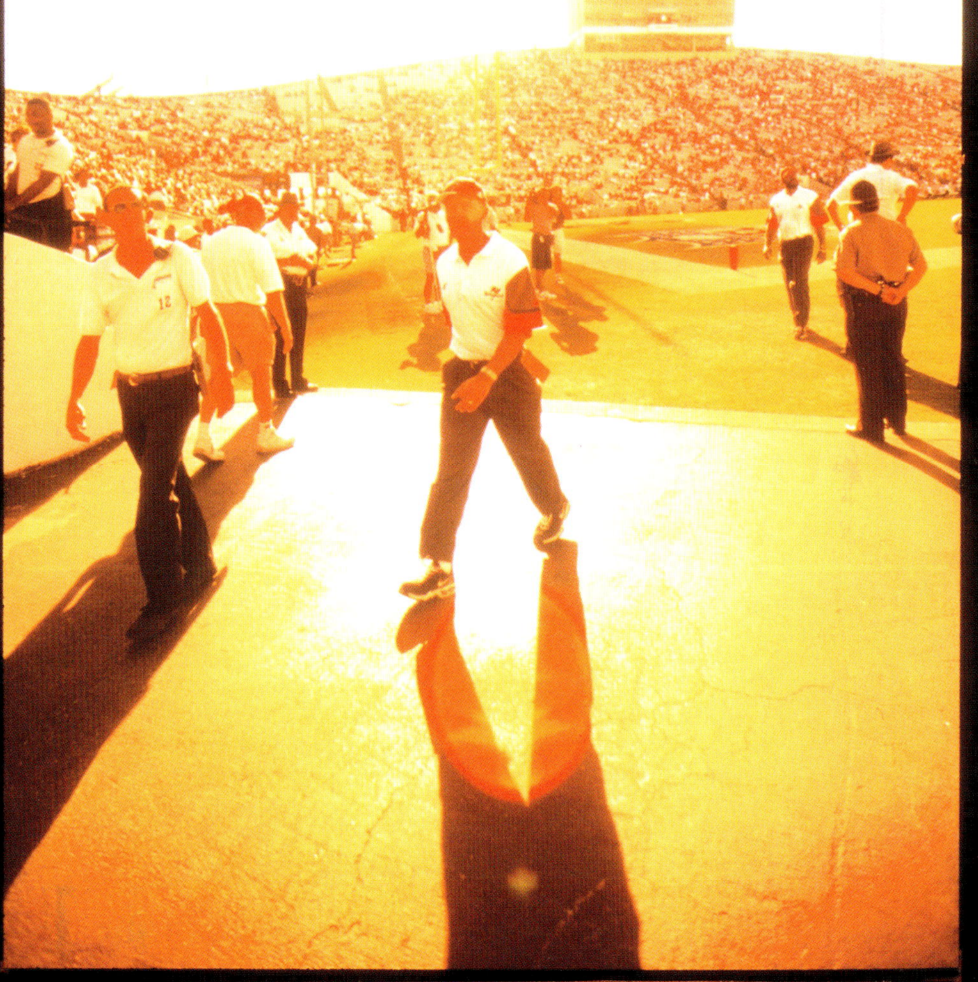

test-tube baby!

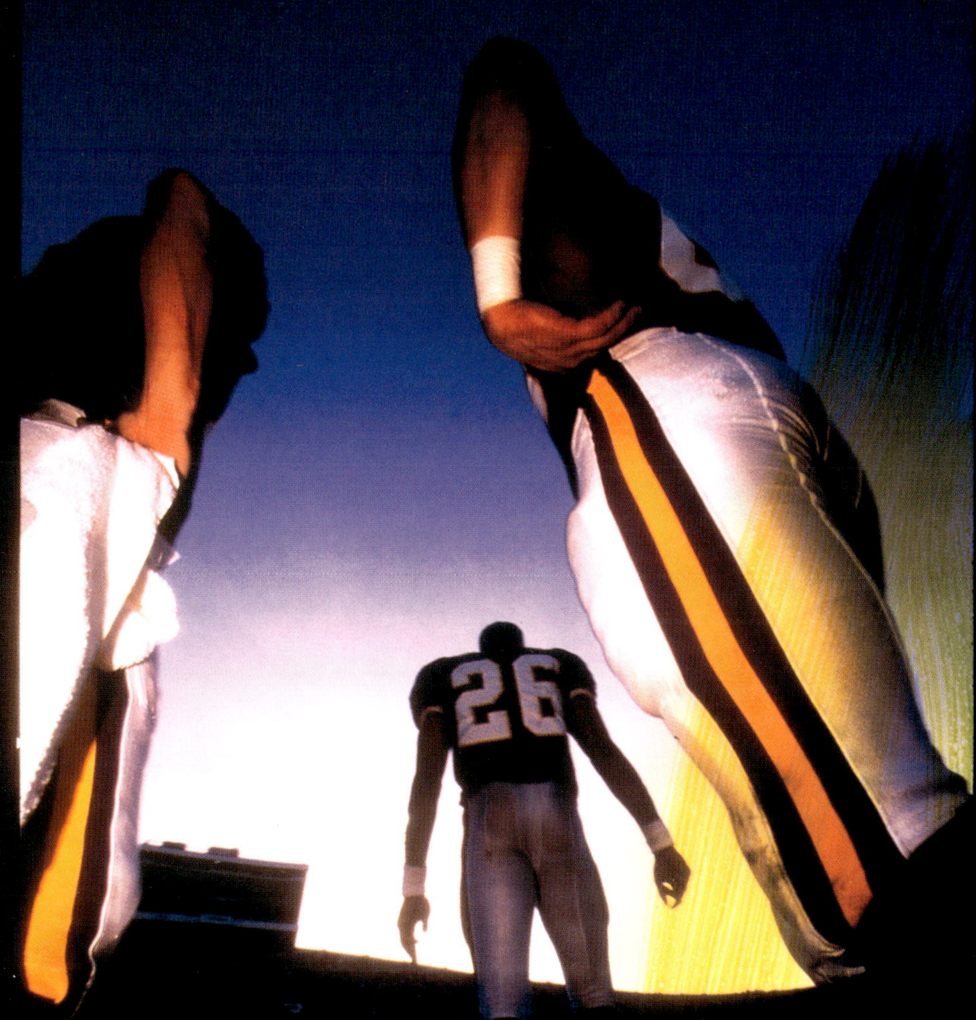
EW FACE!
Stop Premature Ejaculation
Plastic surgeon tells:
Celebs battle the bottle…
26
Baby Is Left in Box; Mother Is 12, Note Says

PLANET MONTAUK ~ JULY, 19, 1997 ~ PHOTO OF EDDIE GEORGE ...

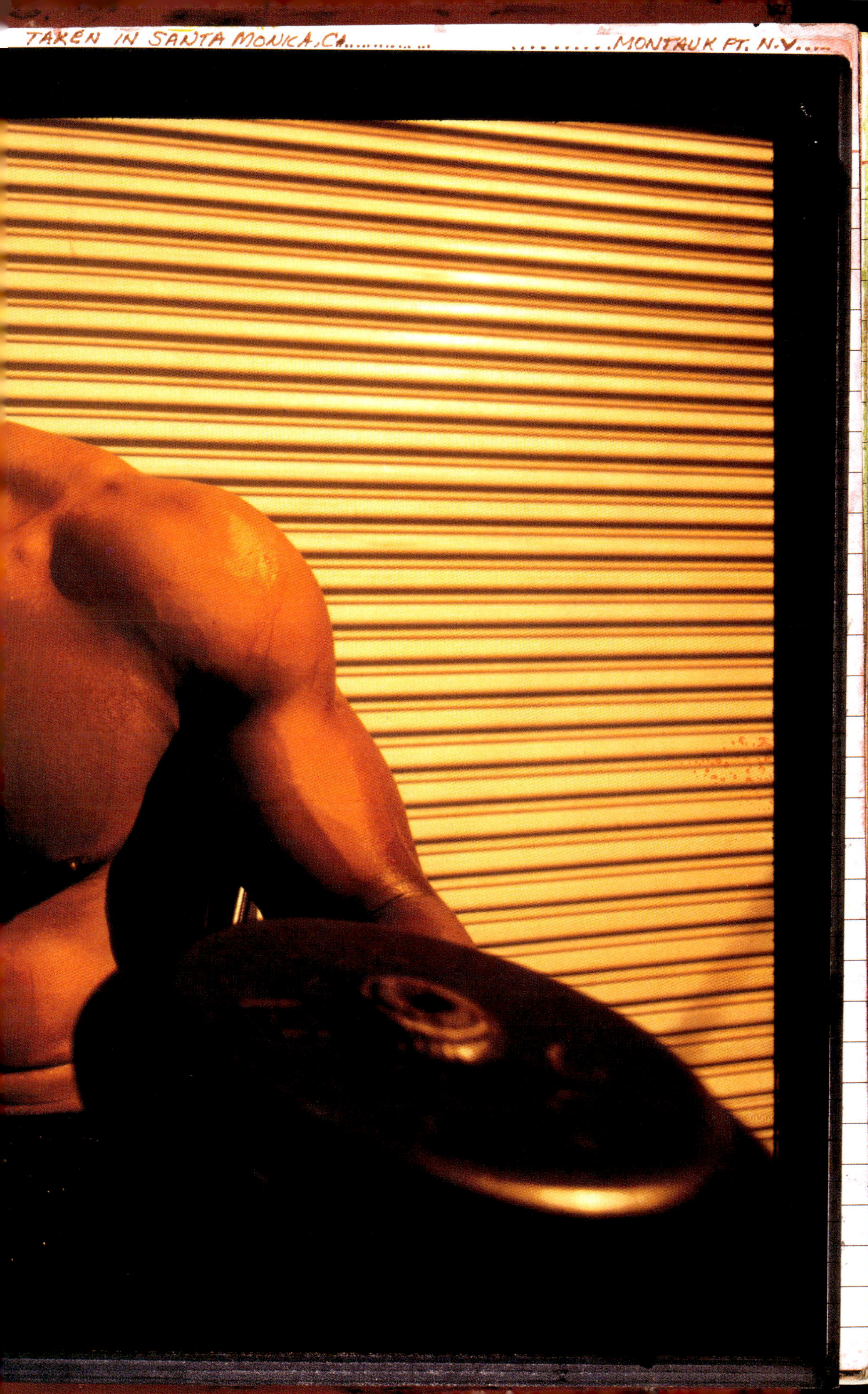
TAKEN IN SANTA MONICA, CA..............
..........MONTAUK PT. N.Y.....

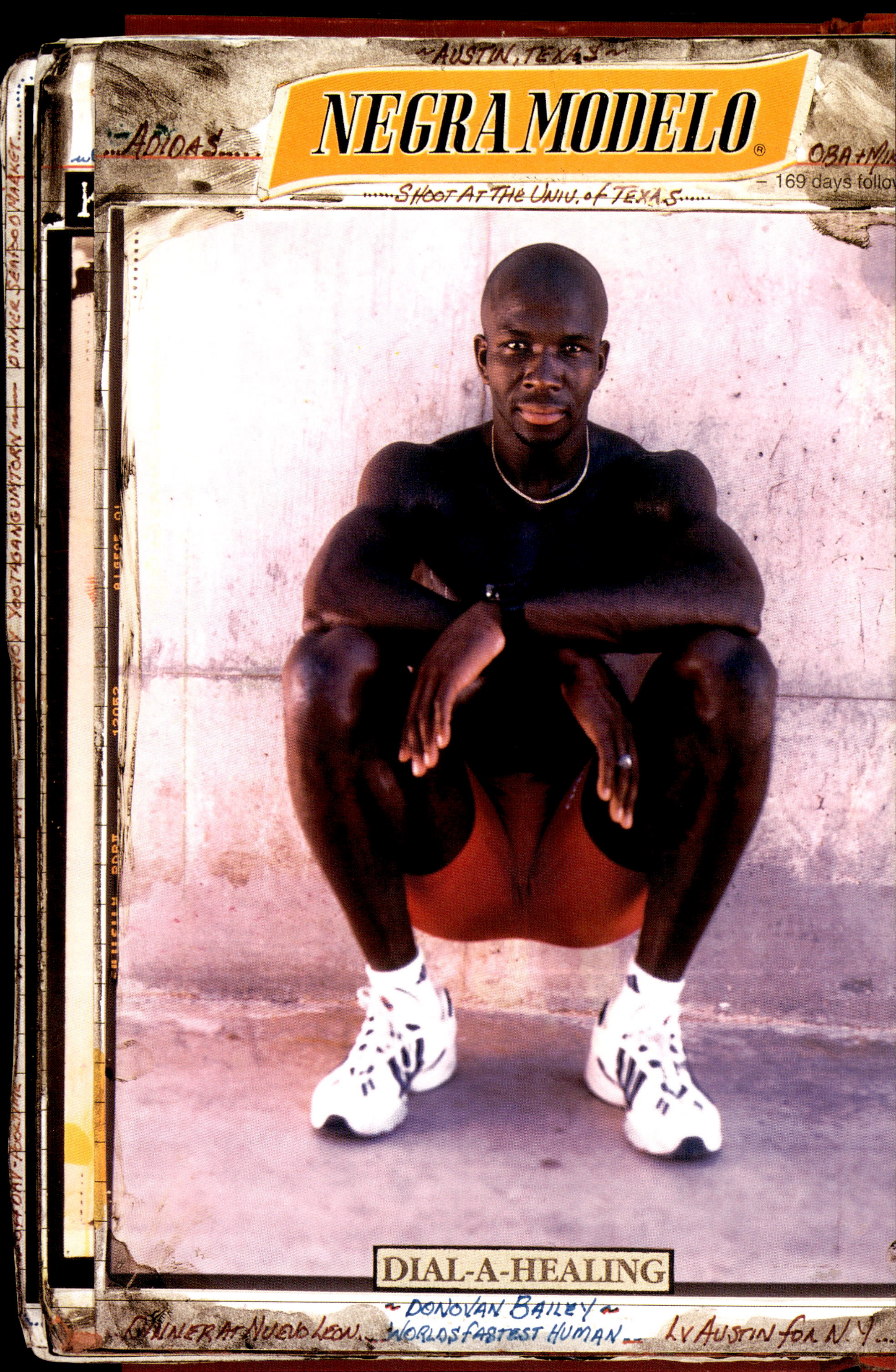

~AUSTIN, TEXAS~

NEGRA MODELO®

...ADIDAS.....

.....SHOOT AT THE UNIV. of TEXAS.....

– 169 days follo

DIAL-A-HEALING

~DONOVAN BAILEY~

DINNER AT NUEVO LEON... WORLDS FASTEST HUMAN... LV AUSTIN FOR N.Y....

RIVERDALE ..... WEDNESDAY **16** JULY

GOODWILL GAMES SHOOT. N.Y.C. ..... SUSHIZEN

1997 197th day – 168 days follow

Marriott 216 696-9200

ROOFTOP SHOOT. 43 FL. ON 3RD + 46TH ST. OZONE ALERT + AIR INVERSION ALMOST ELIMINATES SKYLINE .....

CALL A.D. IN ATLANTA – STOCKS GO CRAZY!

..... SHOOT LASTS FOR 1 HOUR. COLIN + NO JOB ASSIST. ..... TWO FILM CREWS + 15 PEOPLE ON ROOFTOP. DINNER WITH JIM McD. .....

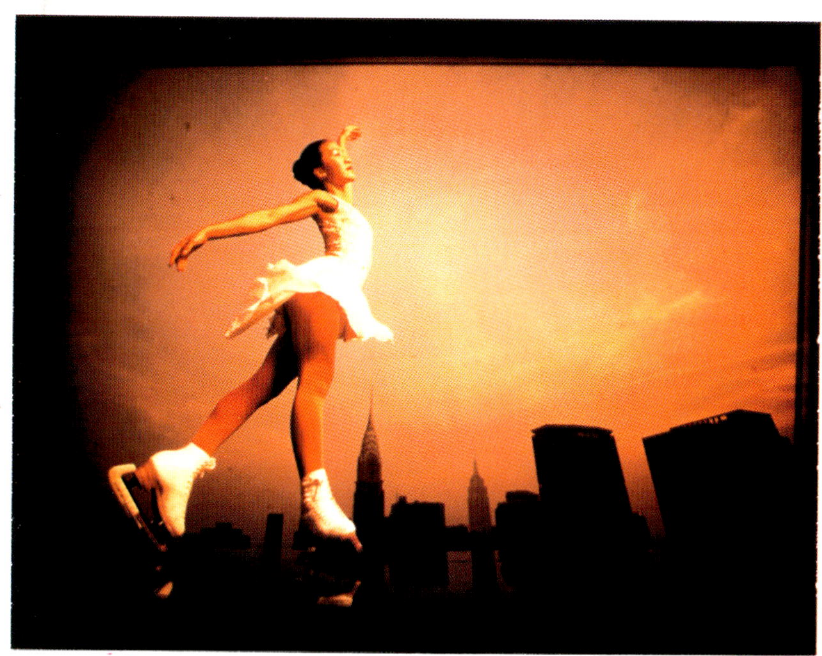

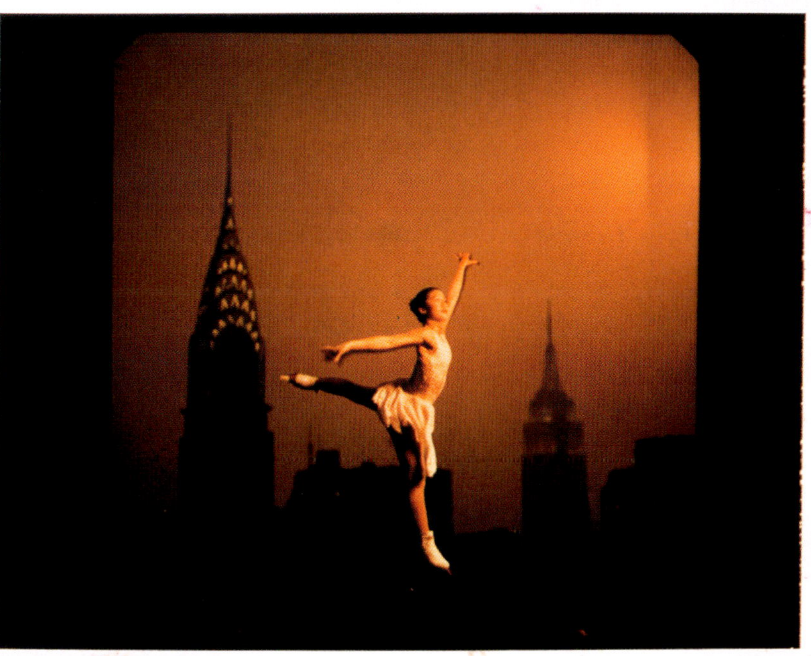

~ MICHELLE QUON ~

STANDARD DIARY®

NYPD TORTURE SCANDAL

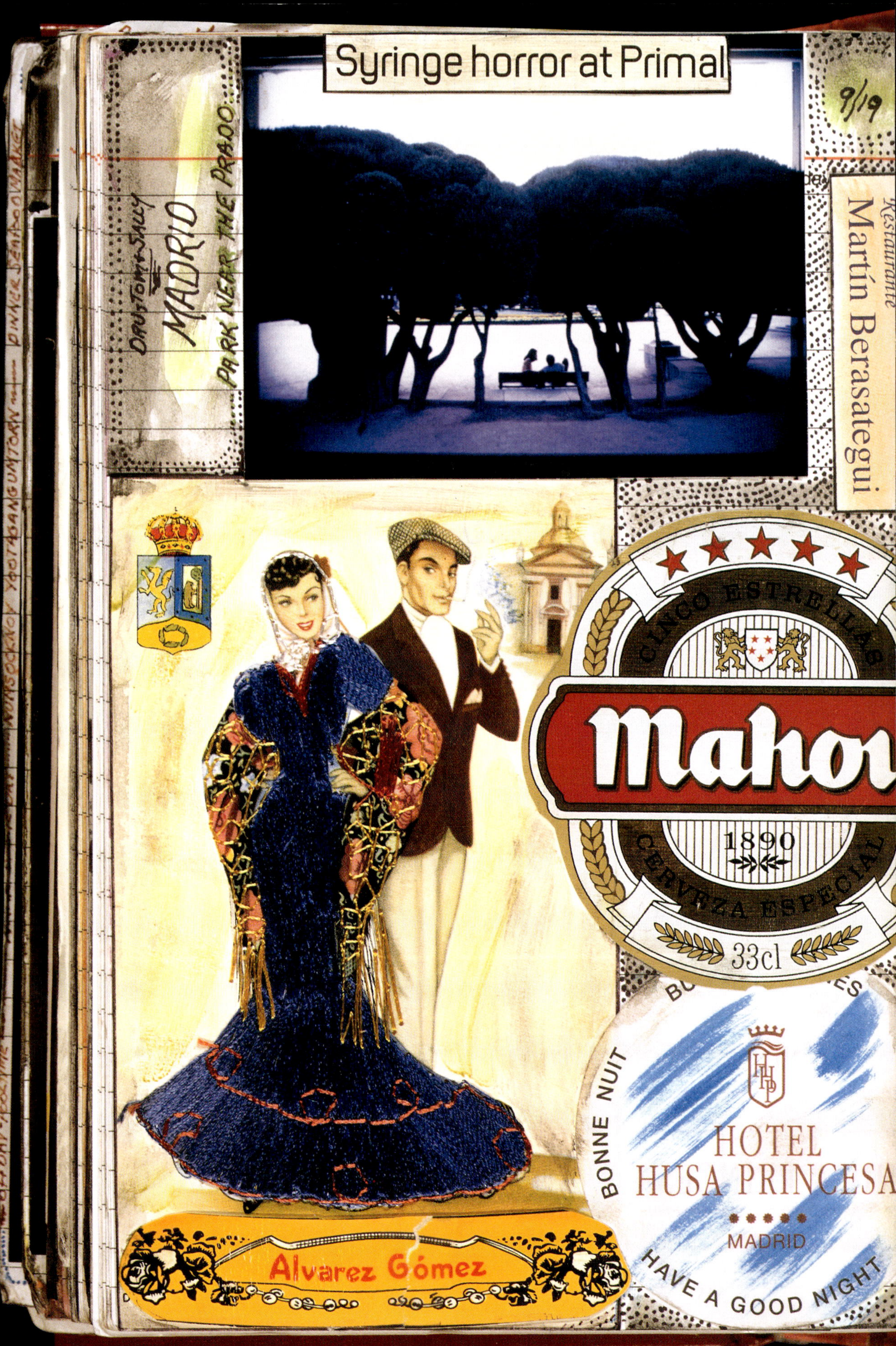

Syringe horror at Primal
9/19
DAVID, TOM & SALLY
MADRID
PARK NEAR THE PRADO
Restaurante
Martín Berasategui
CINCO ESTRELLAS
Mahou
1890
CERVEZA ESPECIAL
33cl
BONNE NUIT
HOTEL
HUSA PRINCESA
MADRID
HAVE A GOOD NIGHT
Alvarez Gómez

MADRID.....

MEET SEXY LOCALS!
Try it FREE! code 2244. 18+
212-813-0520 OR 201-498-0700

ARRIVE AT STADIUM 7:30AM.
...PRADO MUSEUM

20 SEPTEMBER

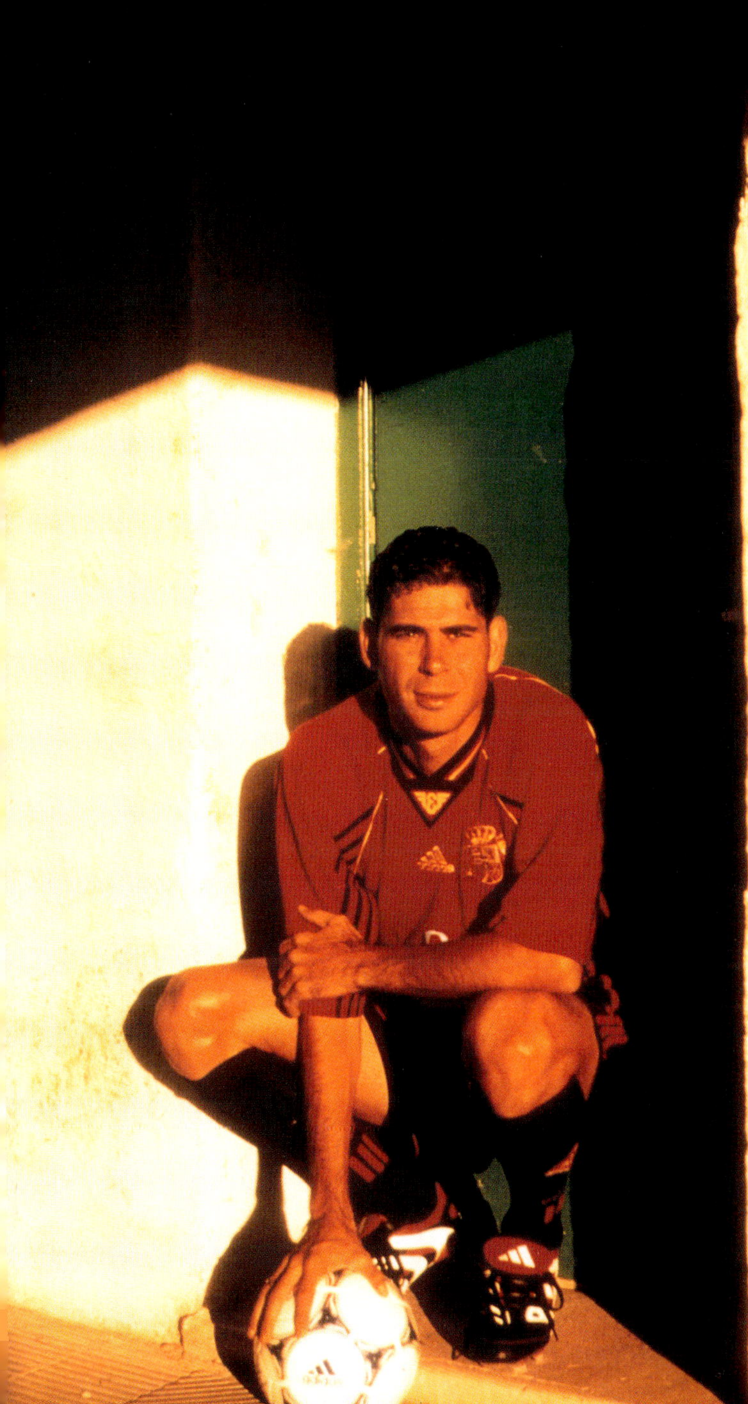

.......HIERRO.......

LV. FOR J.F.K.......

adidas

Riverdale...

Brain-dead woman to be kept alive for fetus

s follow

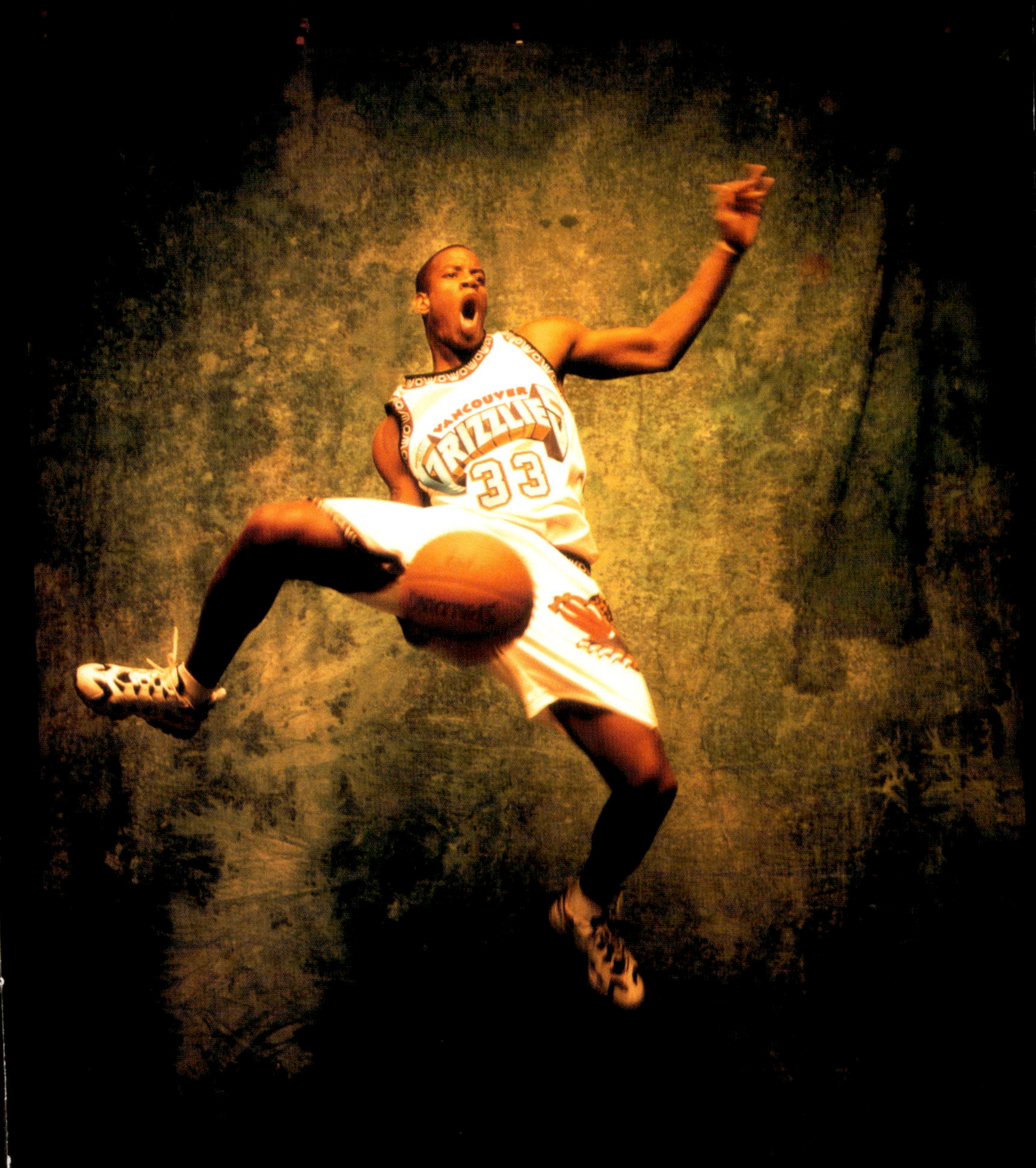

...Antonio Daniels...

Shoot Day-Upperdeck, N.B.A. Rookie Shoot. Chantilly, Va... Fly H

..Sushi...

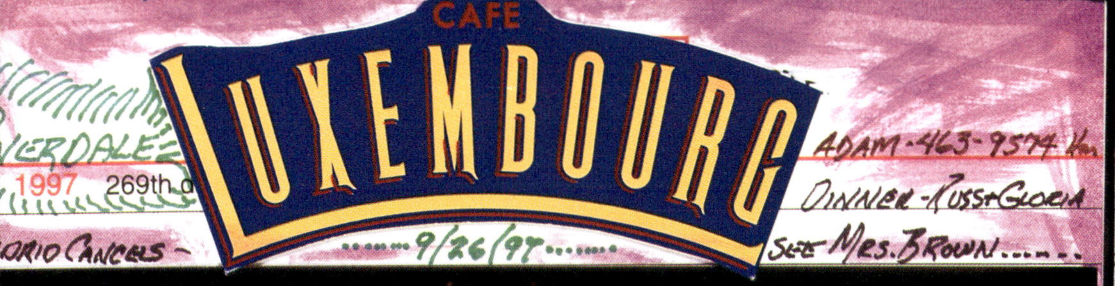

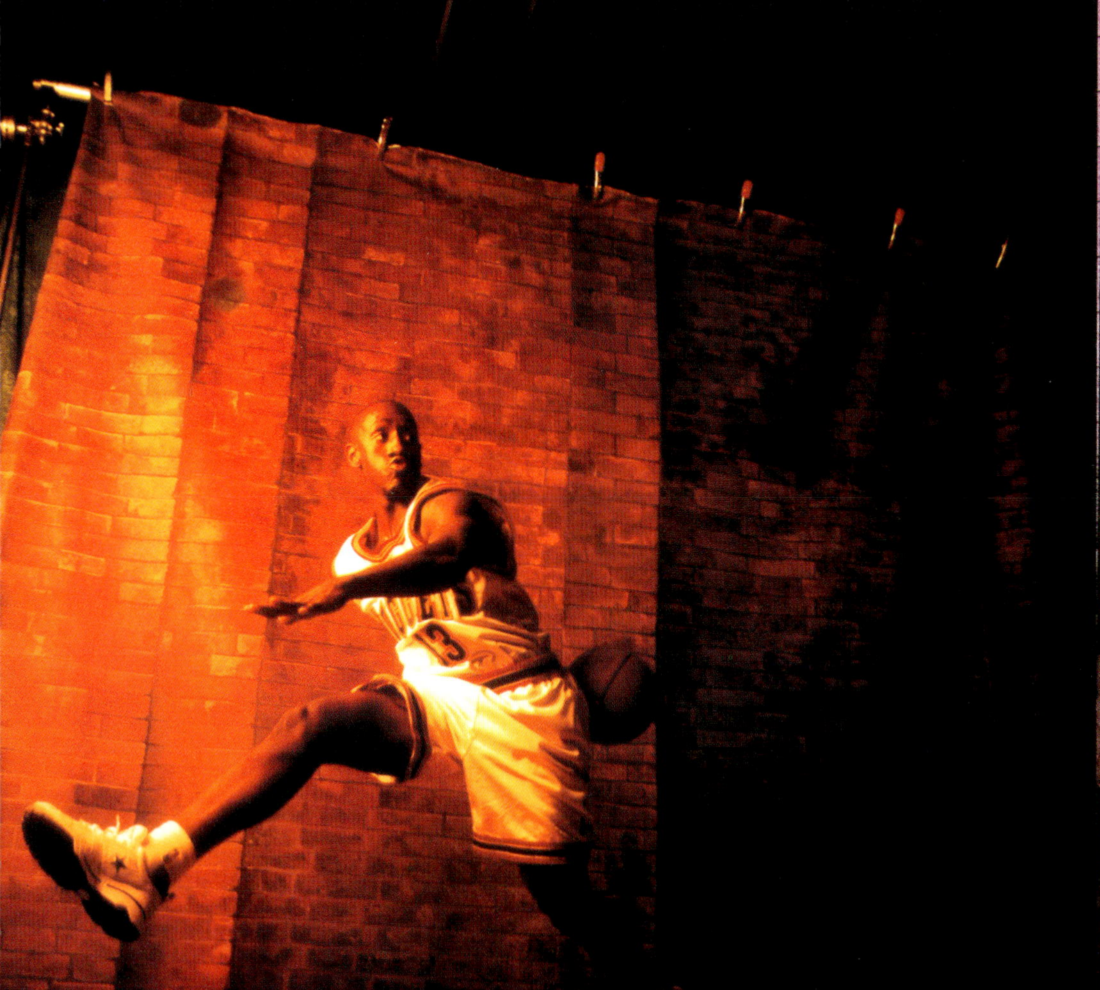

N.B.A. Fines Players Over Length of Shorts

Deaf Mexicans Seen —BOBBY JACKSON

...RIVERDALE ~ 4/20/97 ...VISIT ALI AT THE SHERATON ON 7th AVE AT 10:PM WITH BJORN + NEIL LEIFER
≈ ALI FIRST GETS HIS HAIR CUT AND WE THEN DO AN INKING SESSION WITH HIS HANDS.
WE LEAVE AT 12:15A.M.....

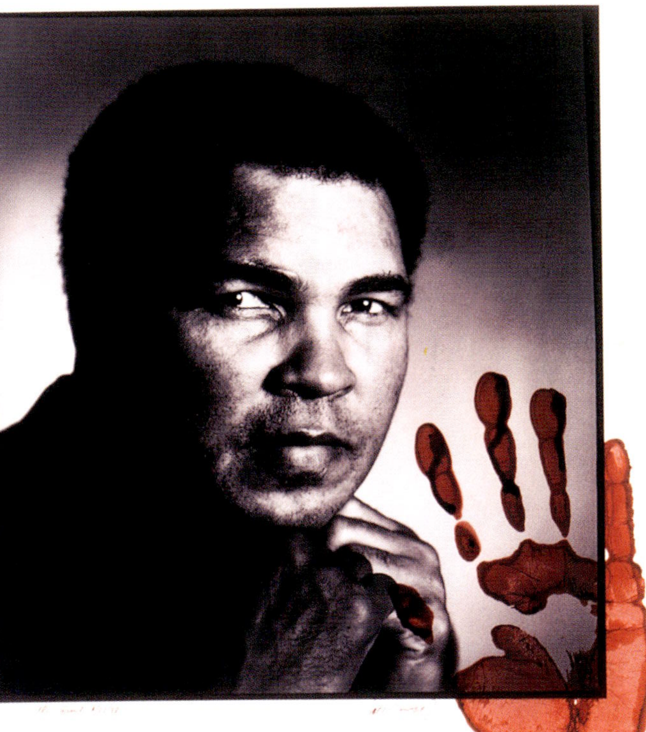

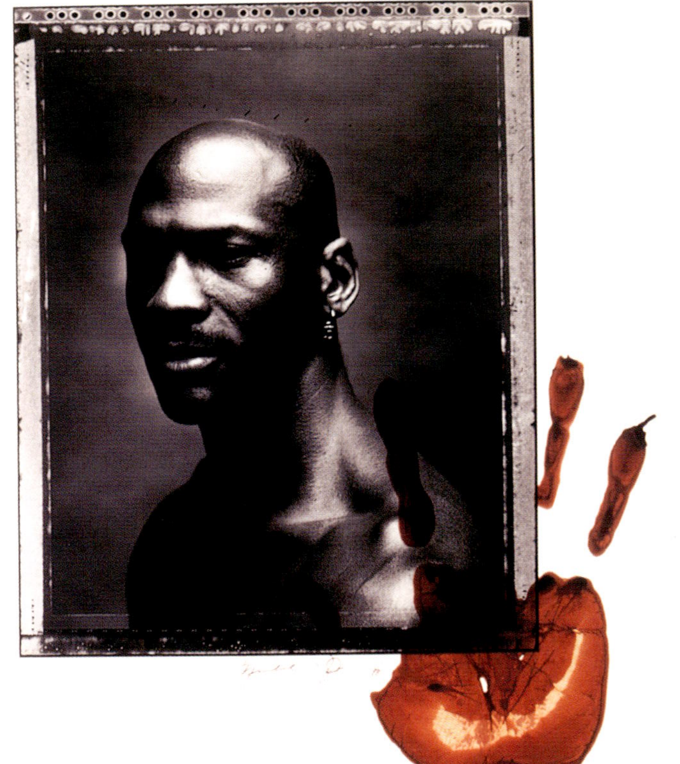

....ALI + AIR....

....RIVERDALE....

TUESDAY 21 APRIL

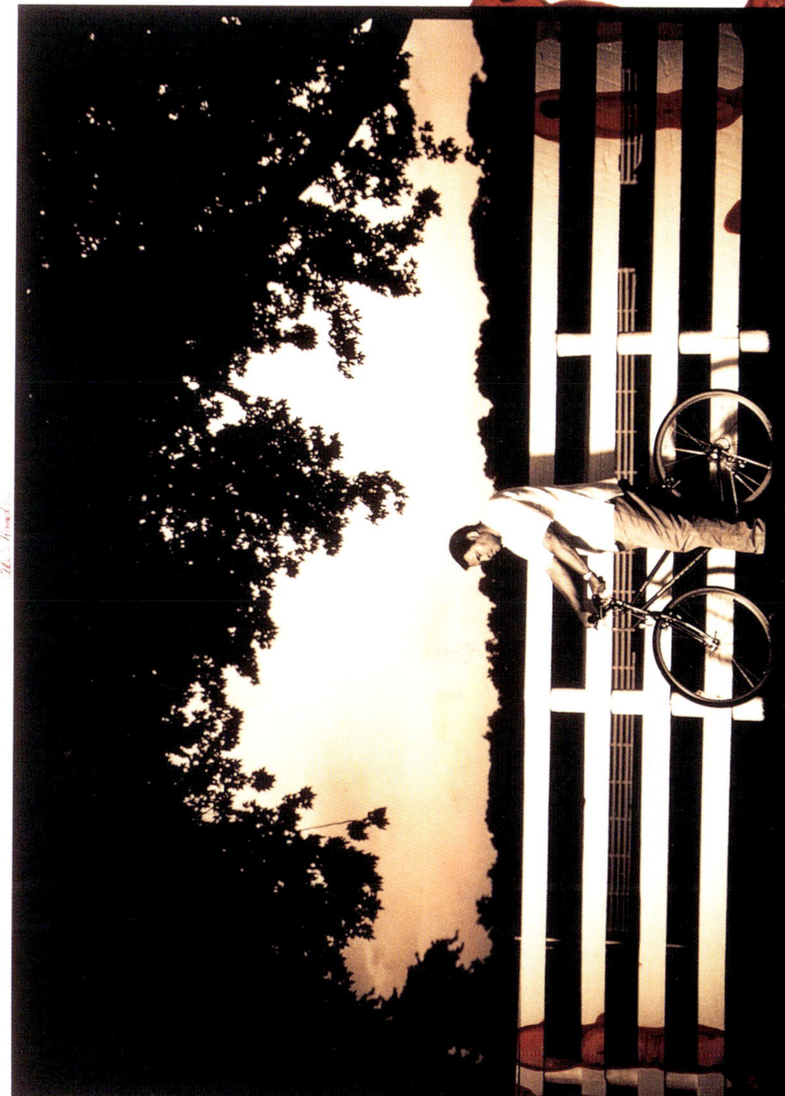

JANUARY 4

KAUAI'S CALL

HANALEI BAY, KAUAI

....POST SURF SESSION AT MIDDLES.....

...ON THE ROAD to HANALEI....

North Shore

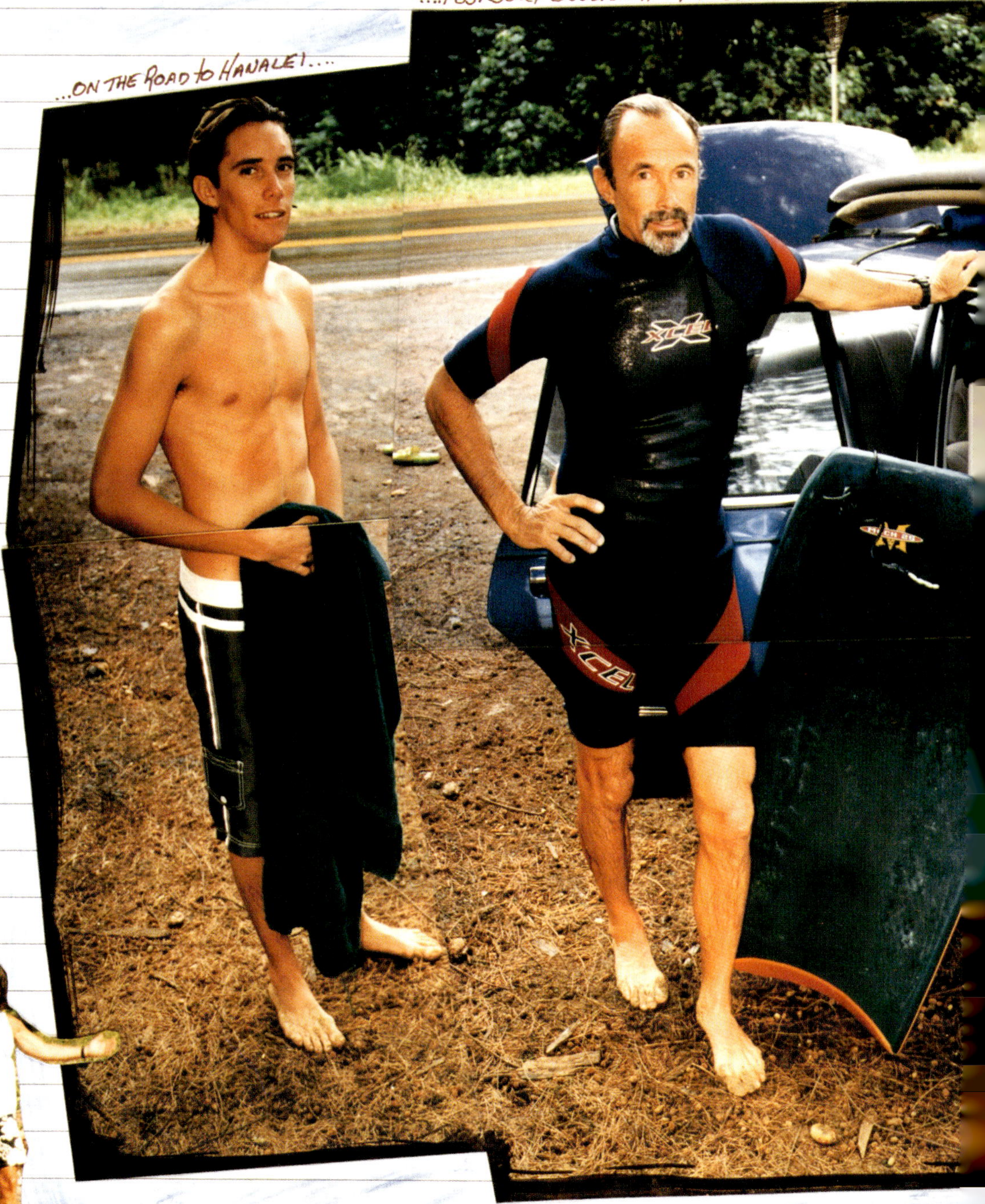

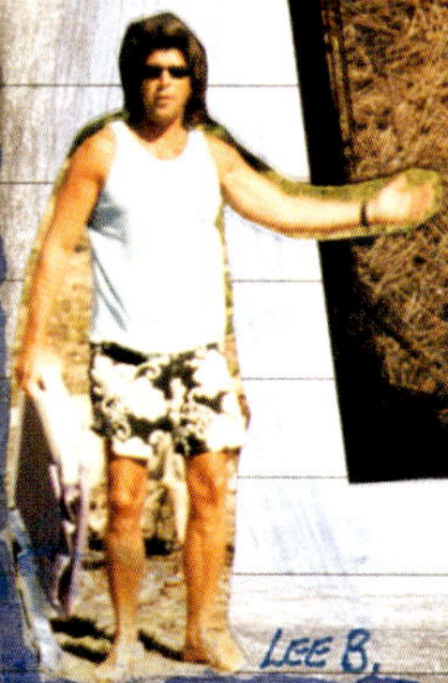

LEE B.

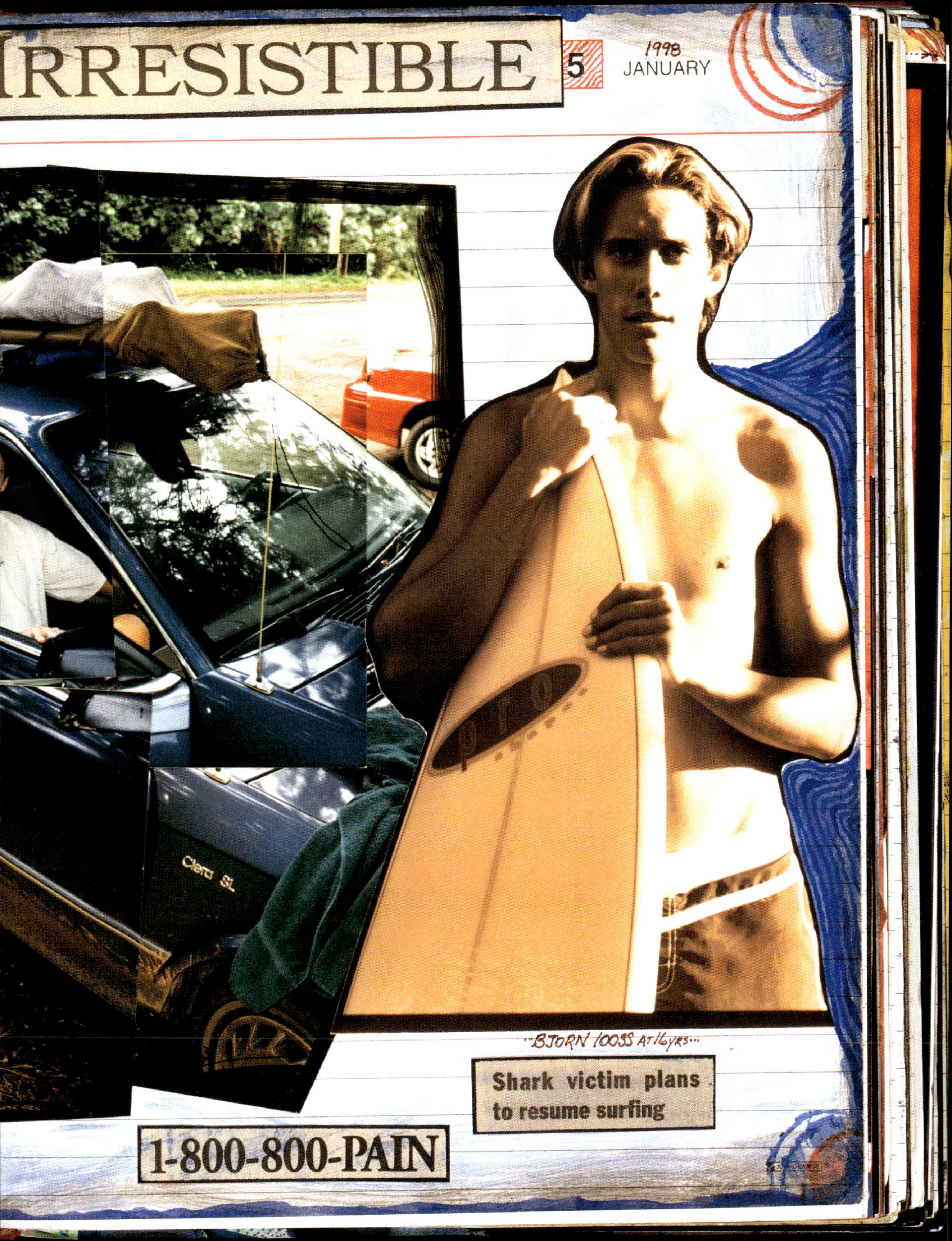

IRRESISTIBLE

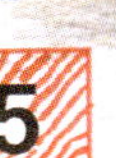

1998
JANUARY

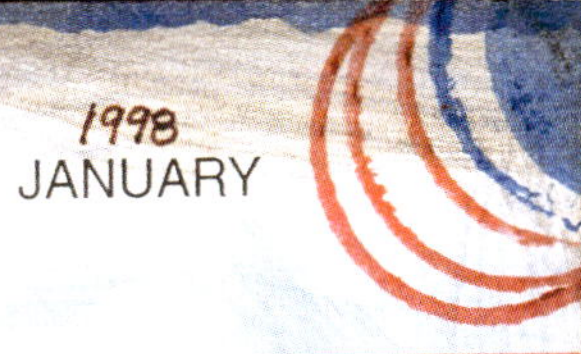

"BJORN IOOSS AT 16 YRS"

Shark victim plans to resume surfing

1-800-800-PAIN

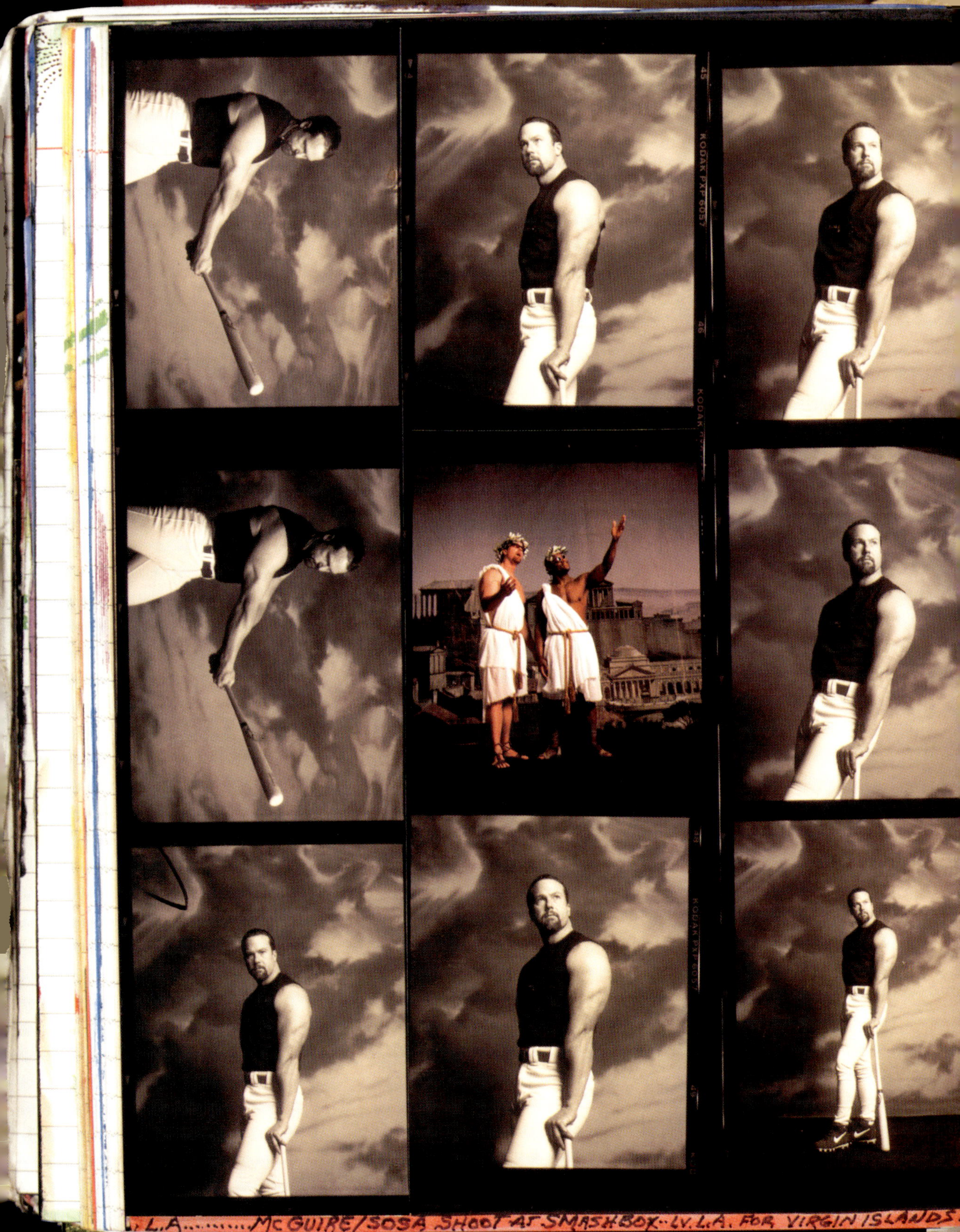
KODAK PXP 6057
L.A........ McGUIRE/SOSA SHOOT AT SMASHBOX.. LV. L.A. FOR VIRGIN ISLANDS.

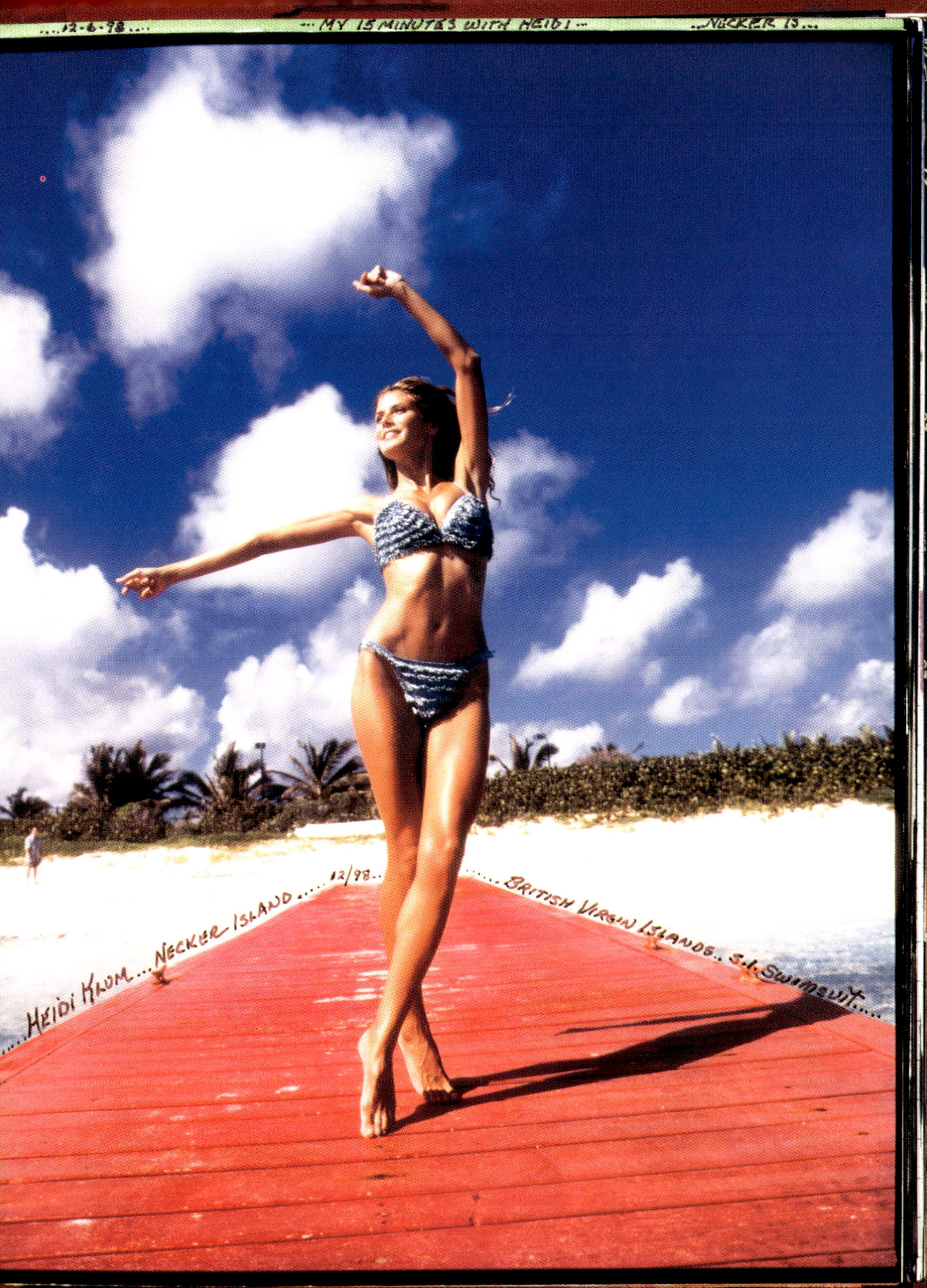
....12-6-98....
...MY 15 MINUTES WITH HEIDI...
...NECKER IS...
....HEIDI KLUM....NECKER ISLAND......12/98......
....BRITISH VIRGIN ISLANDS.. S.I. SWIMSUIT....

VIAGRA: The Love Drug

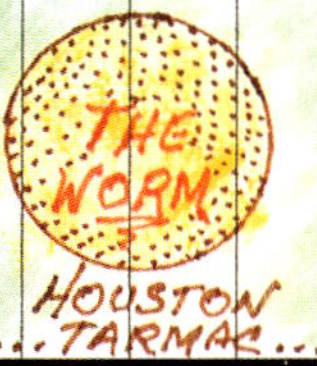

HOUSTON TARMAC

...TORTURED POWERLIFTER... BERTO CENTER...

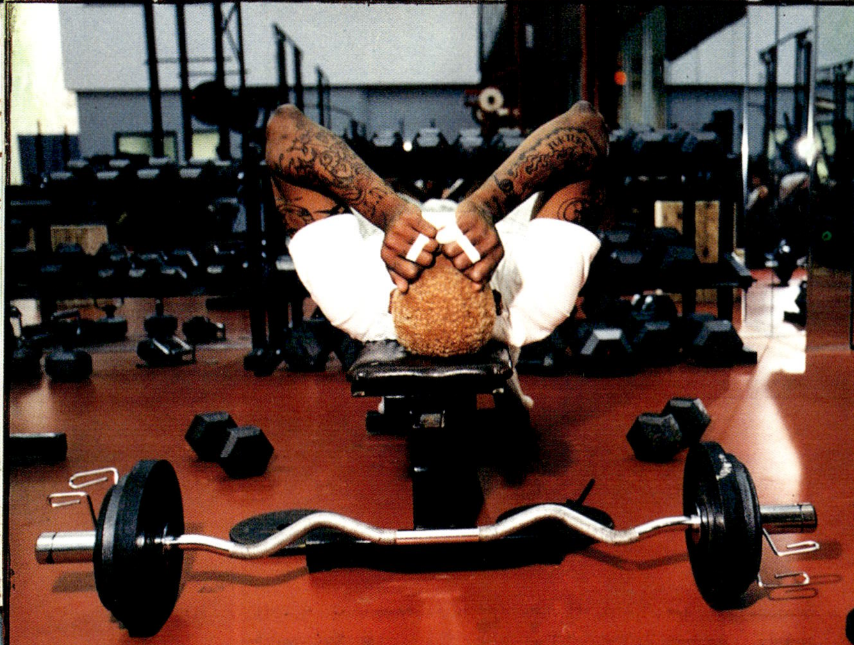

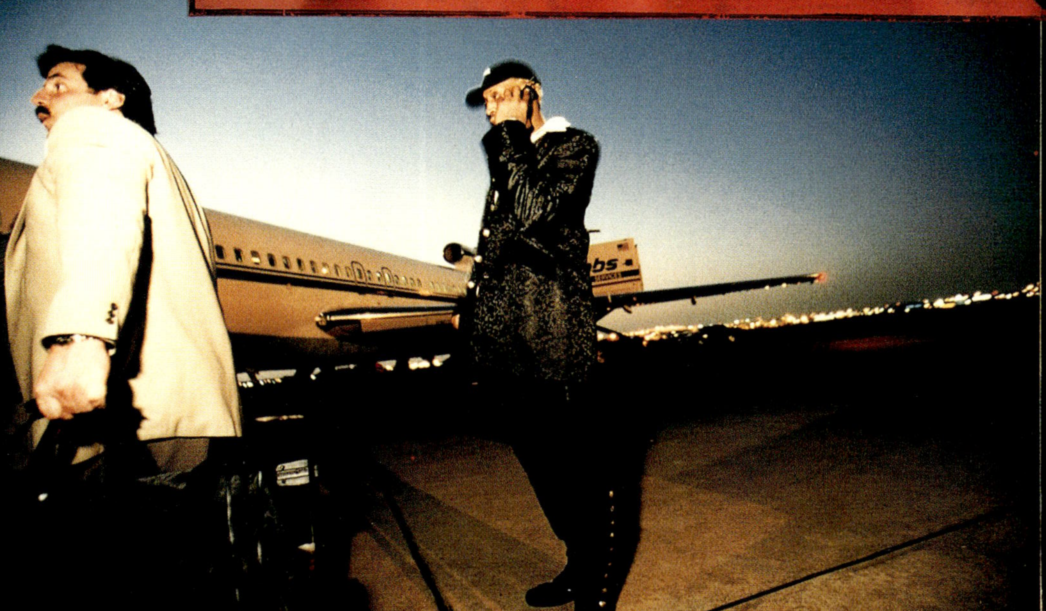

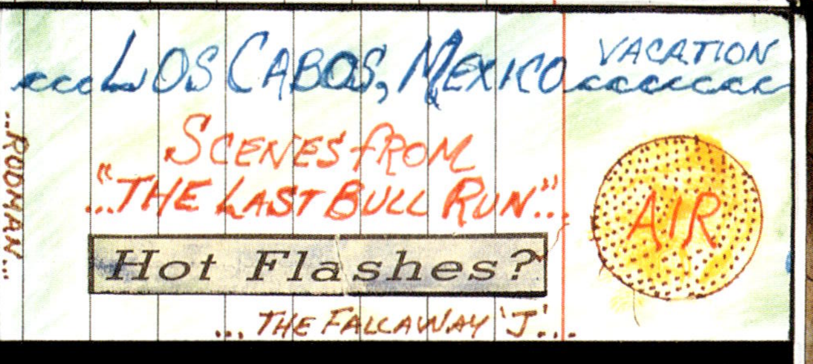

...RODMAN...

... THE FALLAWAY 'J'...

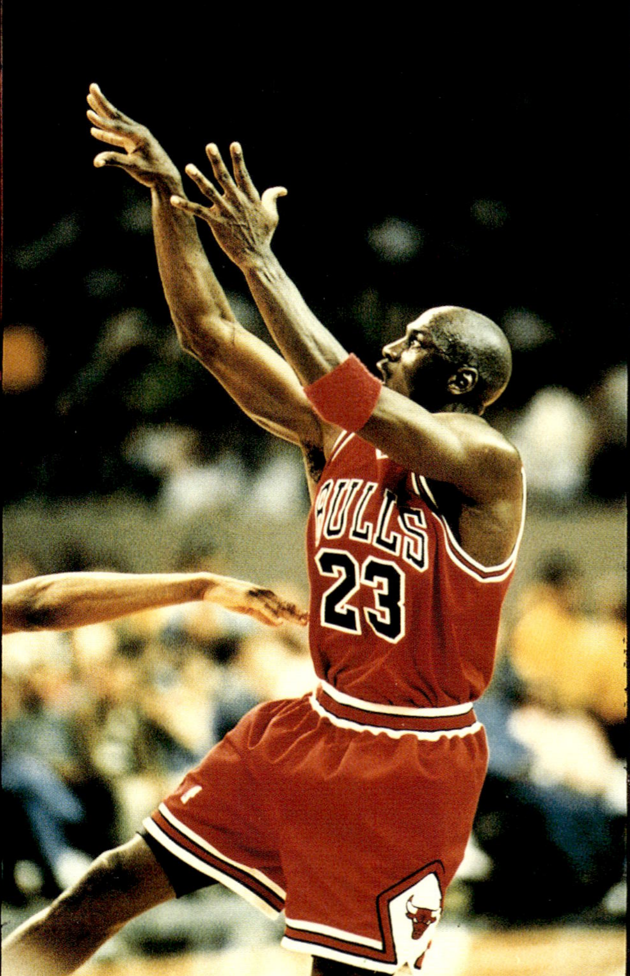

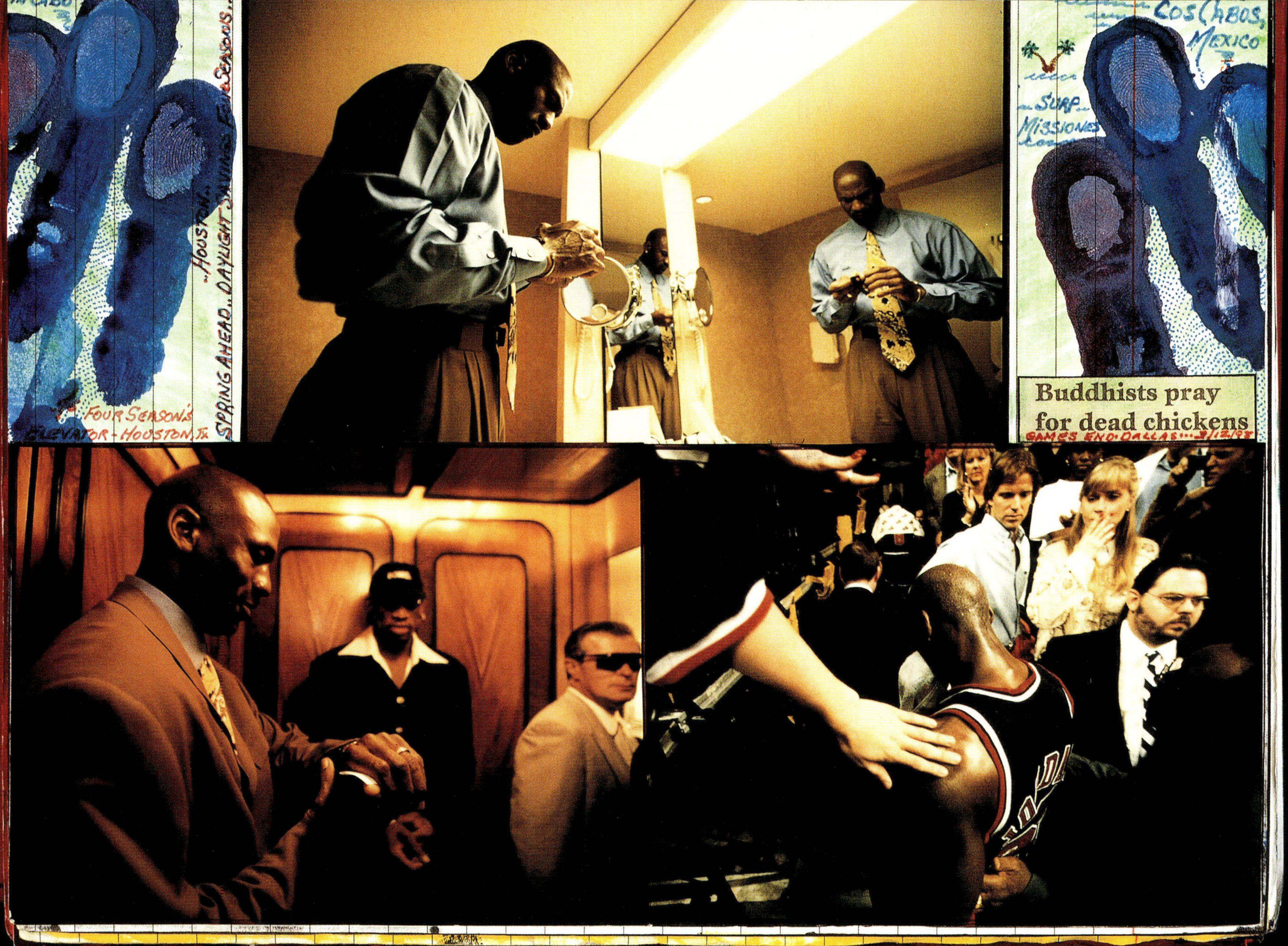
"HOUSTON"
SPRING AHEAD... DAYLIGHT SAVINGS FOUR SEASONS...
FOUR SEASON'S
ELEVATOR-HOUSTON, TX
COS CABOS, MEXICO
SURF
MISSIONES
Buddhists pray
for dead chickens
GAMES END: DALLAS...3/12/98

..CHICAGO...3/5/98...."THE WONDERFUL ACCIDENT"... TAKEN AT MICHAEL'S HOME FOR HIS FAIRWELL BOOK.......

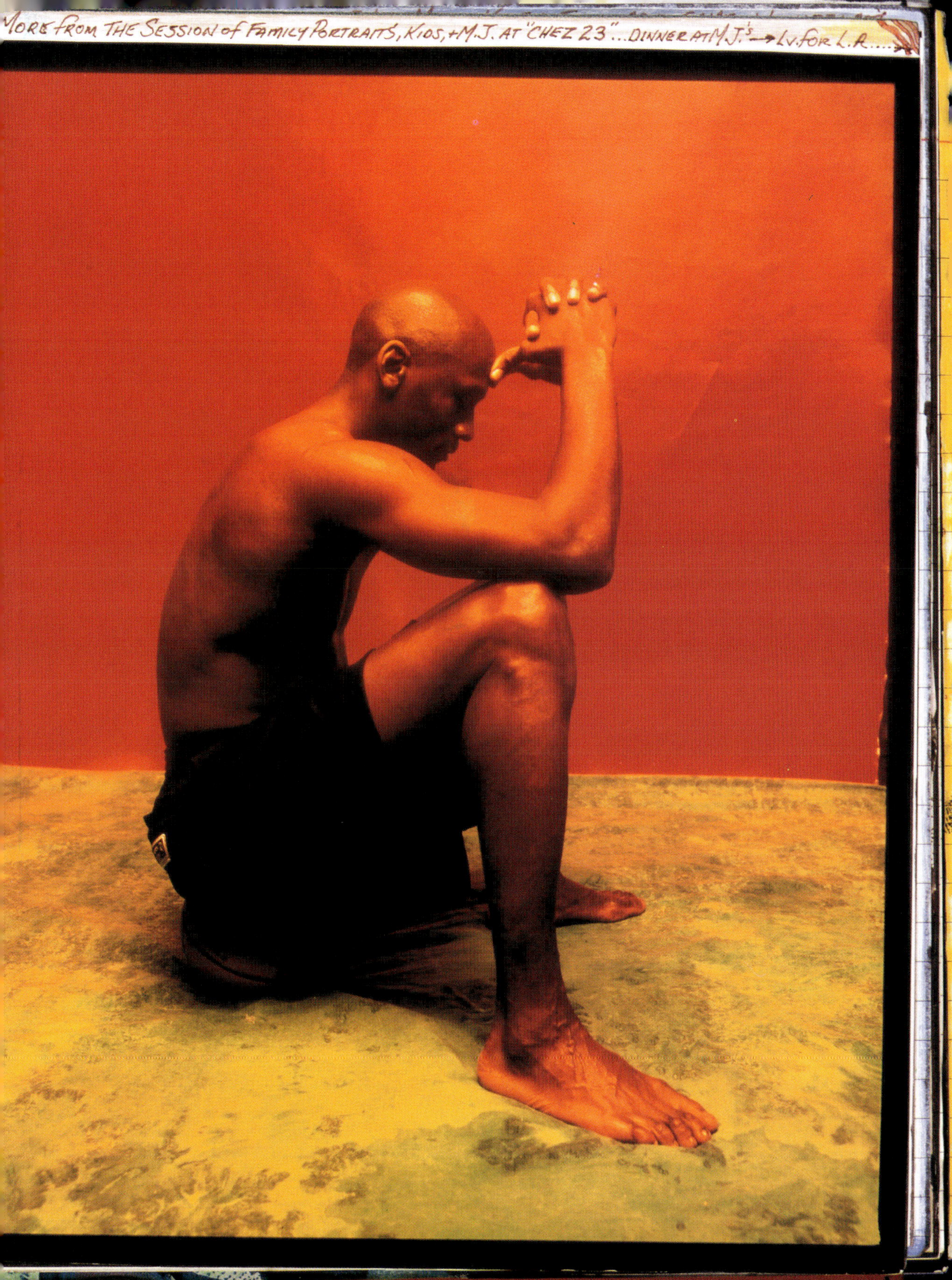
MORE FROM THE SESSION of FAMILY PORTRAITS, KIDS, + M.J. AT "CHEZ 23"... DINNER AT M.J.'s → Lv. FOR L.A....

ADIDAS
OCTOBER 21
1998

Voodoo Burn Case

4th day

...VISIT MAN RAY EXHIBIT BEFORE DINNER AT TINTERO...

Tintero
INTERNATIONAL FISH MARKET

~TURIN, ITALY~

~DEL PIERRO~

~FLYING HEADER~

SEX ✦ SPORTS ✦ BEER

...SHOOT WITH ZADANE FOR 1½ HOURS

MILANO

TAN at HOME!
For as Low as $20/Month

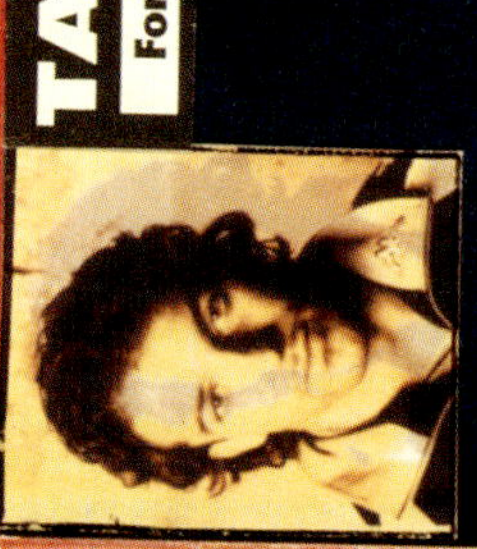

...LV. HOTEL AT 6:30 A.M. DRIVE TO TURIN FOR STUDIO...

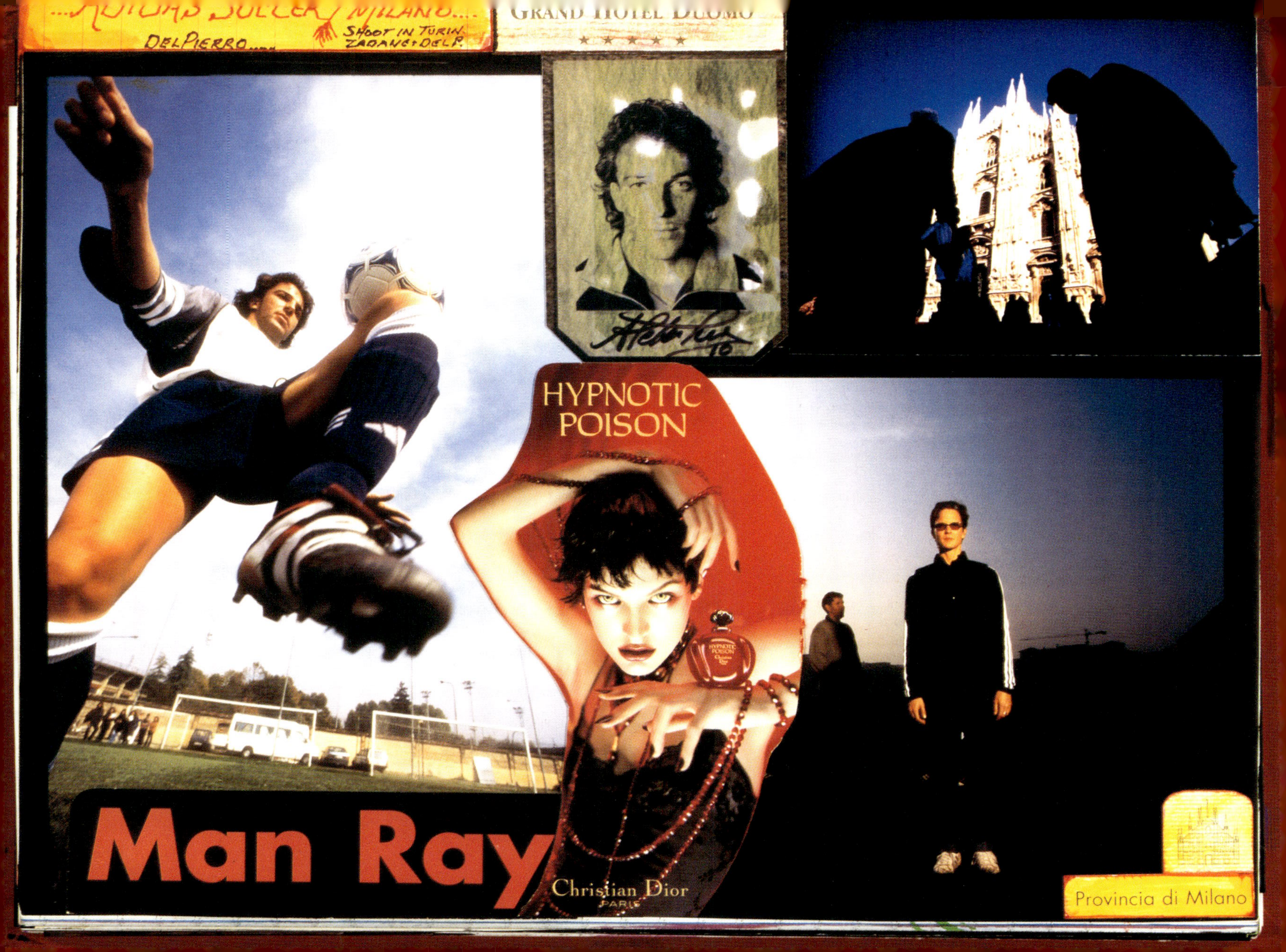

MILANO...

DEL PIERRO....

SHOOT IN TURIN.
ZADANE + DEL P.

GRAND HOTEL DUOMO

HYPNOTIC
POISON

Man Ray

Christian Dior
PARIS

Provincia di Milano

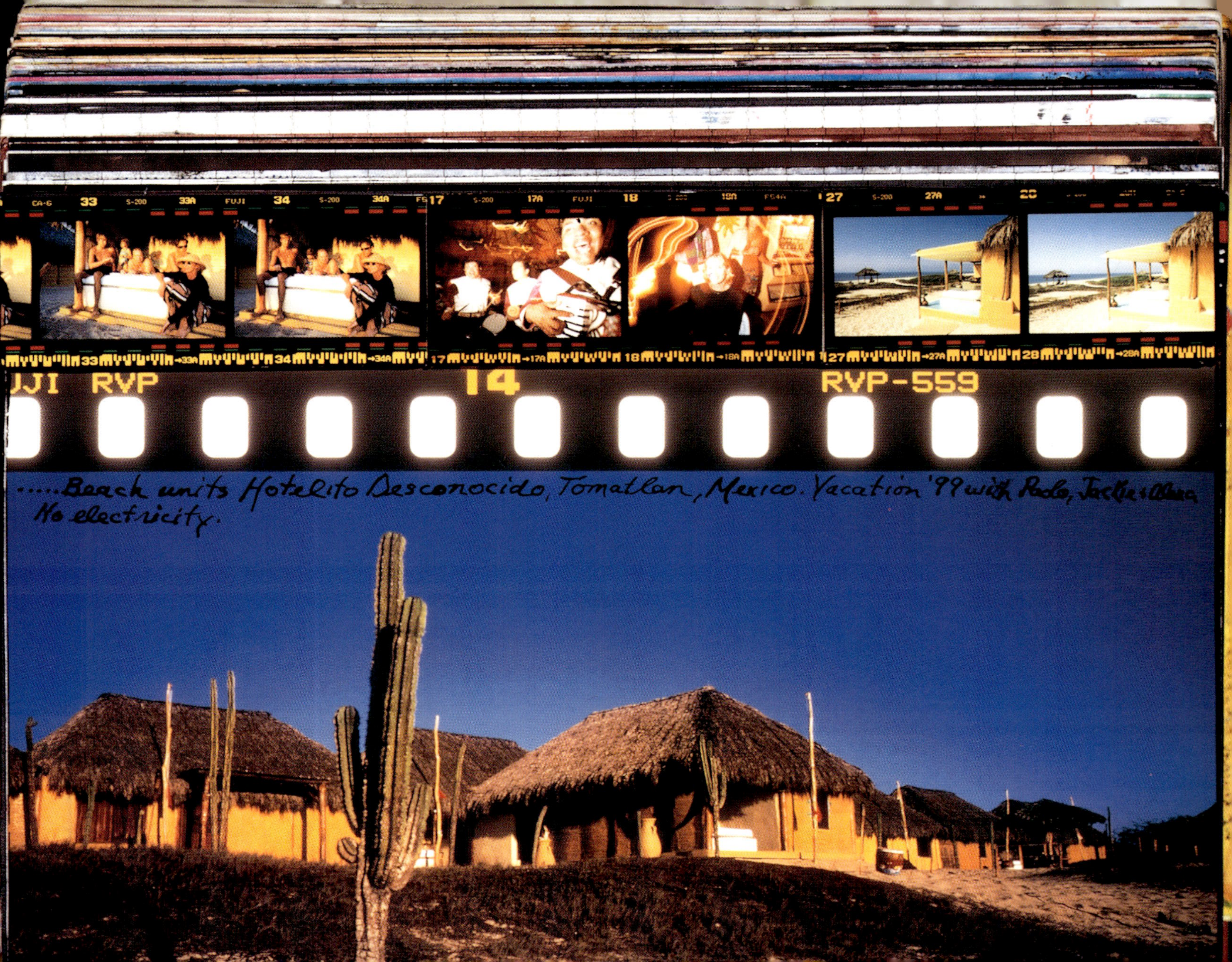
UJI RVP
14
RVP-559
.....Beach units Hotelito Desconocido, Tomatlan, Mexico. Vacatión '99 with
No electricity.

Christian drops into the pit to get worked.

Todays Schedule:

- sneak surf -
- Coffee in bed -
- breakfast -
- ride bike -
- swim or surf -
- Lunch -
- siesta -
- work on diary -
- swim -
- Don Julio Blanco time
- Shower -
- Read -
- dinner -
- Margarita's -
- Bed -

TEQUILA
100% AGAVE

VIBRATOR
STARTER PACK
Never ordered a vibrator before? Or feeling adventurous? Don't know what to choose? How about 3 of our most popular ones? You get:
1 x TEXTURED VIBRO (20cm / 8") | 1 x SMOOTH VIBRO (17cm / 7") | 1 x BENDY VIBRO (17cm / 7")
Also BATTERIES FOR ALL 3
ALL FOR AN INCREDIBLE £18.95 THAT'S A SAVING OF OVER £20
ON CATALOGUE PRICES! ORDER CODE 170
PRODUCTS INFO TEL:
0991 106 191 (24 HOURS)
FREE 32 PAGE SEX TOY CATALOGUE
CHEQUE/PO's TO: MAGIC MOMENTS DEPT DMVP
HASTINGS, EAST SUSSEX. TN35 4JW or
ACCESS / VISA ORDER TEL:
01424 853366

HOTELITO DESCONOCIDO

MONEYLINE
intel
BEATS THE STREET
CNN

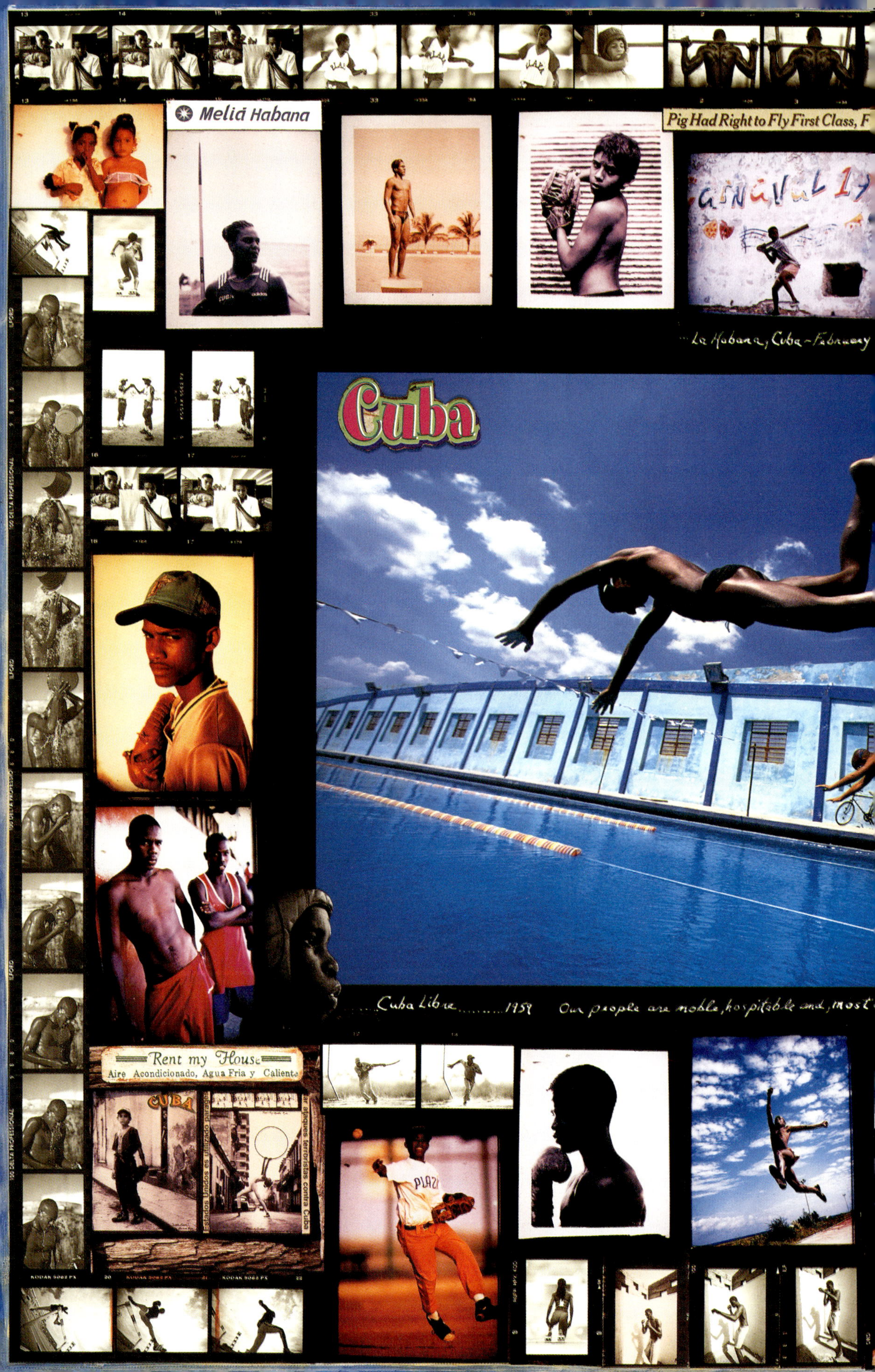

Meliá Habana
Pig Had Right to Fly First Class, F
...La Habana, Cuba-February
Cuba
...Cuba Libre.........1959   Our people are noble, hospitable and, most
Rent my House
Aire Acondicionado, Agua Fria y Caliente
CUBA
Estados Unidos es culpable de los ataques terroristas contra Cuba
PLAZA

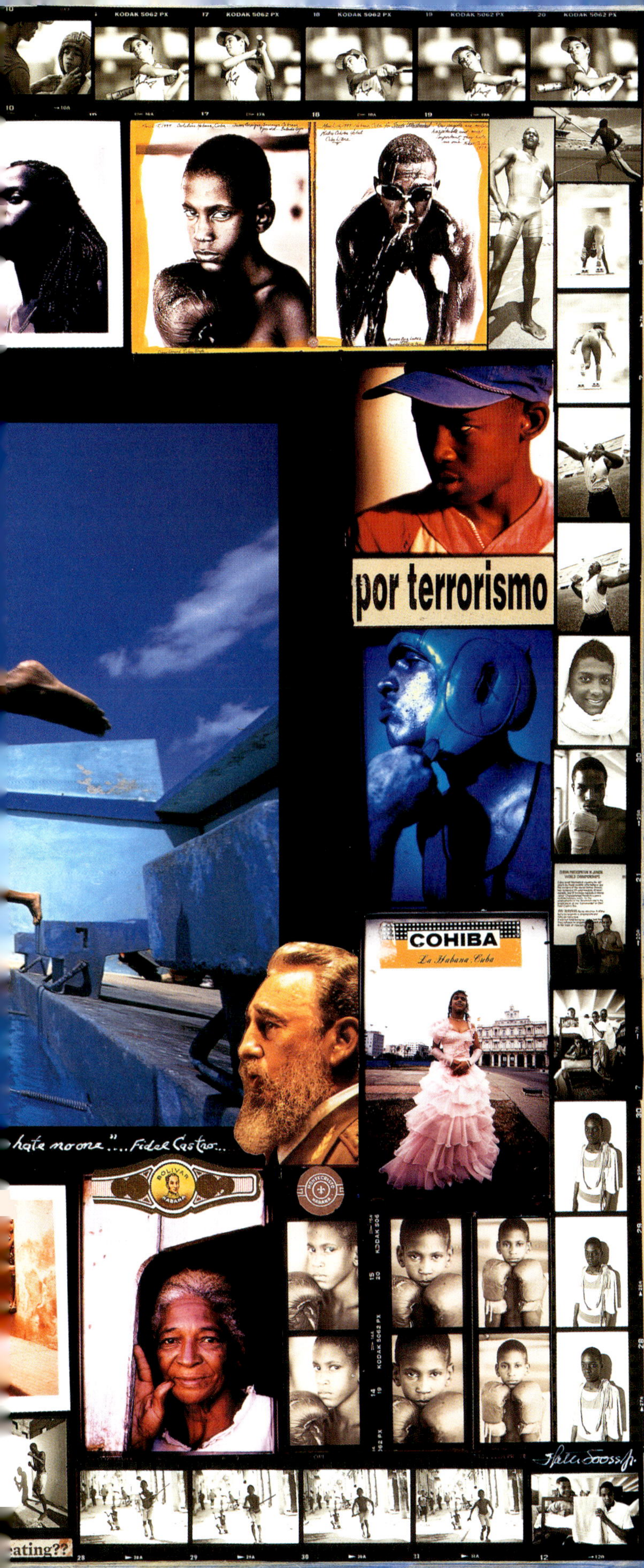
por terrorismo
COHIBA
La Habana Cuba
"hate no one"... Fidel Castro...
BOLIVAR
HABANA
eating??

Viagra in the beef sauce lands French chef in hot water

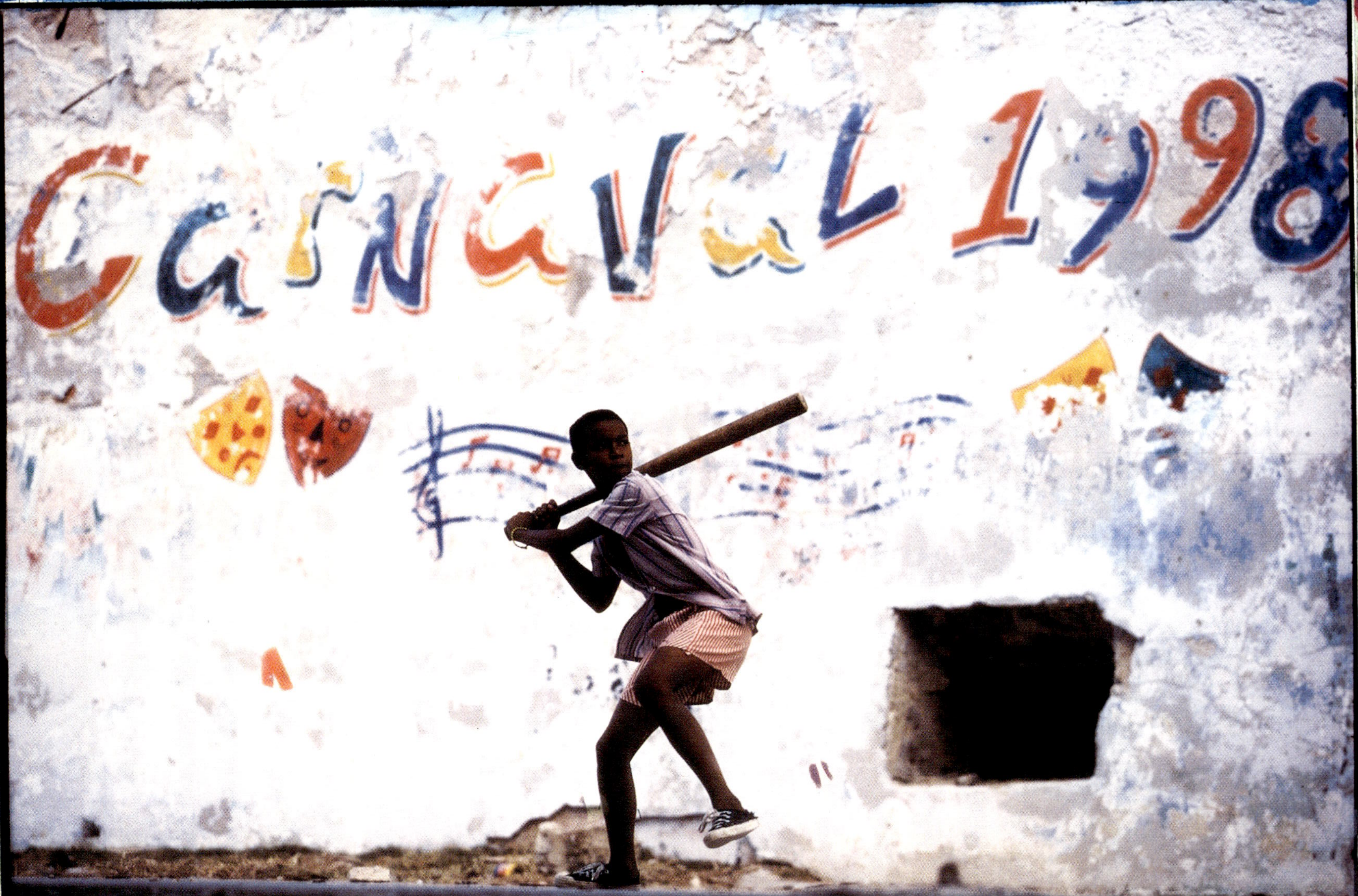

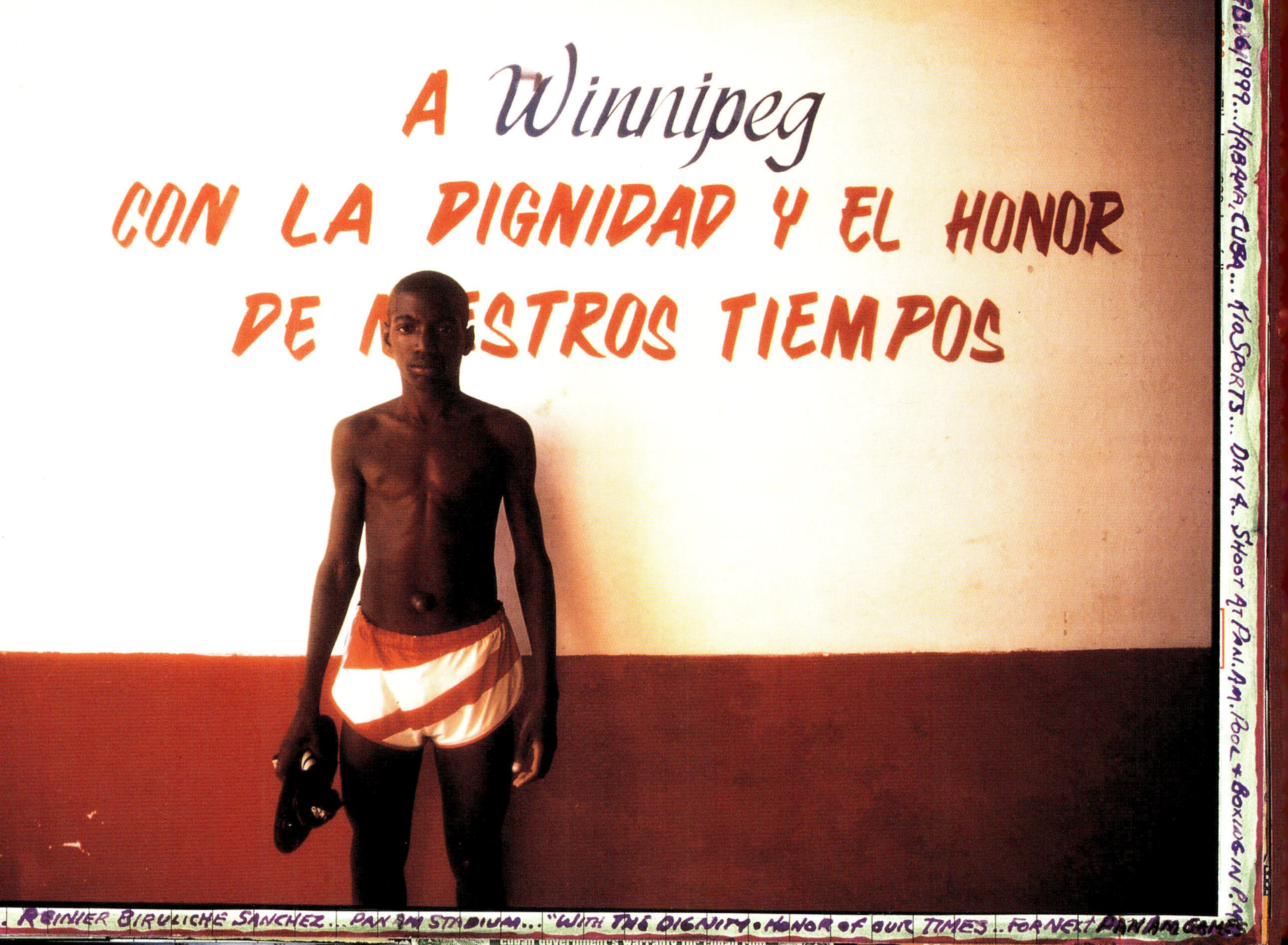
A Winnipeg
CON LA DIGNIDAD Y EL HONOR
DE NUESTROS TIEMPOS
FEB.6/1999... HABANA, CUBA... KIO SPORTS... DAY 4.. SHOOT AT PAN. AM. POOL + BOXING IN P.M.
... REINIER BIRULICHE SANCHEZ.. PAN AM STADIUM... "WITH THE DIGNITY + HONOR OF OUR TIMES.. FOR NEXT PAN AM GAMES
... THE THREE GREATEST FAILURES OF THE REVOLUTION - BREAKFAST, LUNCH, DINNER
Cuban government's warranty for Cuban rum

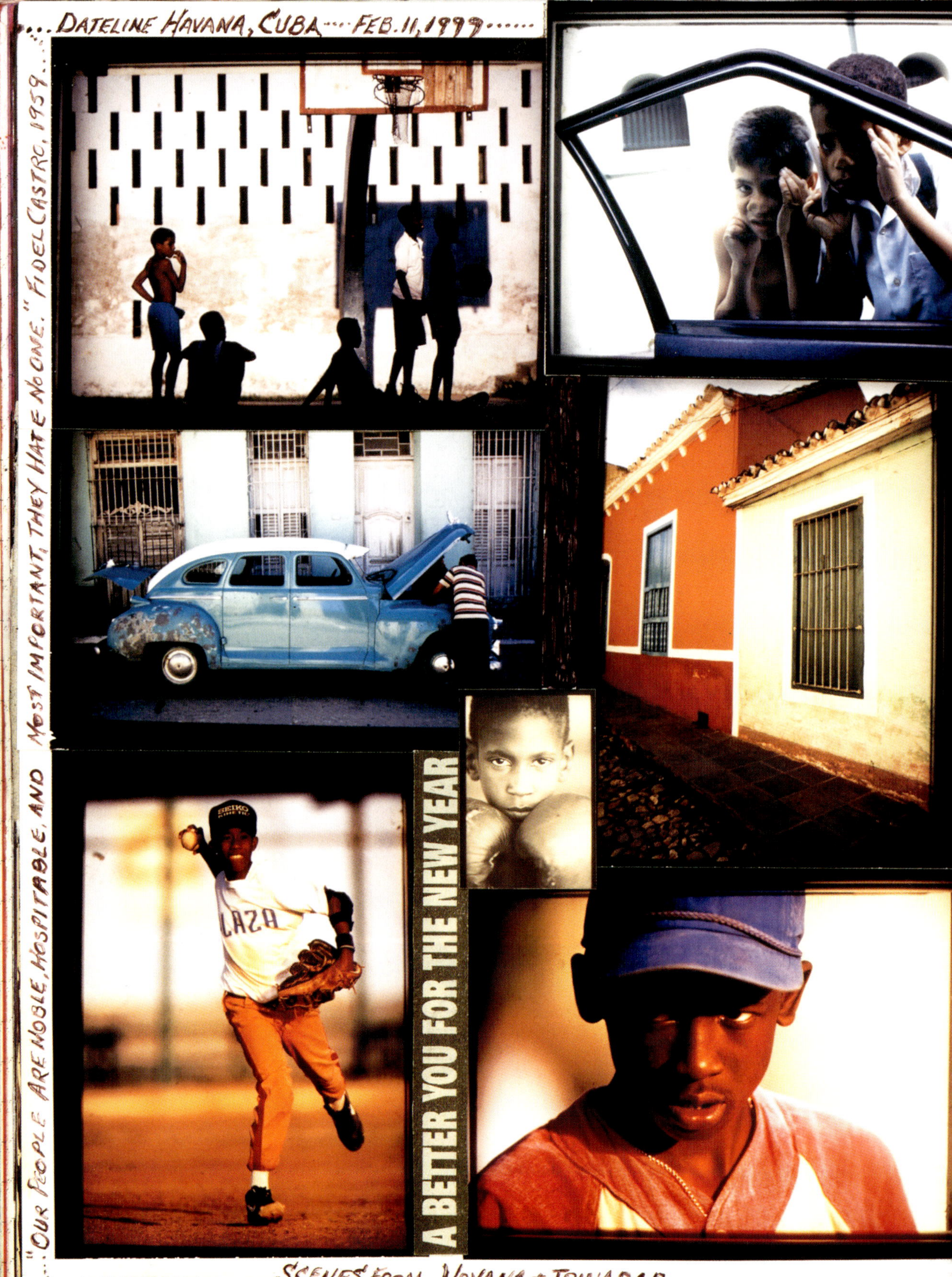

DATELINE HAVANA, CUBA FEB. 11, 1999
"OUR PEOPLE ARE NOBLE, HOSPITABLE, AND MOST IMPORTANT, THEY HATE NO ONE." FIDEL CASTRO, 1959
SEIKO KINETIC
LAZA
A BETTER YOU FOR THE NEW YEAR
SCENES FROM HAVANA + TRINADAD

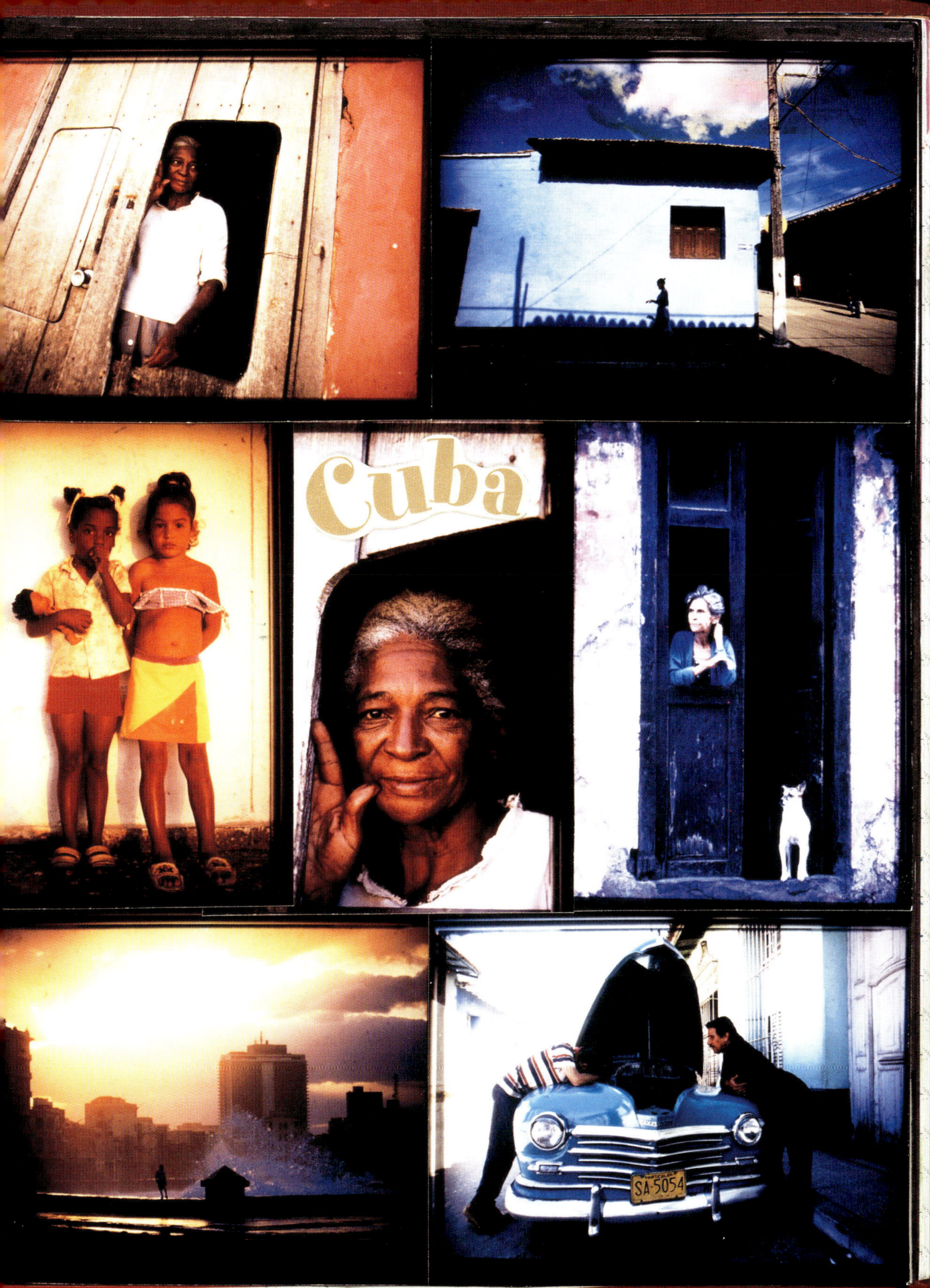
Cuba
SA-5054

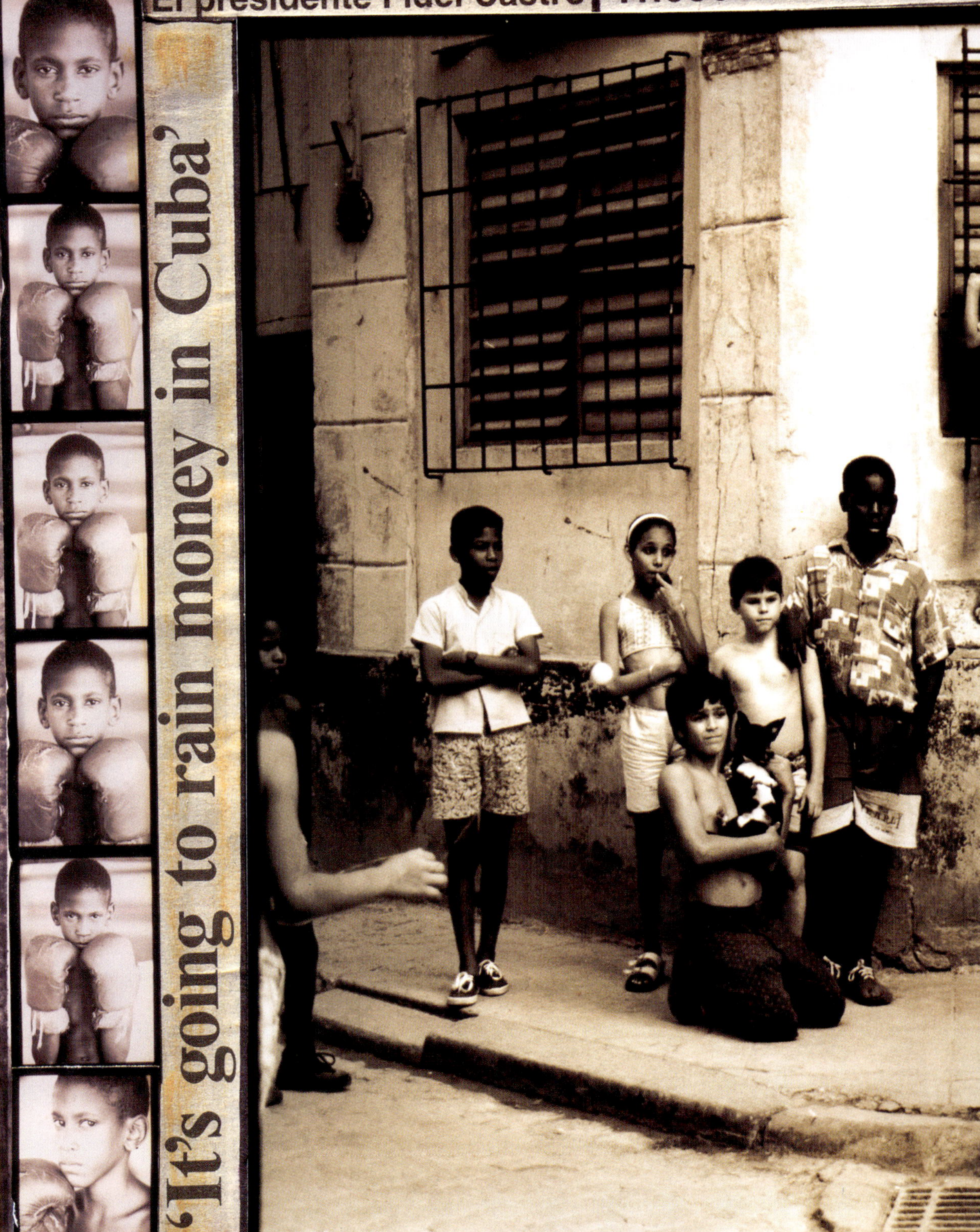

March 13, 1999.... Habana, Cuba.....
Sports Illustrated... Return Tri
El presidente Fidel Castro
These events coul
'It's going to rain money in Cuba'
CUBA EN EL MUNDO
BANANA WARFARE
MEJOR PELICU

SHOOT STREET BASEBALL IN HABANA VIEJO / SWIM MEET AT NOON / HOOPS IN STREET.........

have taken place without the complicity of U.S.

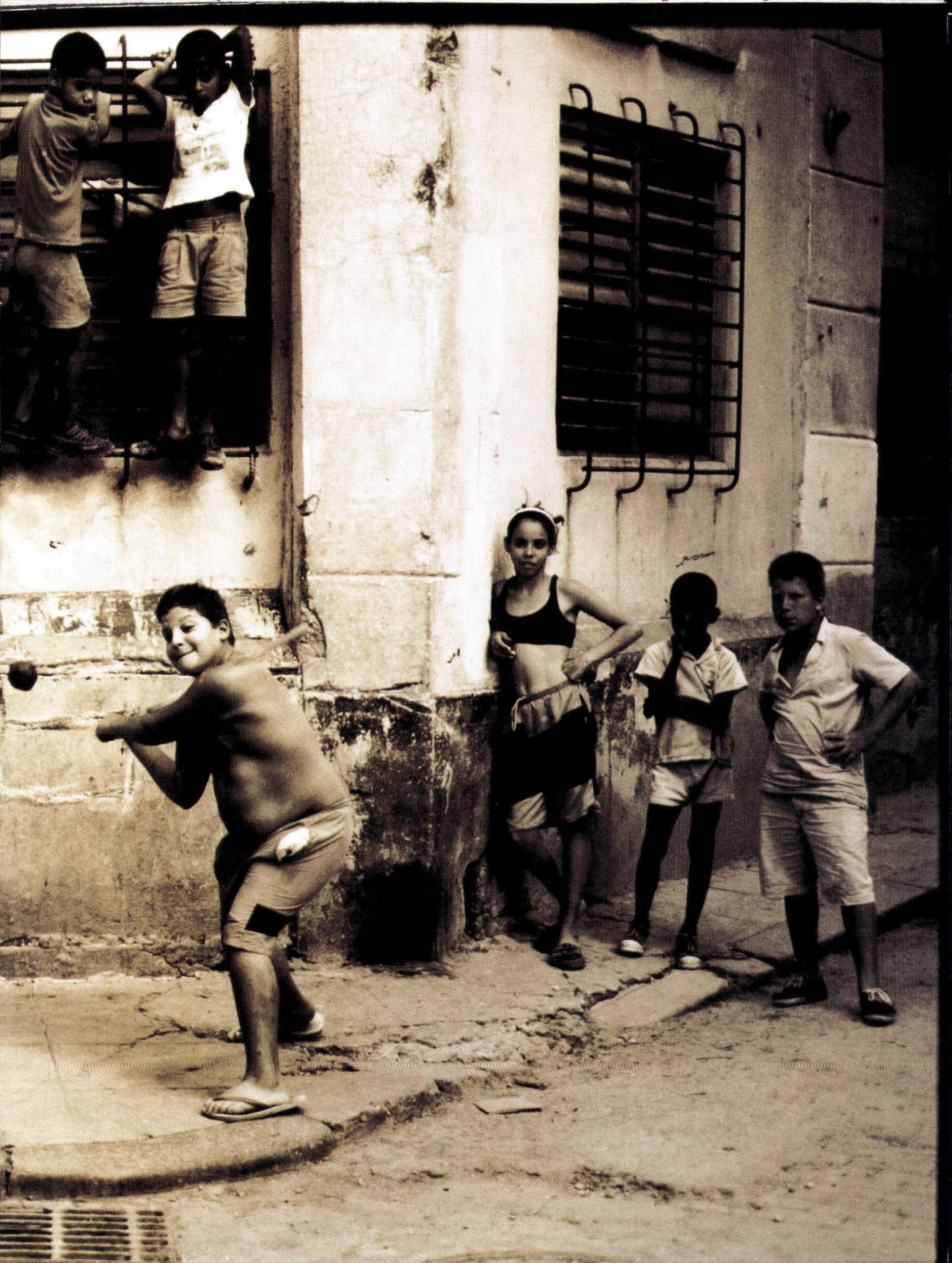

Cuba's truth
Fidel calls
Meliá Cohiba

GANO OFICIAL DEL COMITE CENTRAL DEL PARTIDO COMUNISTA DE CUBA

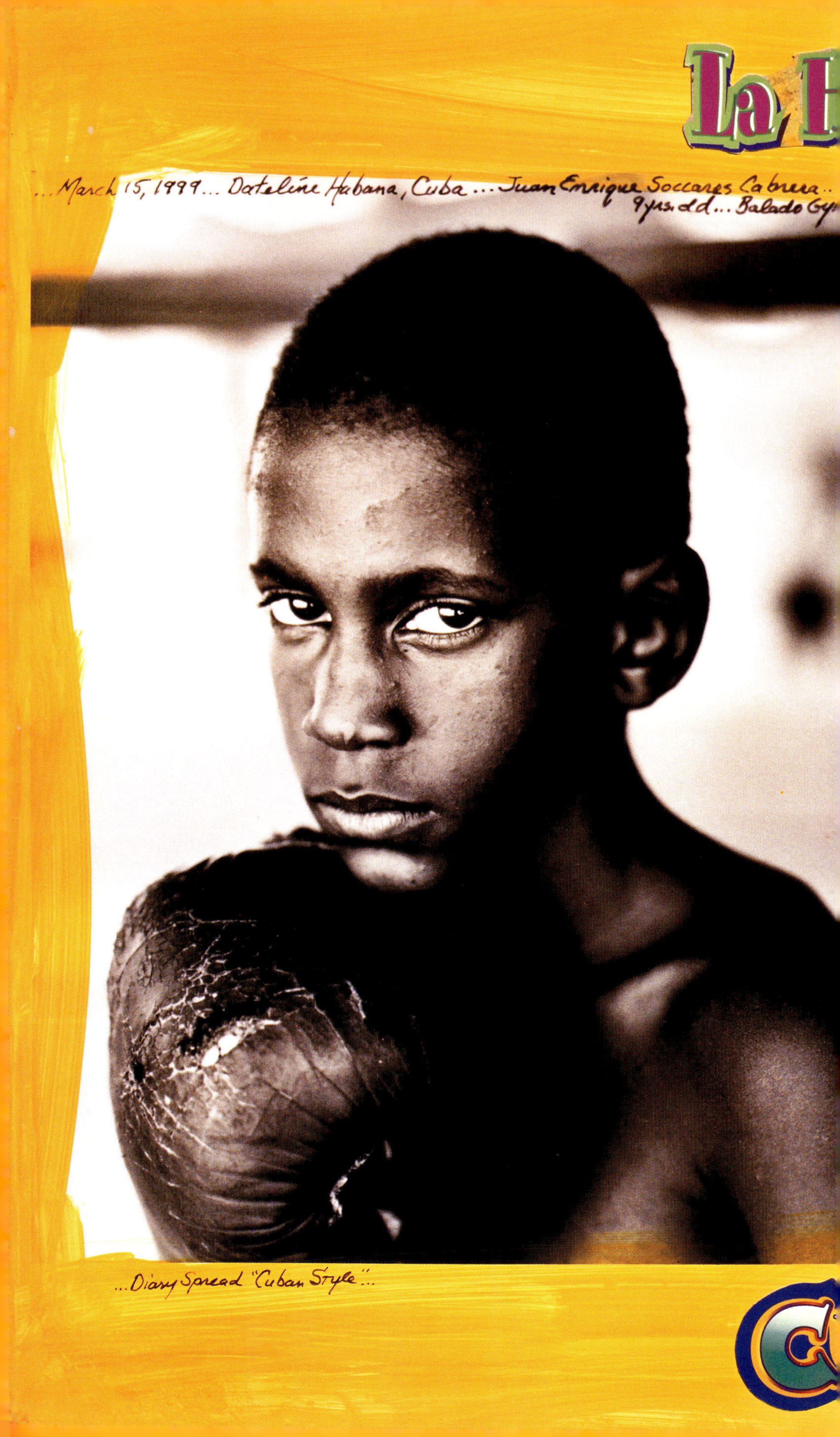

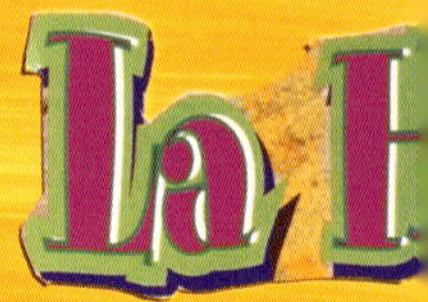

...March 15, 1999... Dateline Habana, Cuba... Juan Enrique Soccares Cabrera.. 9 yrs. old... Balado Gy

...Diary Spread "Cuban Style"...

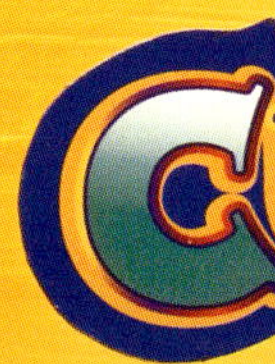

bana,

March 16, 1999, Habana, Cuba for Sports Illustrated.. "Our people are noble, hospitable and, most important, they hate no one." Fidel Castro 1959

Melia Cohiba Hotel
...Cuba Libre...

..Reiner Ruiz Lopez...
15 yrs.
Pan Americano Pool

...Steven Scoss...

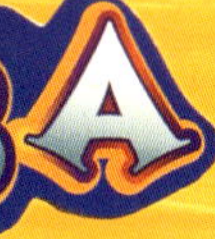

MONTAUK ... SEPTEMBER 17, 1999 ... SHOOT - Spts Ill ...

The Majestic and Mysterious

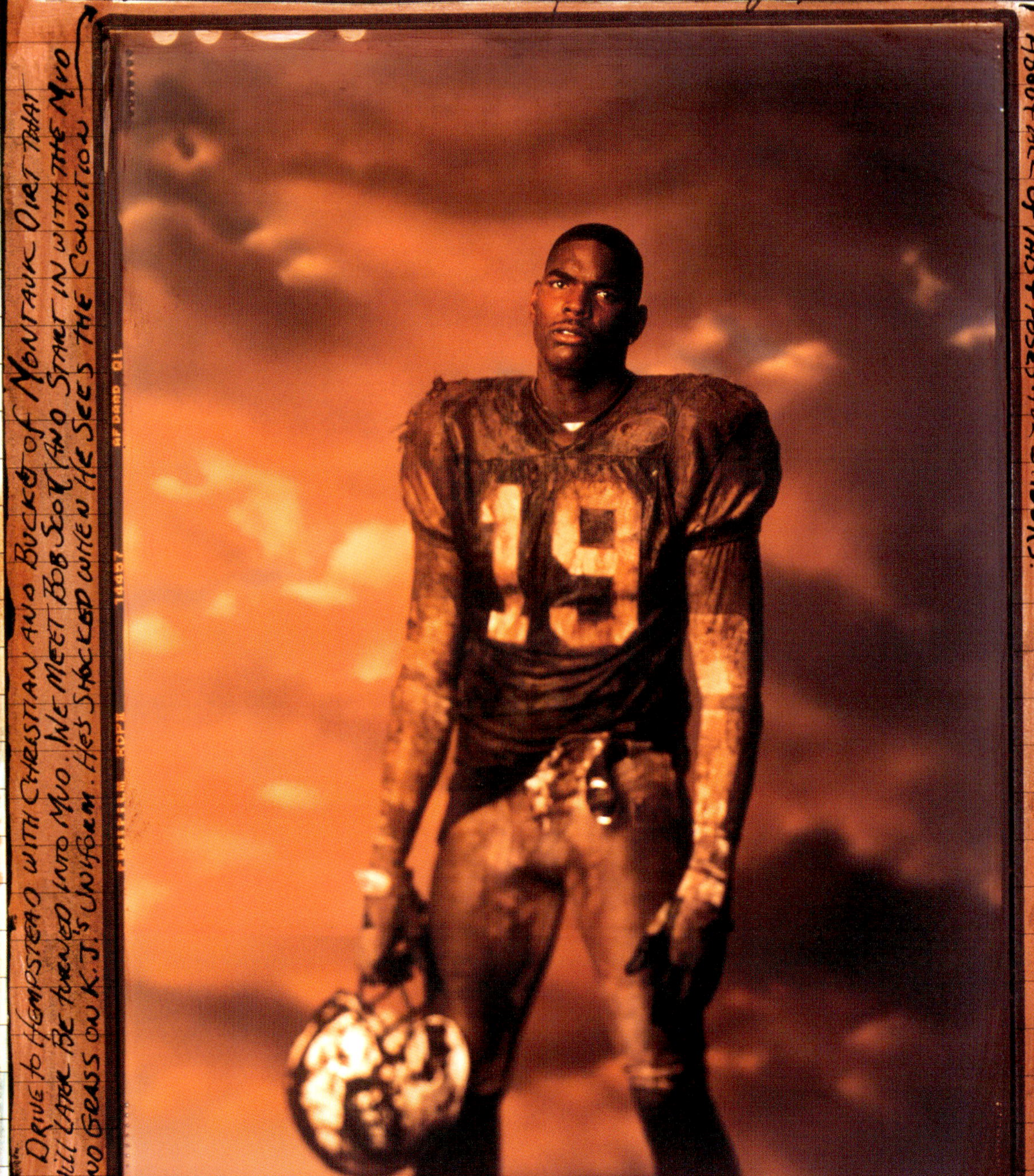

DRIVE to HEMPSTEAD WITH CHRISTIAN AND BUCKETS OF MONTAUK DIRT THAT WILL LATER BE TURNED INTO MUD. WE MEET BOB SCOTT AND START IN WITH THE MUD AND GRASS ON K.J.'S UNIFORM. HE'S SHOCKED WHEN HE SEES THE CONDITION OF HIS UNIFORM AND HOW IT WILL FEEL TO PUT ON. K.J. IS GOOD NATURED ABOUT ALL OF THIS + POSES FOR 3 HOURS.

... KEYSHAWN JOHNSON ...

· N.Y. JETS ·

... DINNER WITH CHRISTIAN at Nick + Toni's ...

TALK

POLAR OPPOSITES: YES, K.J. HAS AN EGO, BUT HE'S A CHARMING, SMILING, BRIGHT MAN, READY TO WORK.

MR+MRS K.J.

STUDIO MUD BOWL SHOTS

9/13/99

Emily SN// Katy - 503-797-4046// Second ass't in Turino// Book charter from Montauk// Tracy Shiro - Canon Ad

- Action Chi conf. -

PRACTICE FIELD, HOFSTRA

BANKERS BACKDROP

BRODERSON SKY

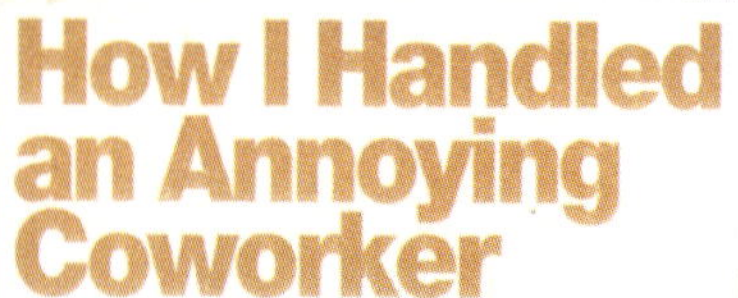

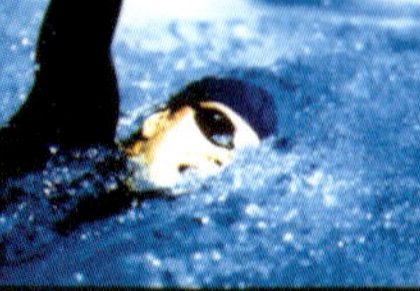

TACO BELL DOG
CUSTODY WAR

EROTIC STIMULATION
TREATMENT

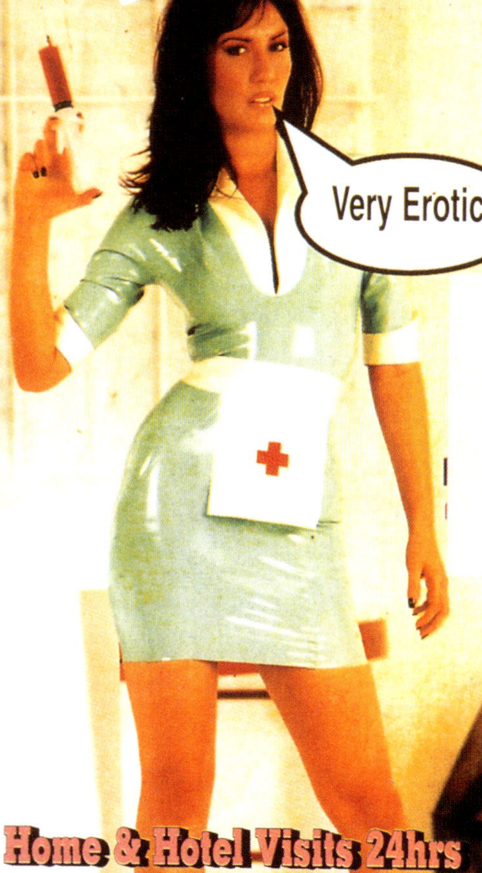

0171 565 8336

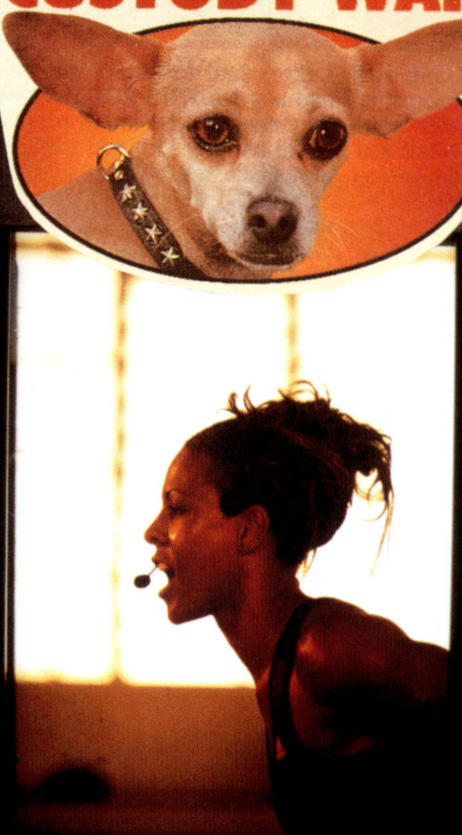

YOUR COMPLETE GUIDE TO
THE NATIONAL GALLERY

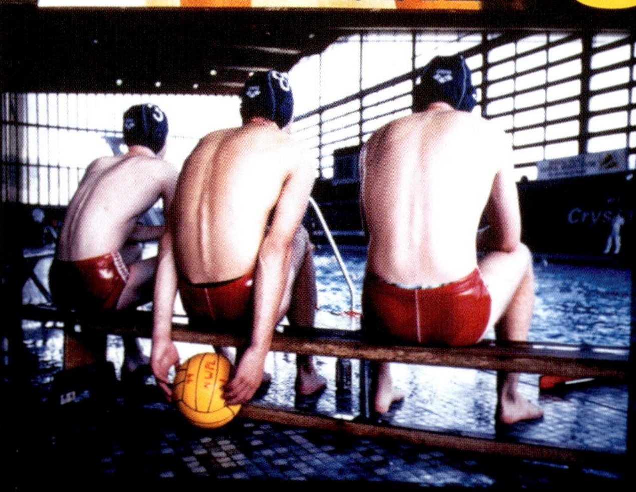

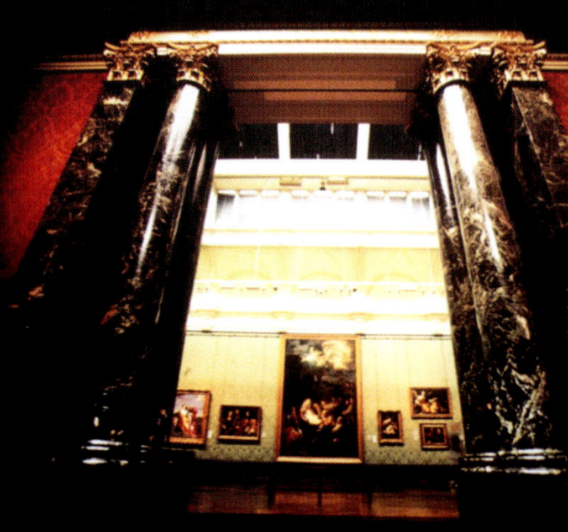

September 4, 1999 - London, England... Ru-Tee, Personal-Trainer.

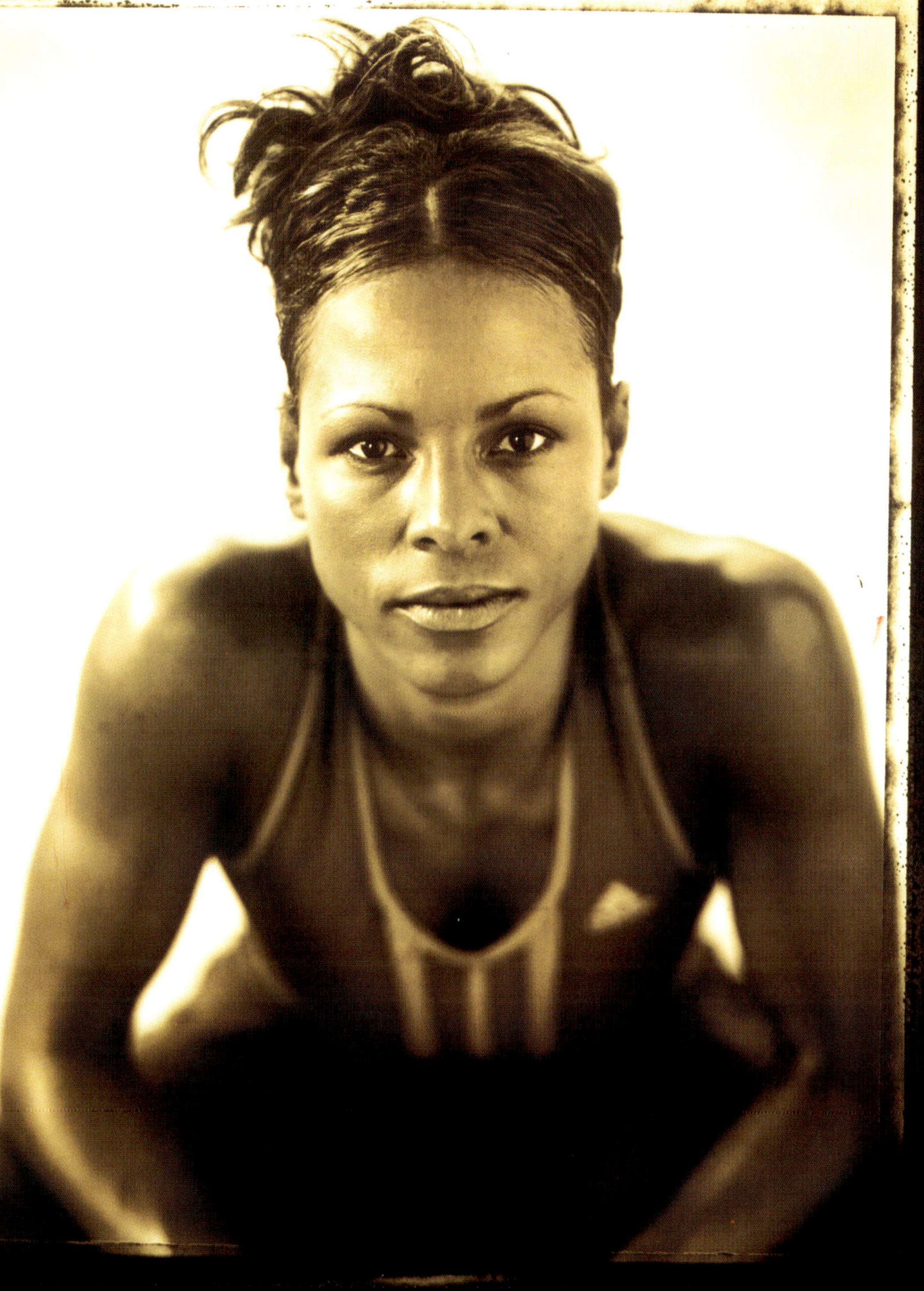

..ADIDAS..

Tiger Stadium, baseball's oldest park, on its last legs, soon to be demolished into the games history books. Memories of 88 Seasons soon to be a pile of rubble, come October.
6/19/99

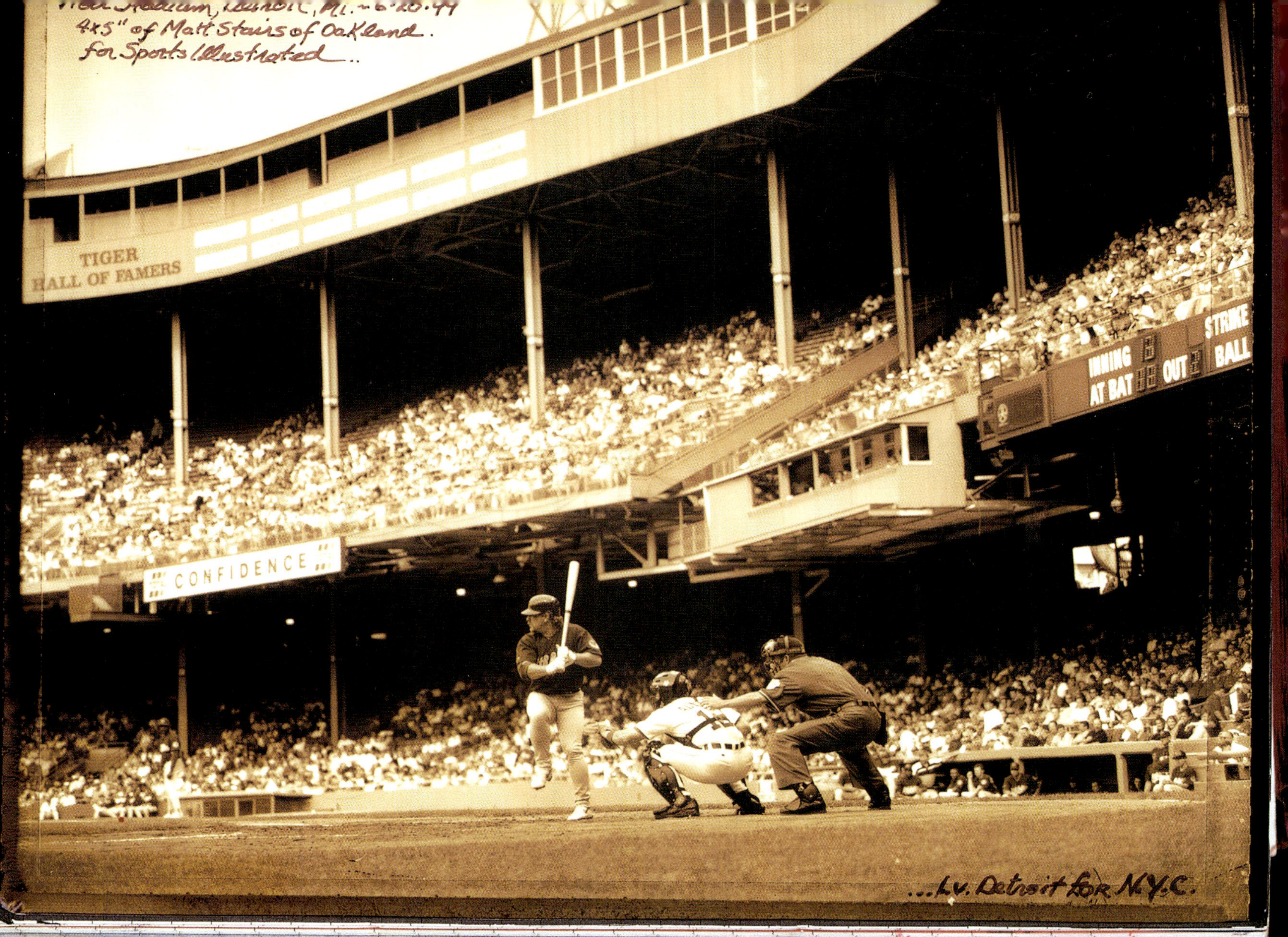
4x5" of Matt Stairs of Oakland.
for Sports Illustrated..
TIGER
HALL OF FAMERS
CONFIDENCE
INNING
AT BAT
OUT
STRIKE
BALL
...Lv. Detroit for N.Y.C.

....December 2,nd 1999....
20th Century Sports Awards at Madison Square Garden
....Jim Brown....

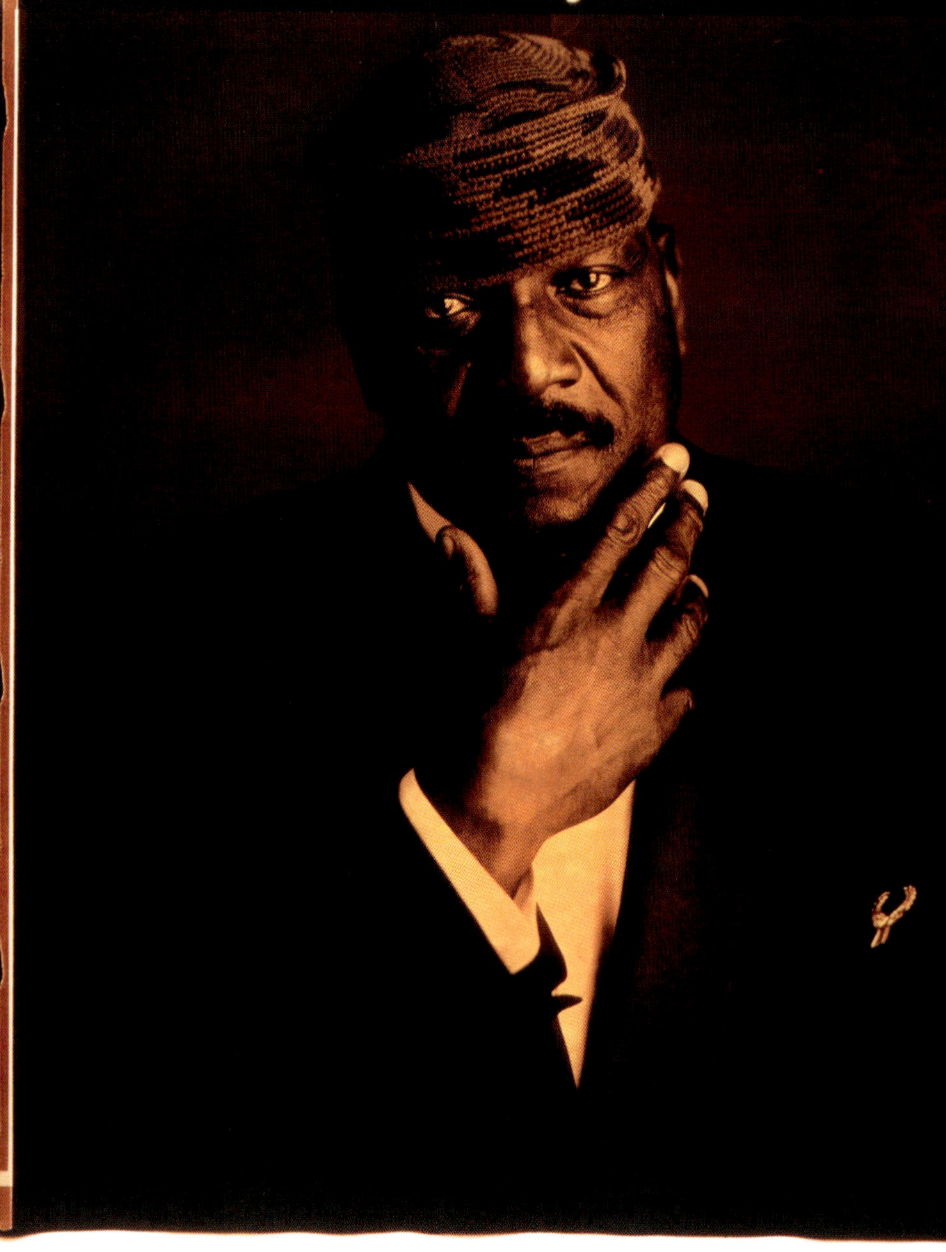

Jim Brown

20"x24" Polaroid camera.. Pose; Russell, Magic, Chrissie, Jackie, Yogi, Jack
... Joe, Evander, Elway, Oscar
Billy Crystal, Al Pacino...

....ARNOLD PALMER.....

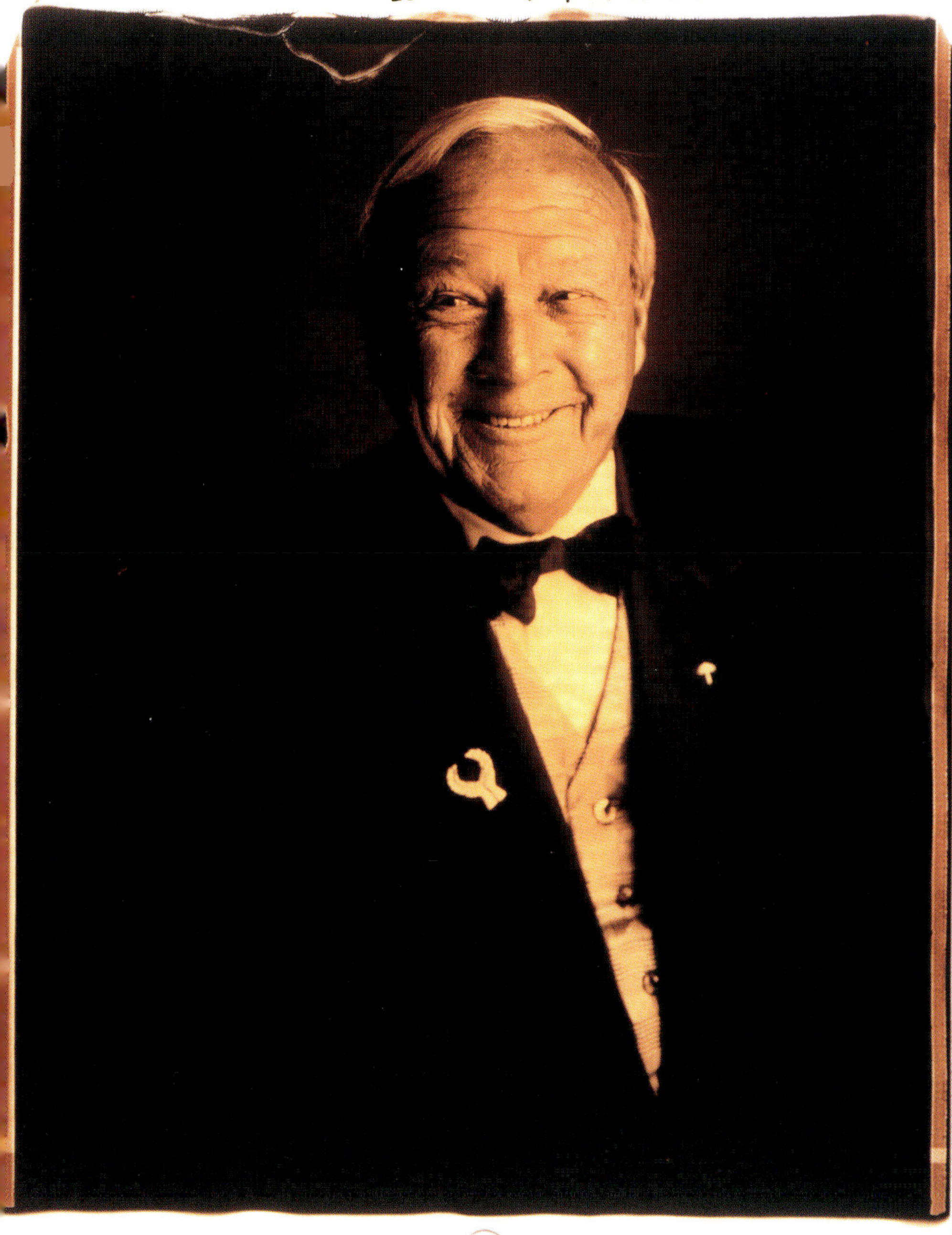

Arnold Palmer

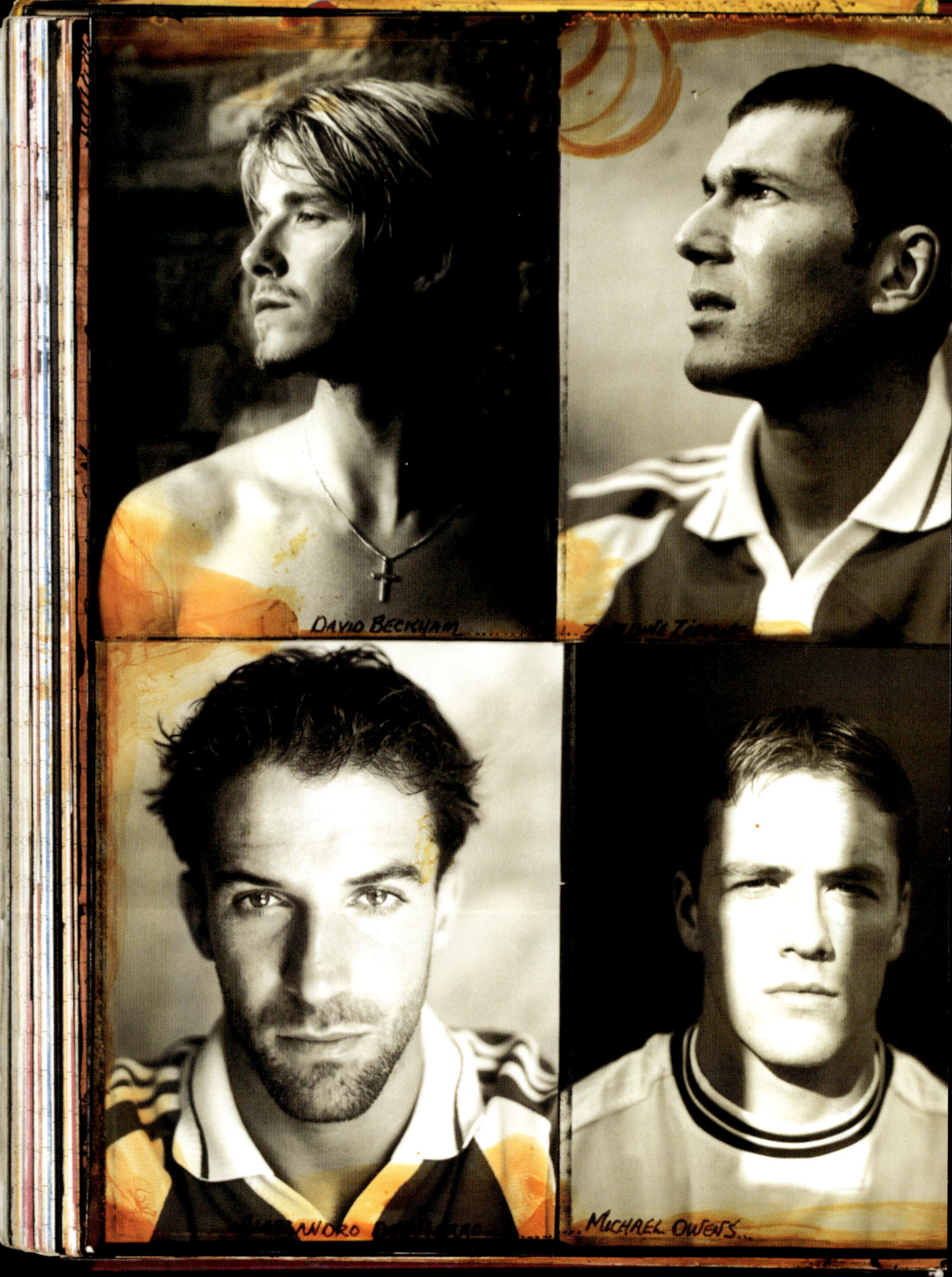
DAVID BECKHAM
MICHAEL OWENS...

1999 263rd day – 102 days follow
Yom Kippur

MONDAY 20 SEPTEMBER

LV. FOR TURIN

E-Mail From Milan

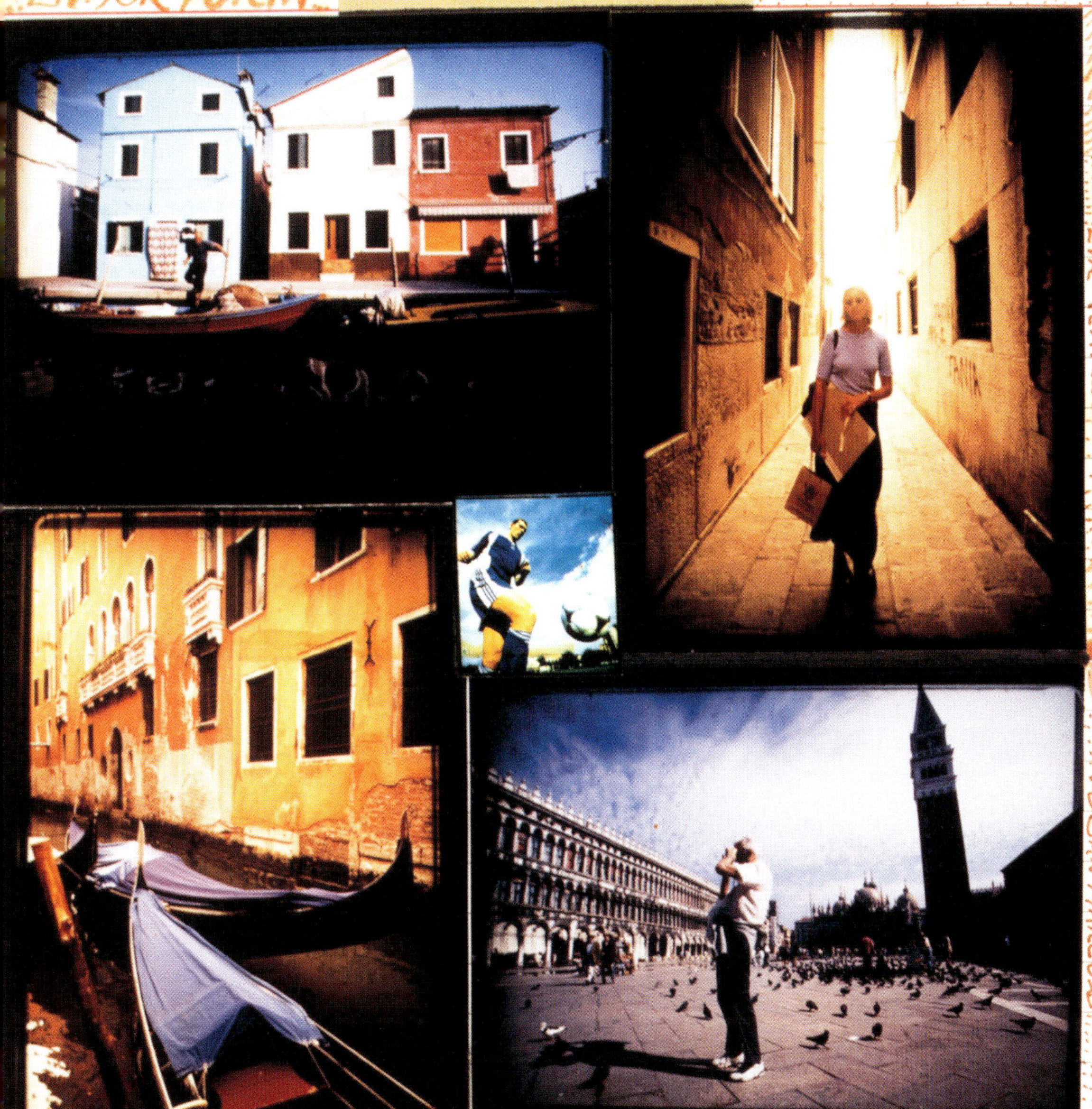

EVA ~ VENICE

SAN MARCO

Eva and I start our Italian adventure. We fly by charter, Montauk to Farmingdale, taxi to J.F.K., J.F.K. to Milano, and Milano to Turino by Taxi! Unfortunately I don't bring a bag containing my film, as this trip is not solely a holiday but an Adidas shoot. We scramble to get the film from Montauk to Italy, Concord aided, to save me, but to no avail, as customs refuses to release it. We're able to purchase film in Turino, cash only, and barely scrape through, since ATMs wouldn't accept my card.

AT-A-GLANCE®

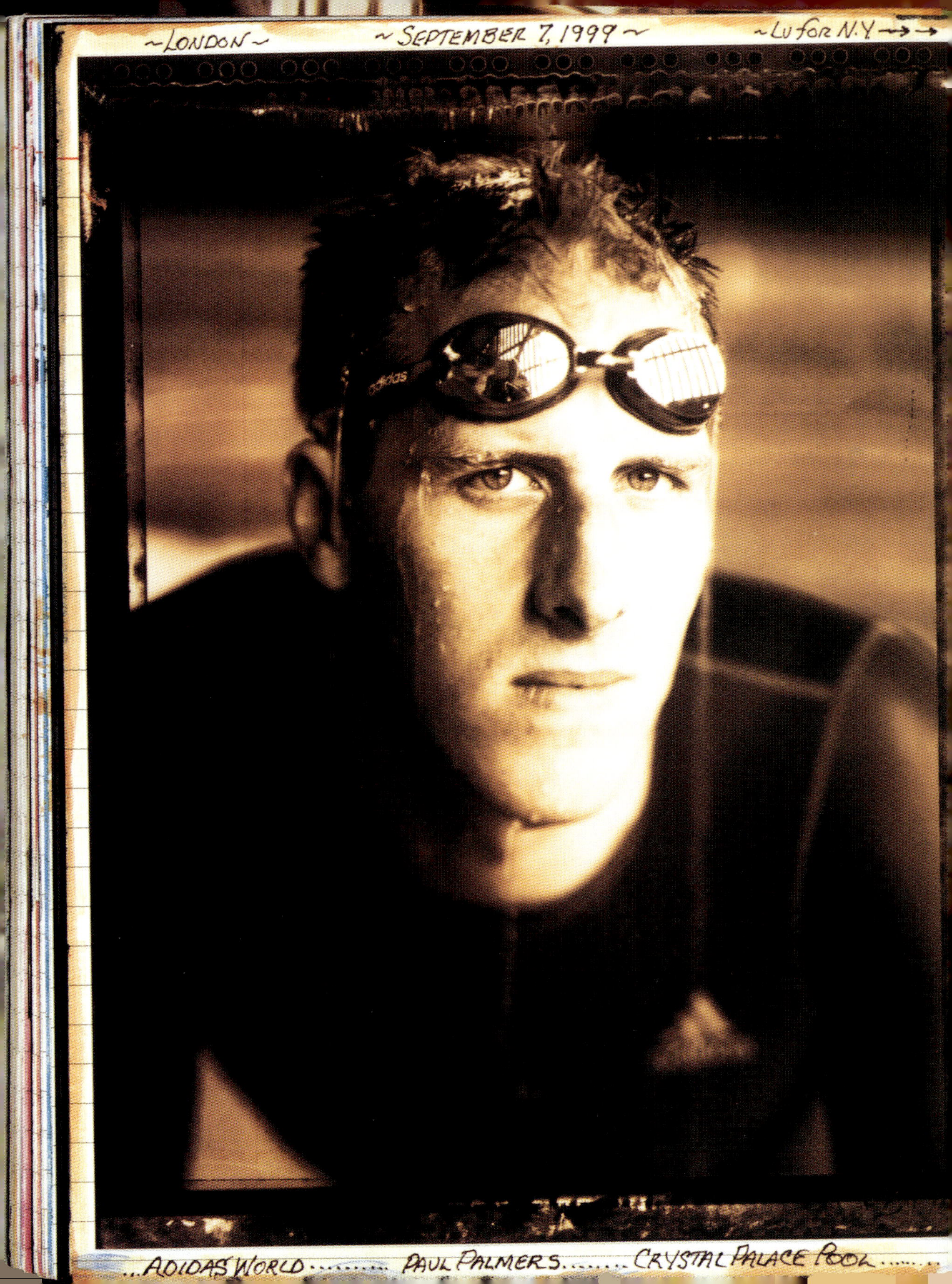
~LONDON~
~SEPTEMBER 7, 1999~
~LU FOR N.Y →→
adidas
...ADIDAS WORLD......... PAUL PALMERS........ CRYSTAL PALACE POOL......

~Montauk Pt.~ ~September 8, 1999~ ~Surf Ditch~

~Sue Rolph~

SEPTEMBER

VENICE

Eva and I spend
day in Venice, knowing
only day, since the
is unable to extend
all the other hotels
We start
swim in the
saltwater
Then a
breakfast
ing the lagoon
We soon
San Marco
quickly leav-
throngs
We visit a
filled with
+ Bambinis.
+ cappuccinos and more
clear day. We water
an island filled with
unusually brilliant
Beautiful light + photos.
to San Marco at sunset
boat back to our hotel.
and some succulent
service, and a
Venezia closes.

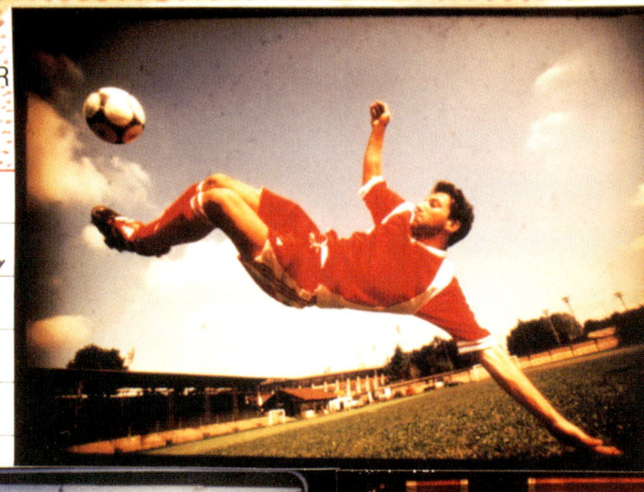

day – 99 days follo

SEPT. 2

one splend
that could be
Cipriani Hot
our stay an
are booked s
the day with

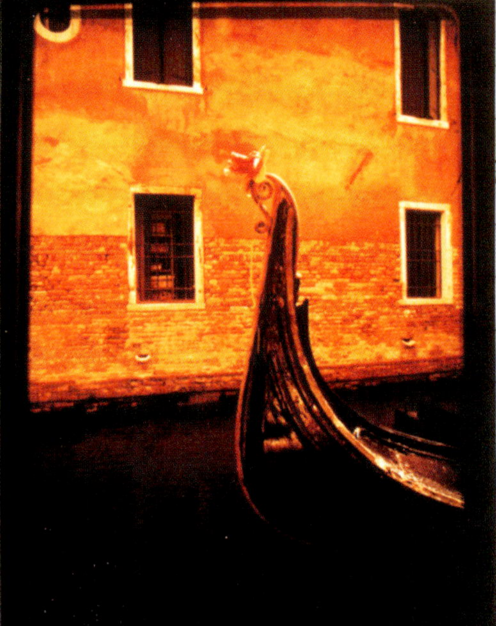

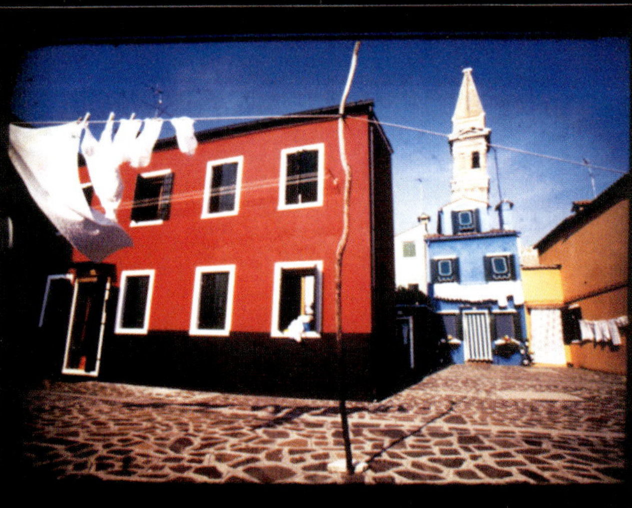

~BURANO~

walking on a
taxi to Bura
homes paint
colors, purple
We water ta
and catch th
One more s
food via r
perfect d
...LV. FOR MILA

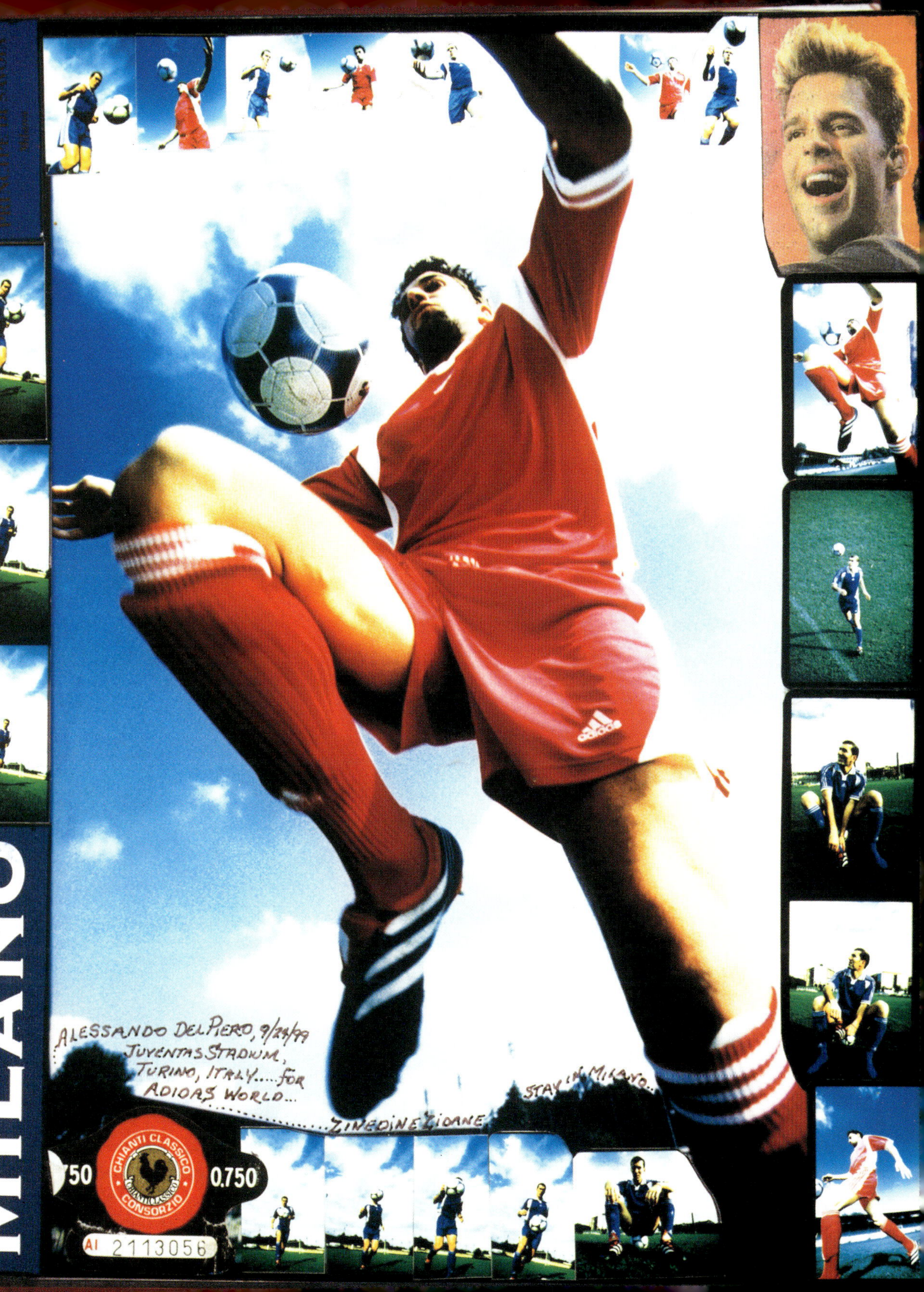
MILANO
ALESSANDO DEL PIERO, 9/24/99
JUVENTAS STADIUM,
TURINO, ITALY.....FOR
ADIDAS WORLD...
STAY IN MILANO...
ZINEDINE ZIDANE
CHIANTI CLASSICO
CONSORZIO
750
0.750
AI 2113056

...TRAVEL DAY--Lv ATLANTA for TAMPA...

_OCTOBER 29, 1999_ADIDAS SHOOT_MARTINA HINGIS_SADDLEBROOK, FL

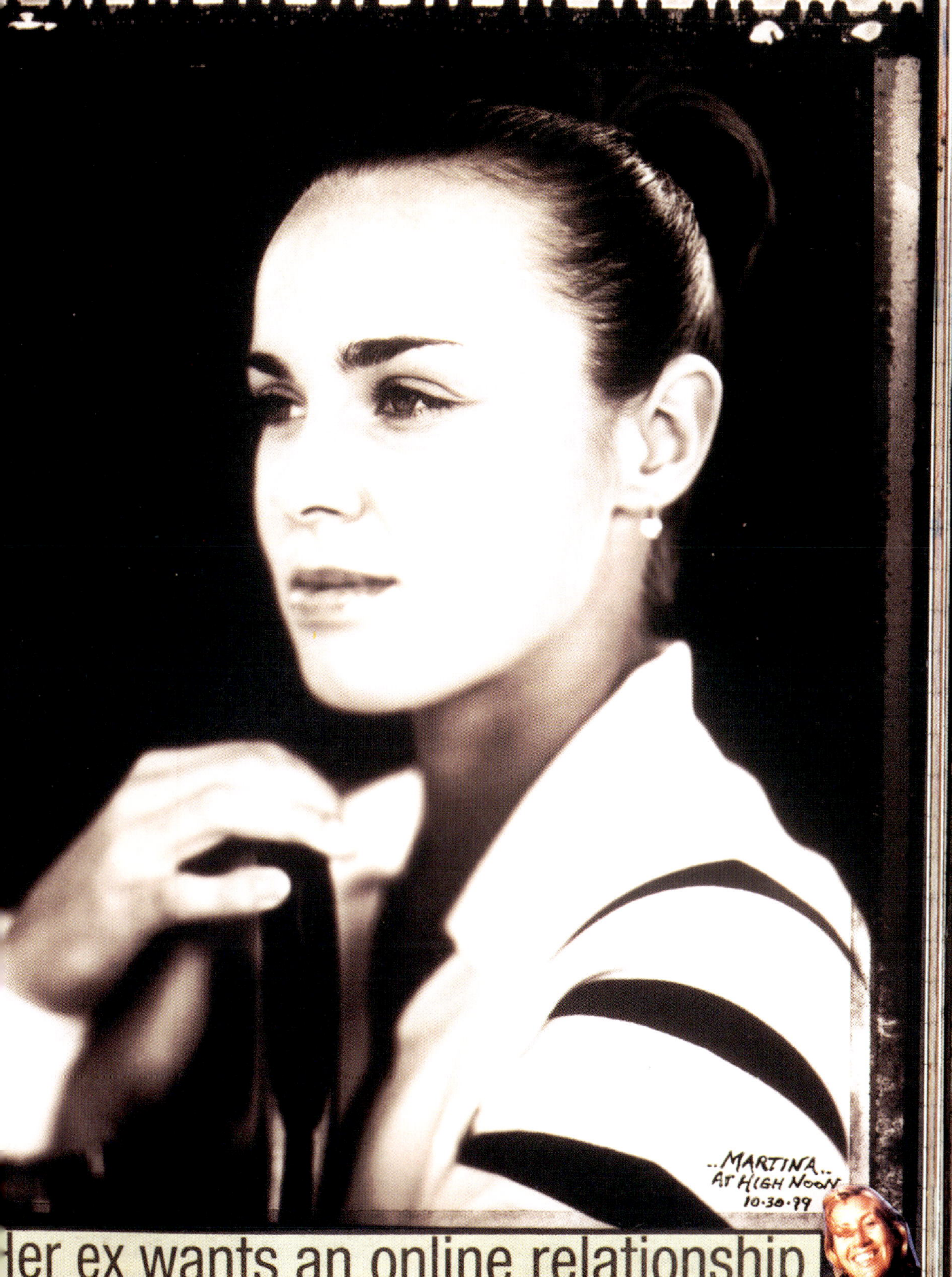
..MARTINA..
AT HIGH NOON
10·30·99
ler ex wants an online relationship

OCT. 15, 1999
SHOOT DAY-2
DAWN AT 3 TABLES

Happiness erupts on island

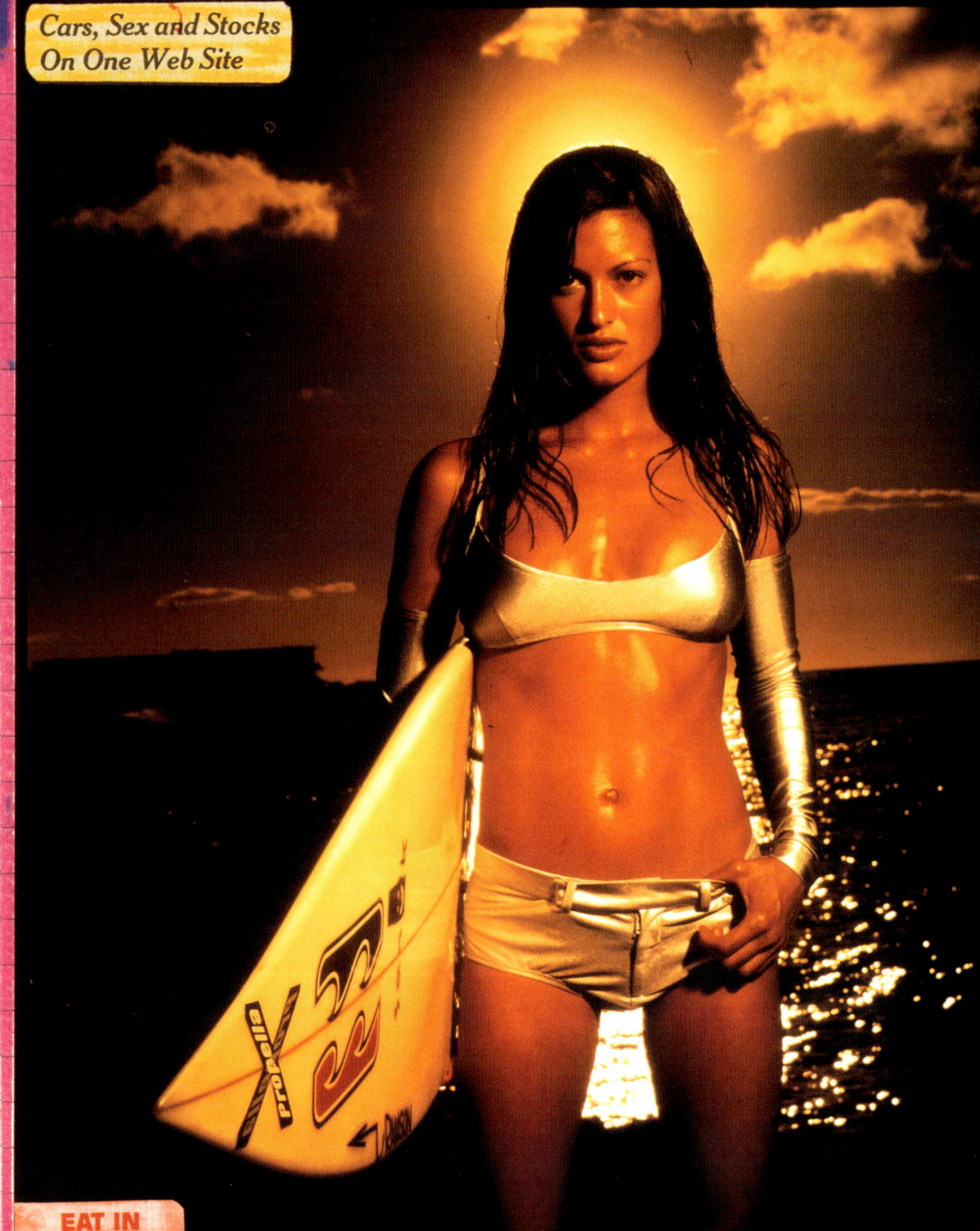

BILLABONG
UNITED STATES

6:00 P.M, F32 ... MALIA JONES - KAHUKU BCH ... DINNER - HAL

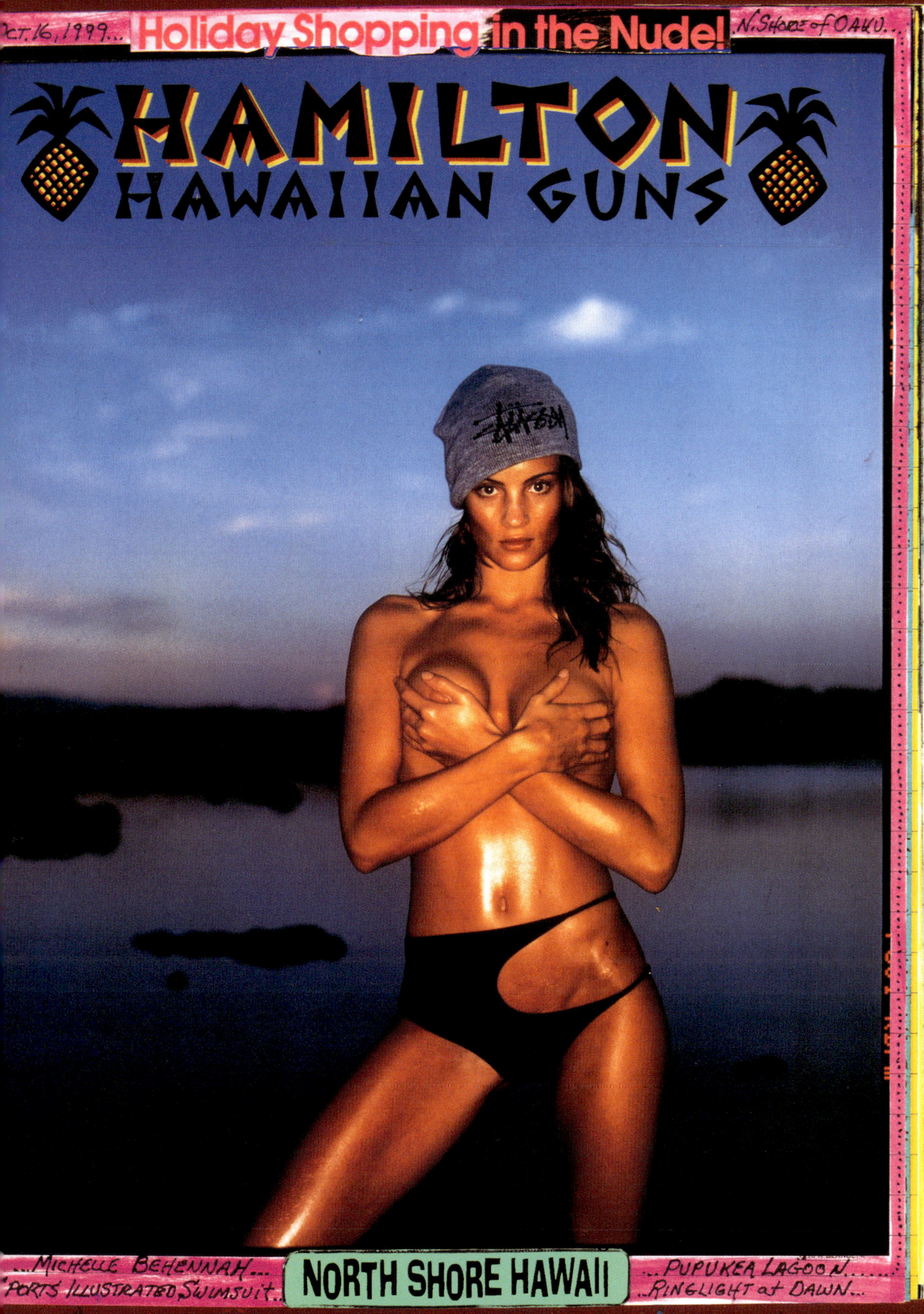

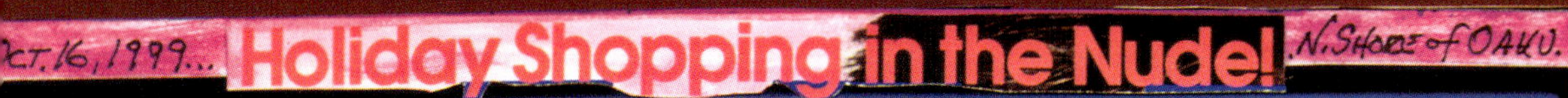

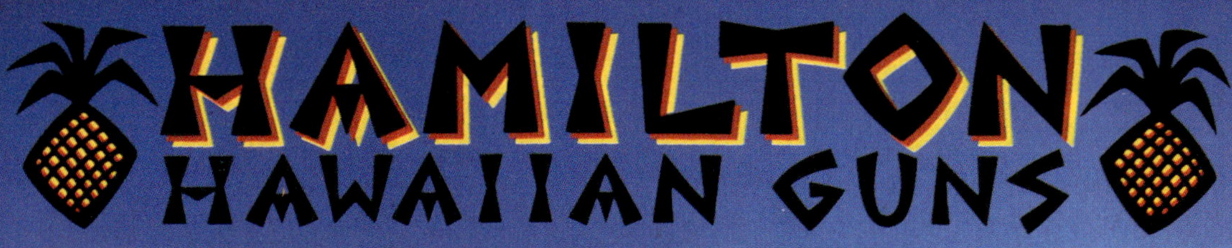

...Michelle Behennah...
Sports Illustrated Swimsuit...

NORTH SHORE HAWAII

...Pupukea Lagoon...
...Ringlight at Dawn...

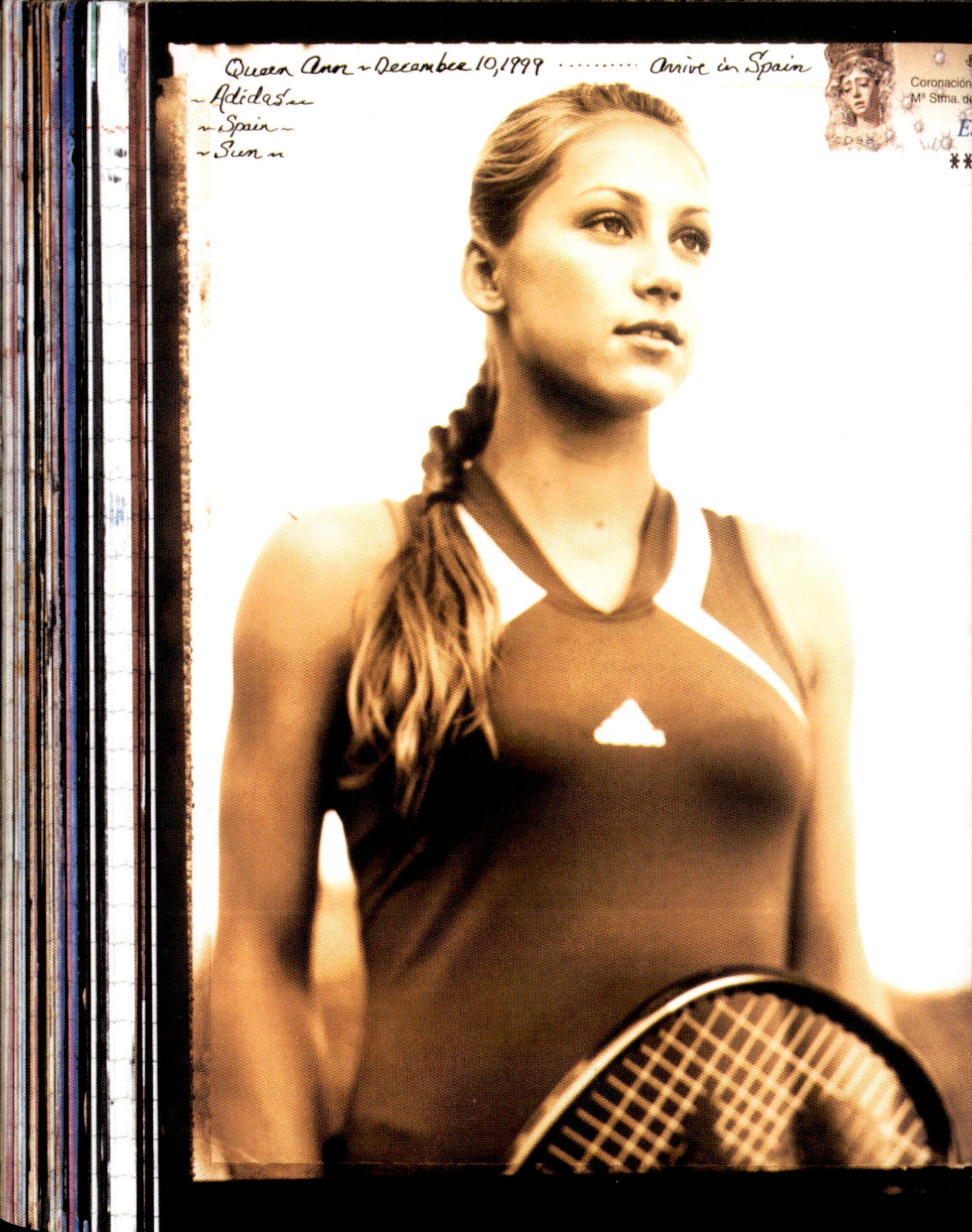
Queen Ann ~ December 10, 1999 .... Arrive in Spain
~ Adidas ~
~ Spain ~
~ Sun ~
Coronación

n't Leave Romance to Chance.

Another quiet day in the deserted vacation town of Playa De Son Moll on the N.E. point of Mallorca. Temparature so low we had to cancel shoot with Anna, eventhough there was a cloudless sky. Too cold for a tennis dress. Have never had to postpone a shoot with such wonderful light. We'll try tomorrow. Our hotel, The Sorreno Palace, is a beautiful building and a 4 star resort with 140 rooms. There are now only 6 rooms that are rented out, and the Adidas crew has 4 of them. This German tourist town feels as if there has been an evac-uation. Actually it has been quite beautiful. Dinner tonight at another bad German seafood restaurant and then back to the hotel for drinks in the empty bar. It all reminds me of the movie "The Shining".

...Buenos Nochea....
The Human Fedex Package......

ANNA KOURNIKOVA .. 12/99.. ...MALLORCA, SPAIN... FOR ADIDAS-WORLD.....

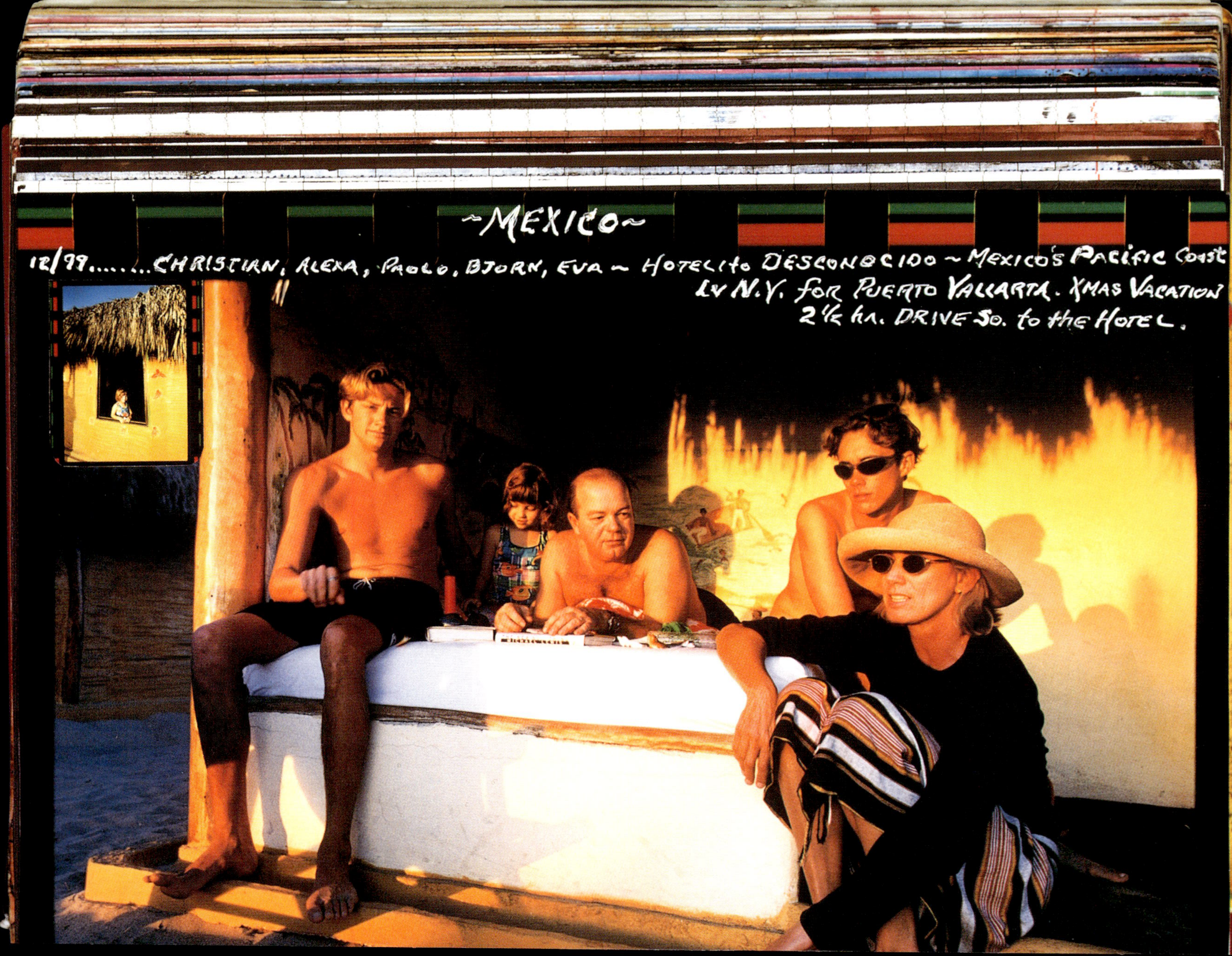
~MEXICO~
12/99.......CHRISTIAN, ALEXA, PAOLO, BJORN, EVA ~ HOTELito DESCONOCIDO ~ MEXICO'S PACIFIC COAST
LV N.Y. FOR PUERTO VALLARTA. XMAS VACATION
2½ hr. DRIVE SO. to the HOTEL.

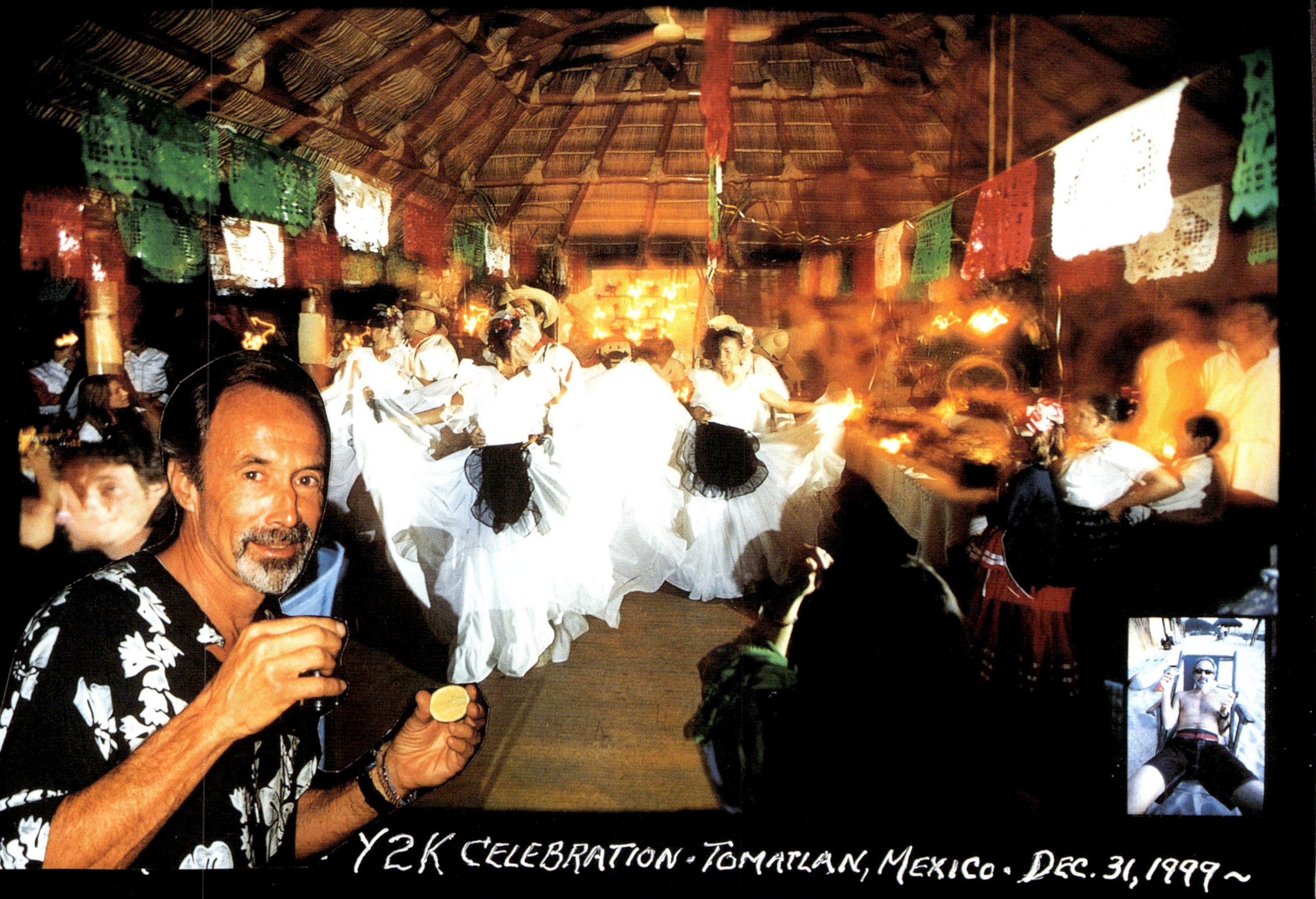
Y2K CELEBRATION · TOMATLAN, MEXICO · DEC. 31, 1999~

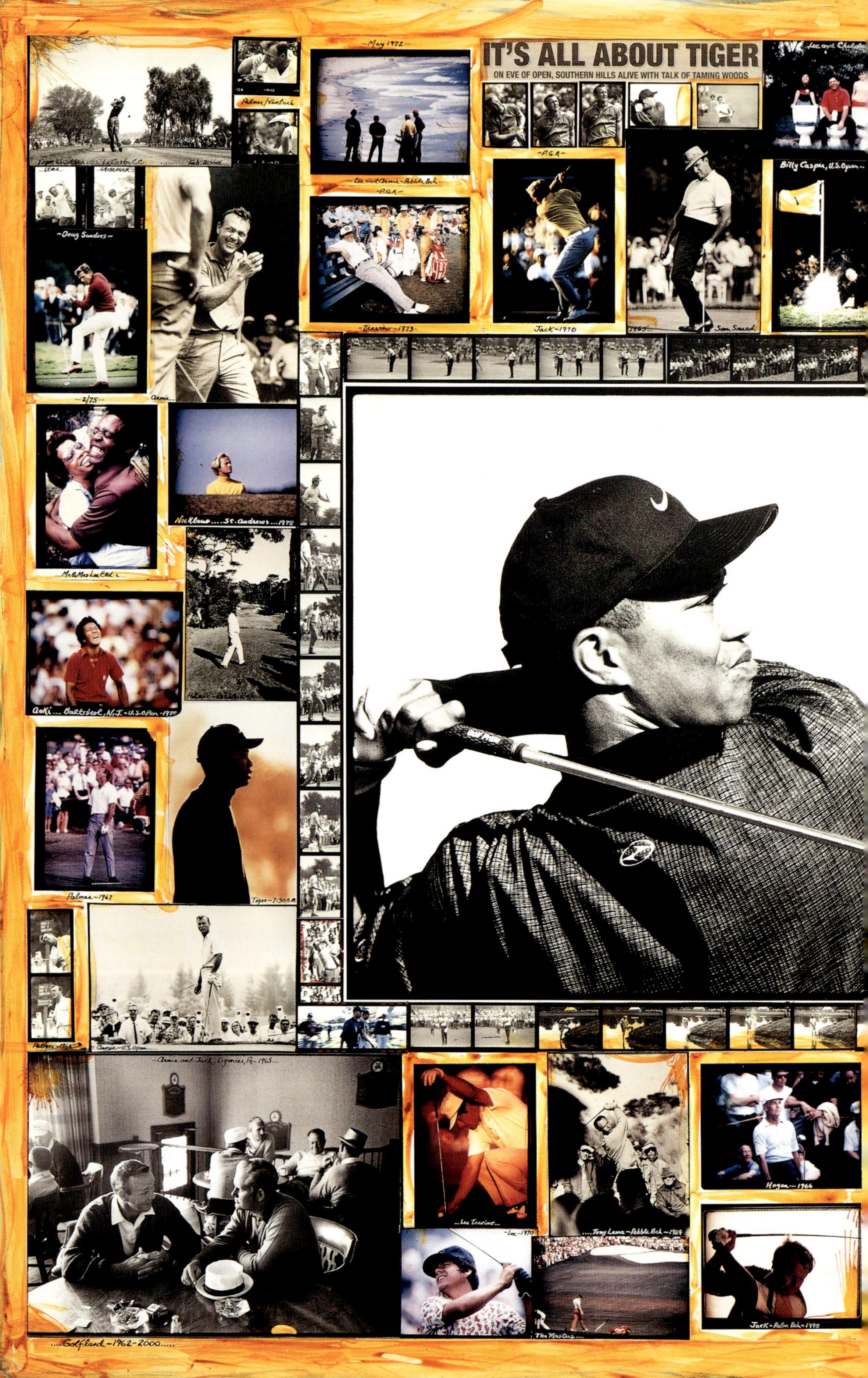

IT'S ALL ABOUT TIGER
ON EVE OF OPEN, SOUTHERN HILLS ALIVE WITH TALK OF TAMING WOODS
~May 1972~
Palmer/Venturi
~Doug Sanders~
Lee and Arnie~Pebble Bch
~P.G.R~
Trevino~1973
Jack~1970
Sam Snead
Billy Casper, U.S. Open
Nicklaus....St. Andrews....1978
Aoki....Baltusrol, N.J.~U.S. Open~1980
Palmer~1967
Tiger~7:30 A.M.
Arnie~U.S. Open
~Arnie and Jack, Ligonier, Pa~1965
...Lee Trevino...
~Lee~1970
....Tony Lema~Pebble Bch~1964
Hogan...1966
The Masters
Jack~Palm Bch~1990
.....Golfland~1962-2000.....

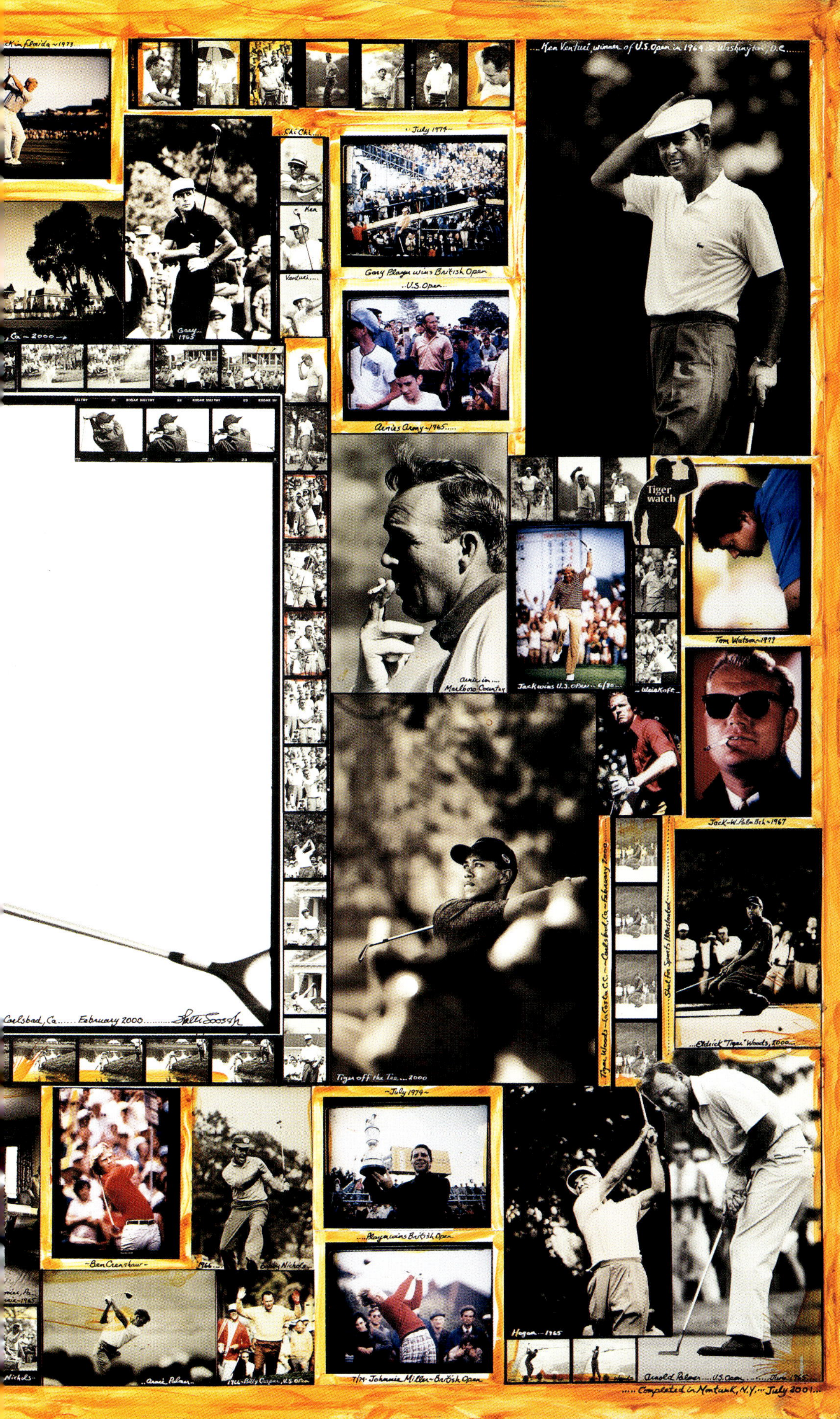
...Ken Venturi, winner of U.S. Open in 1964 in Washington, D.C....
~July 1974~
Gary Player wins British Open
..U.S. Open..
Arnies Army ~ 1965....
Tiger watch
Tom Watson ~ 1977
arnie in.... Marlboro Country
Jack wins U.S. Open... 6/80...
Jack ~ W. Palm Bch ~ 1967
Carlsbad, Ca...... February 2000..........
Tiger off the Tee....2000
...Eldrick "Tiger" Woods, 2000...
Tiger Woods ~ La Costa C.C. ~ Carlsbad, Ca ~ February 2000
Shot for Sports Illustrated
~July 1974~
...Player wins British Open
~Ben Crenshaw~
Bobby Nichols
..Arnie Palmer..
1966 ~ Billy Casper, U.S. Open
7/74 ~ Johnnie Miller ~ British Open
Hogan... 1965
Arnold Palmer.... U.S. Open.... June 1965...
....Completed in Montauk, N.Y.... July 2001...

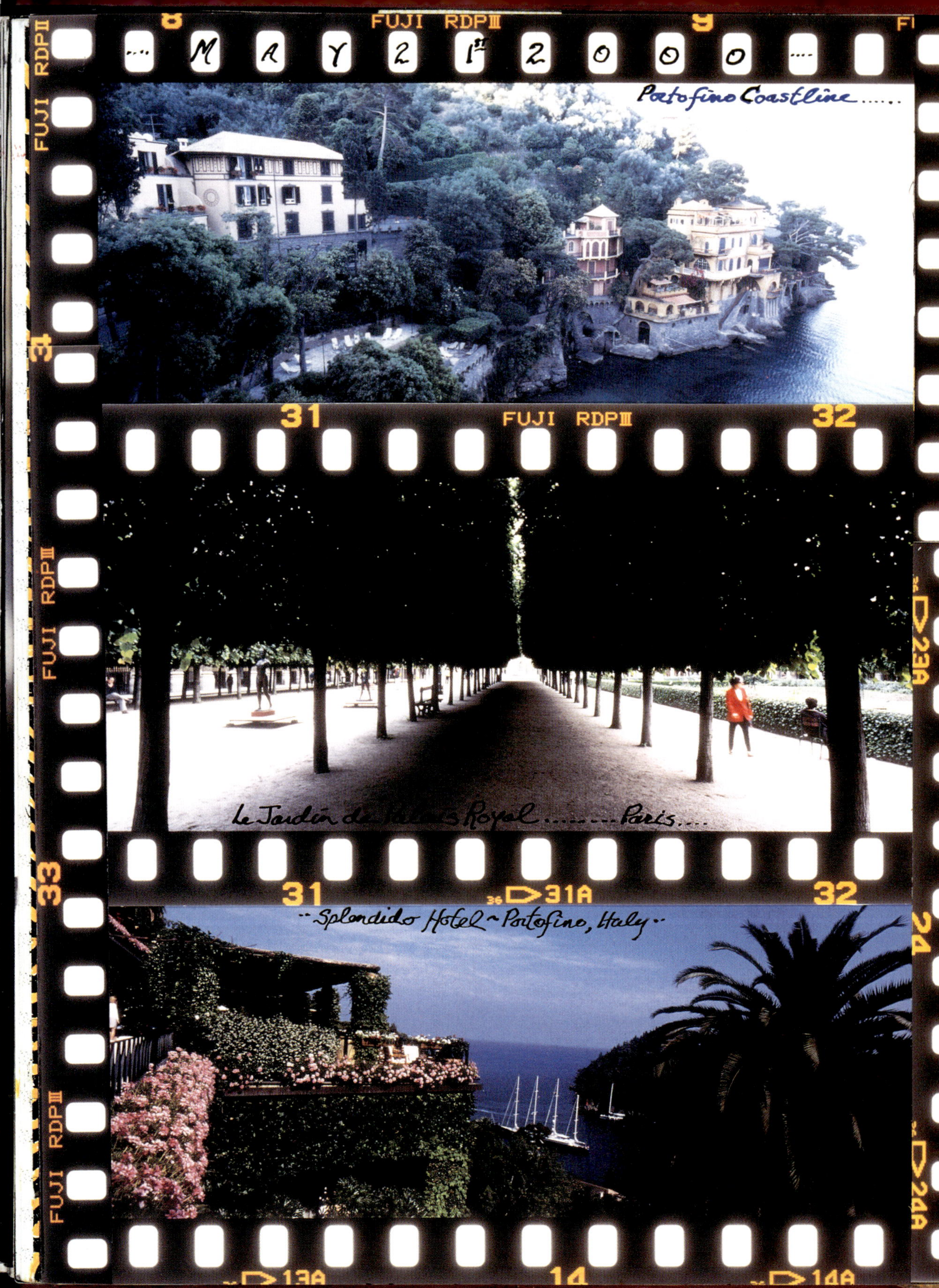

.... MAY 21st 2000 ....
FUJI RDPIII
Portofino Coastline......
Le Jardin de Palais Royal........Paris....
-- Splendido Hotel ~ Portofino, Italy --

~PARIS~ May 22nd, 2000 .....

~Plaza Athenée Hotel~

Lv. hotel at 6:00 A.M for flight to Mallorca for the Anna K. shoot, for Sports Ill., Shoot takes place at the Pula C.C., on the north coast, for 1 hour. Horrible locations at Pula except for this empty spa, Four planes and four taxis later I arrived back in Paris at 12:30 A.M. Film in hand, mission accomplished.

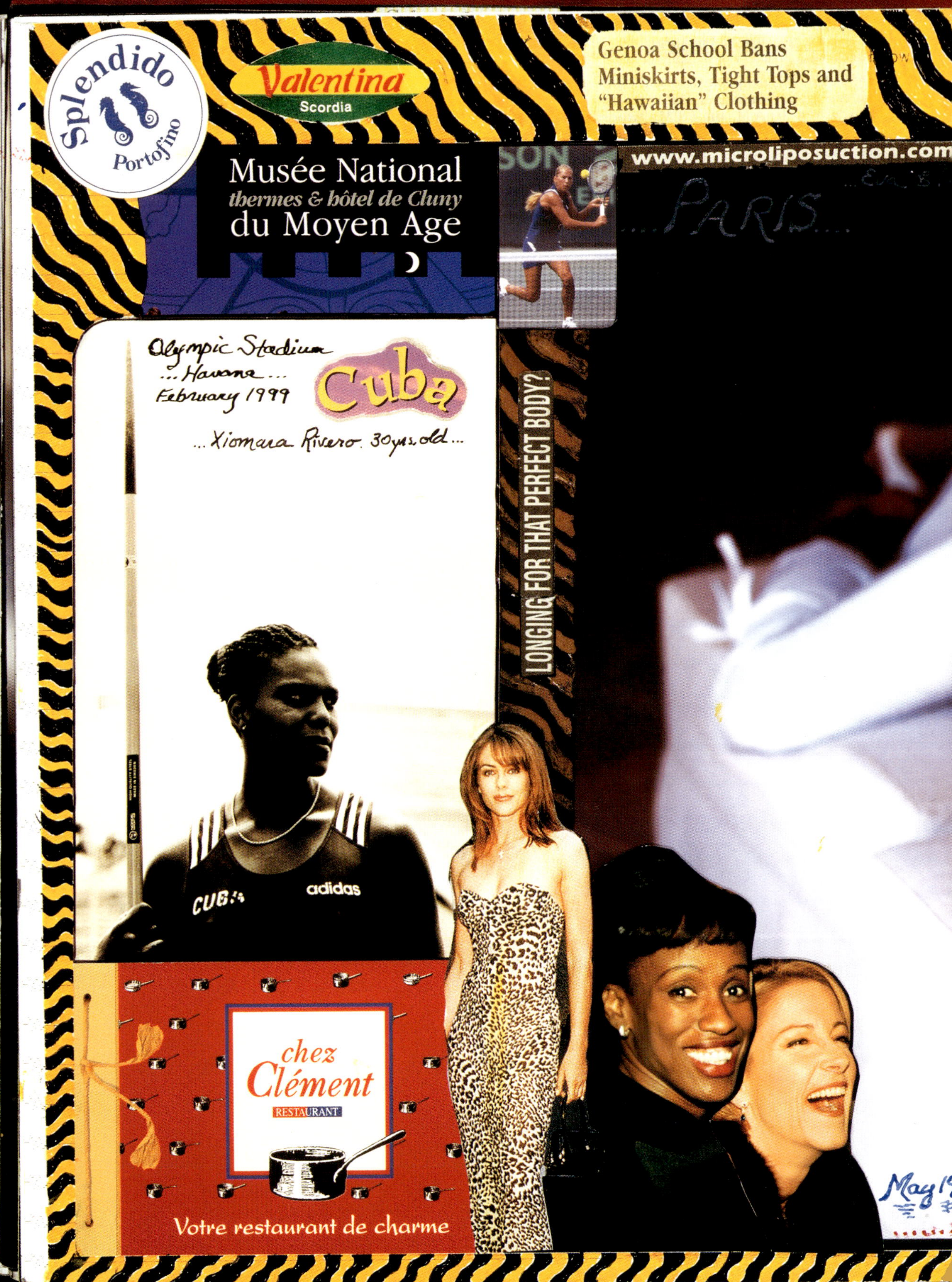

Splendido
Portofino
Valentina
Scordia
Genoa School Bans
Miniskirts, Tight Tops and
"Hawaiian" Clothing
Musée National
thermes & hôtel de Cluny
du Moyen Age
www.microliposuction.com
....PARIS....
Olympic Stadium
...Havana...
February 1999
Cuba
...Xiomara Rivero. 30yrs. old...
LONGING FOR THAT PERFECT BODY?
CUBA
adidas
chez
Clément
RESTAURANT
Votre restaurant de charme

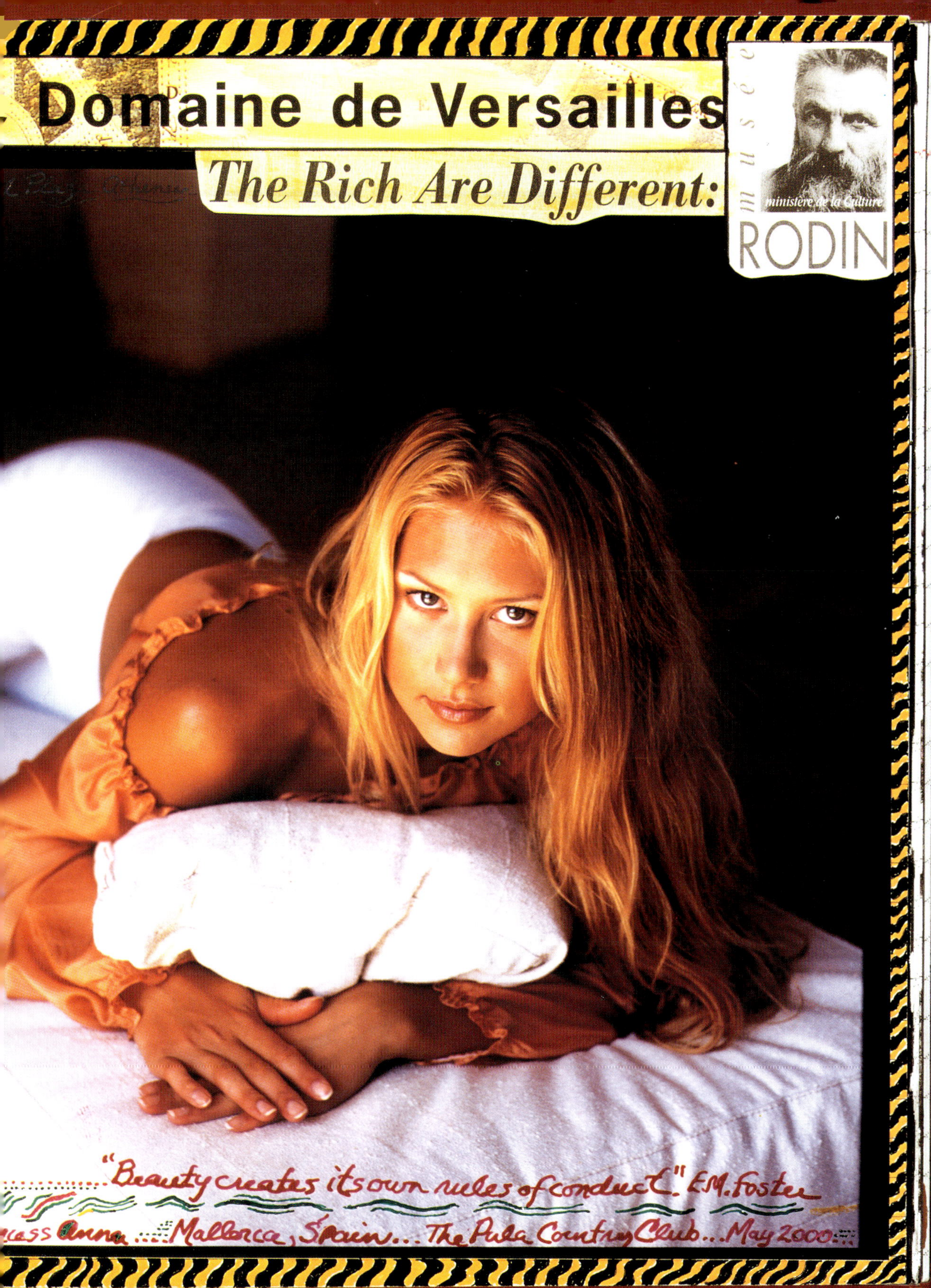
Domaine de Versailles
The Rich Are Different:
musée
ministère de la Culture
RODIN
"Beauty creates its own rules of conduct." E.M. Foster
Anna ... Mallorca, Spain... The Pula Country Club... May 2000

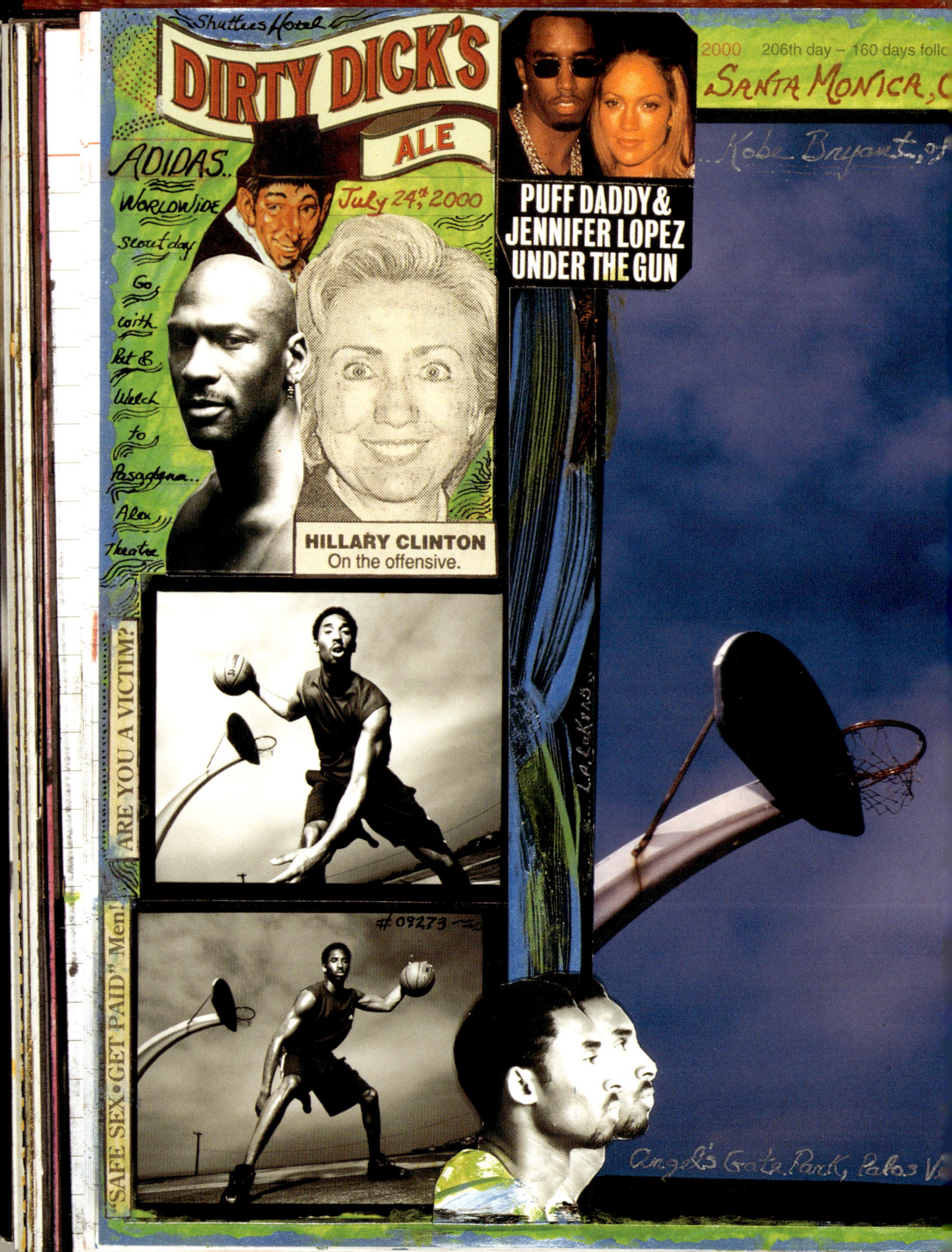
Shutters Hotel
DIRTY DICK'S
ALE
ADIDAS..
WORLDWIDE
scout day
Go
with
Pat &
Welch
to
Pasadena...
Alex
Theatre
July 24th 2000
PUFF DADDY &
JENNIFER LOPEZ
UNDER THE GUN
HILLARY CLINTON
On the offensive.
2000 206th day – 160 days follo
SANTA MONICA, C
..Kobe Bryant
ARE YOU A VICTIM?
"SAFE SEX • GET PAID" Men!
#09273
LA Lakers
Angel's Gate Park, Palos V

Farrakhan: I do like a few Jews

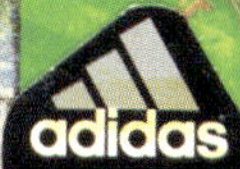

...ld Champion Los Angeles Lakers, at 21 years old.........

NOBU
MALIBU

Sushi Roku

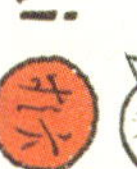

Assist

KATSU3

HOT HORNY HOUSEWIVES
Crave discreet men...

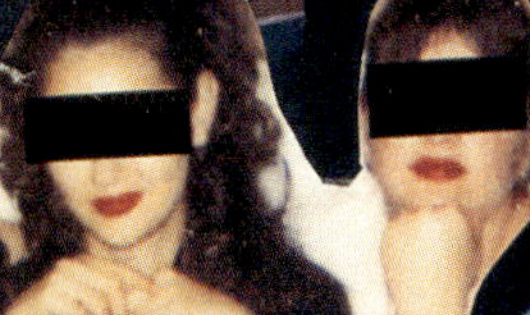

..July 25th, 2000..

.....Dinner with the wonderful adidas crew-Sushi Roku

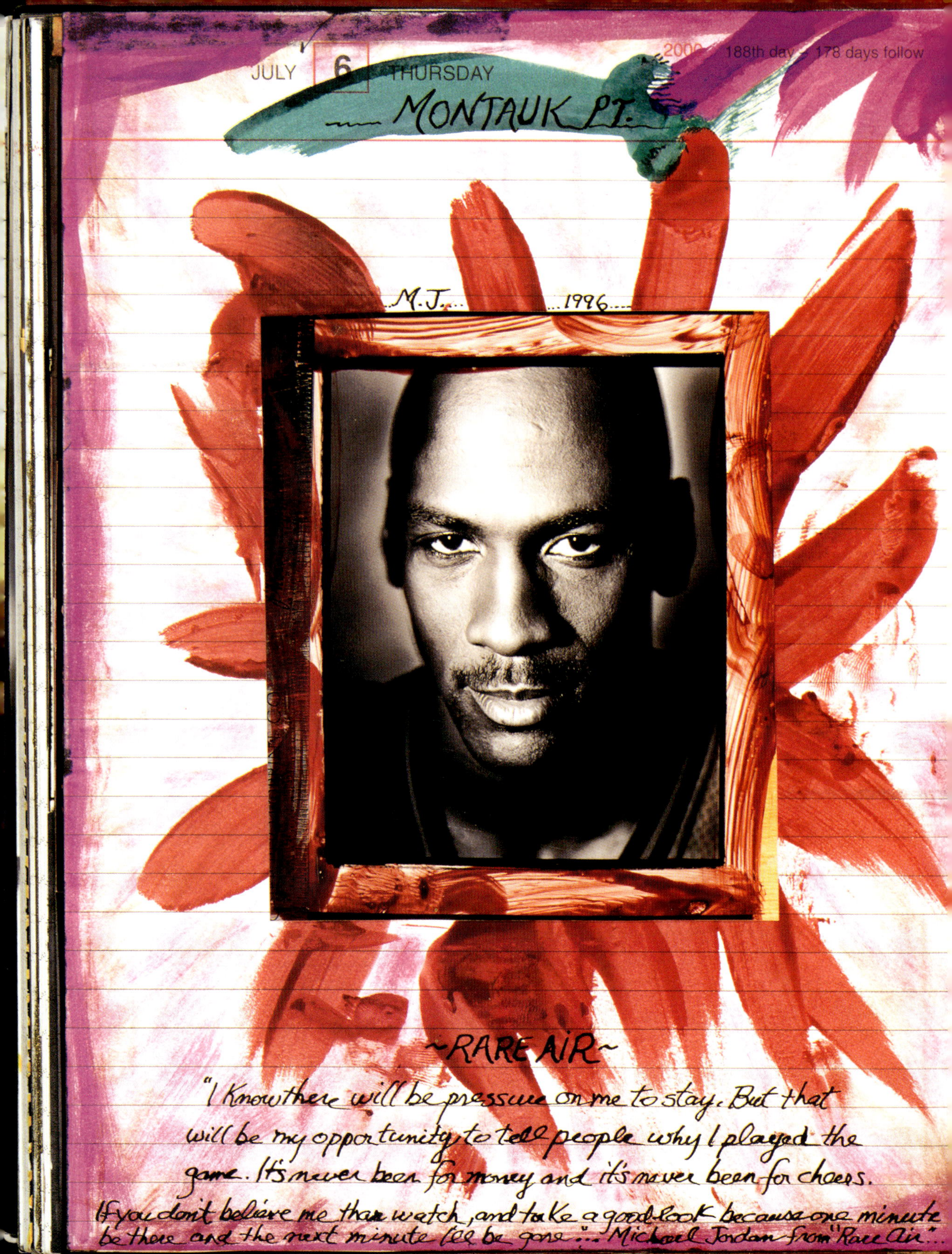

JULY 6 THURSDAY
2000 188th day – 178 days follow
MONTAUK PT.
M.J. 1996
~RARE AIR~
"I Know there will be pressure on me to stay. But that
will be my opportunity to tell people why I played the
game. It's never been for money and it's never been for cheers.
If you don't believe me then watch, and take a good look because one minute
be there and the next minute I'll be gone"... Michael Jordan from "Rare Air"...

....MONTAUK POINT ~~ July 7, 2000 ~~ Surf Ditch ~~ Dinner at Dave's...

"No bird soars too high if he soars with his own wings." William Blake

K.G. ~ Kevin Garnett .... Minnasota Timberwolves.... February 1999....

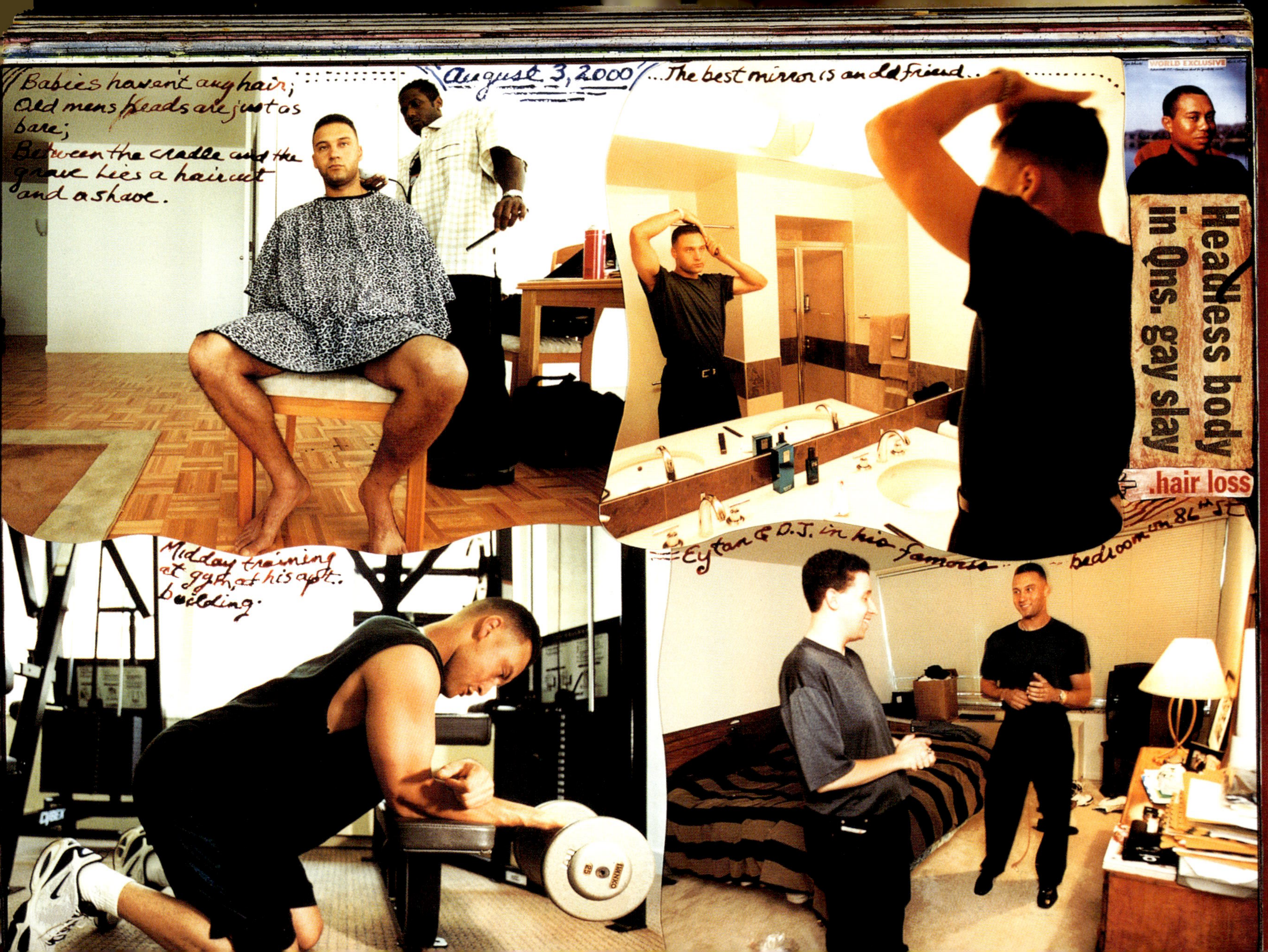
Babies haven't any hair;
Old mens heads are just as bare;
Between the cradle and the grave lies a haircut and a shave.
August 3, 2000
...The best mirror is an old friend...
WORLD EXCLUSIVE
Headless body in Qns. gay slay
.hair loss
Midday training at gym, at his apt. building.
Eytan & D.J. in his famous bedroom on 86th St.

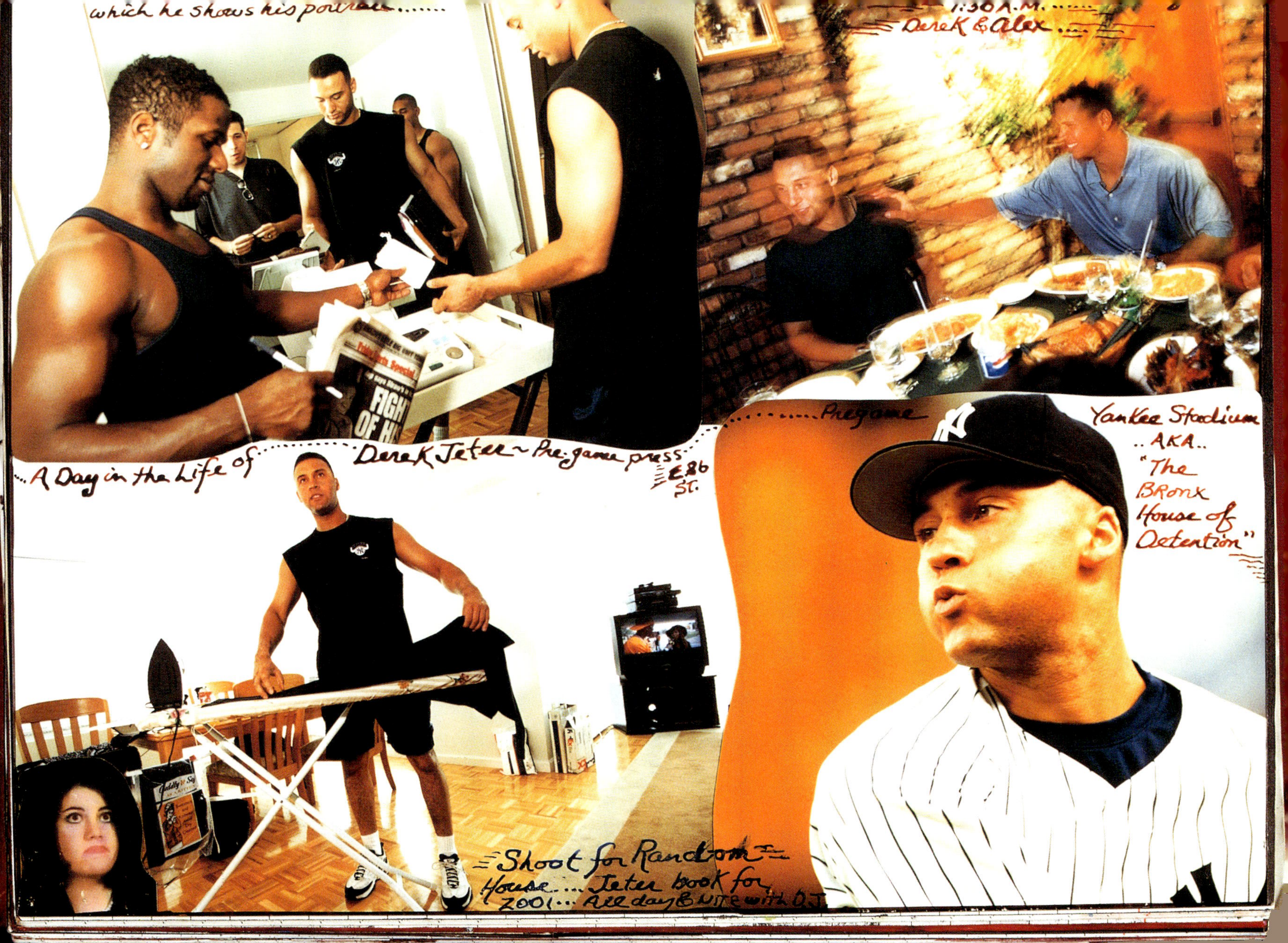
which he shows his portrait......
1:30 A.M. ......
Derek & Alex ......
...A Day in the Life of ...... Derek Jeter ~ Pre-game press E.86 St.
......Pregame
Yankee Stadium ..AKA.. "The Bronx House of Detention"
Shoot for Random House... Jeter book for 2001... All day & nite with D.J.
FIGHT OF HIS

FR@Rage.FR FRED RAGET

AUGUST **25** FRIDAY

QUACK.COM,

MARION'S REP.

2000 238th day – 128 days follow

Dave MINGEY 503-671-3479

d.MINGY@NIKE

Paris

Plaza Athénée

Last shoot day with Lefred for LeCoq Sportif. A.M. shoot at the Beach with Kids soccer at first light. Afternoon session is at and around the Eiffel tower. Good to see Fred & Paris again. The last supper is at a Japonais rest. called Taka. Not bad except for the sm

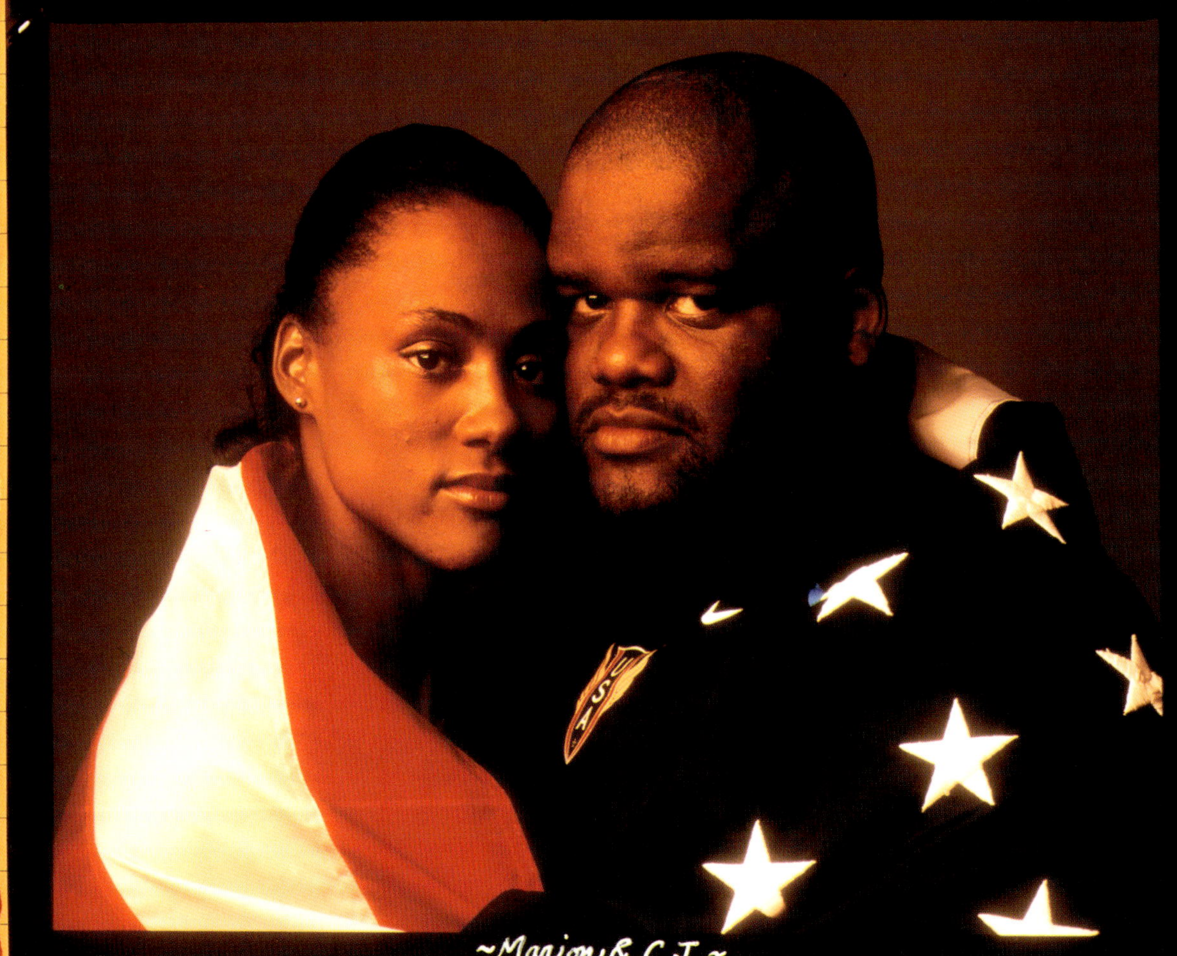

~Marion & C.J.~

Rarely do I meet an athlete with such grace, charm, and personality as a Marion Jones. She arrived, much to my shock, early and waited for us to finalize the set. Early in this case was 45 min. Once we started everything she did, every movement she made was perfection. Alas S.I. did not use the shot for the cover. They thought the image was too Elegant ....

~Mrs. Jones~

Your life is waiting.™

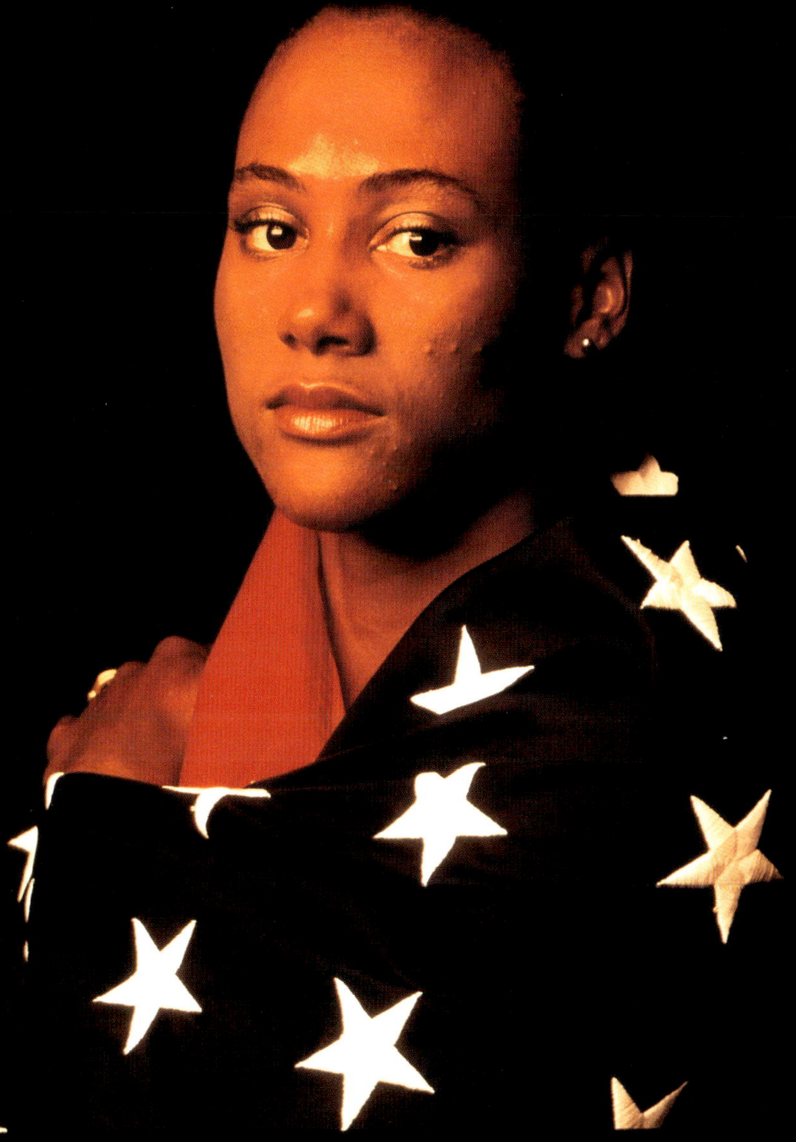

..Lv. Paris for Brussels to shoot Marion + C.J. for Spts. Ill... Stay at Montgomery..

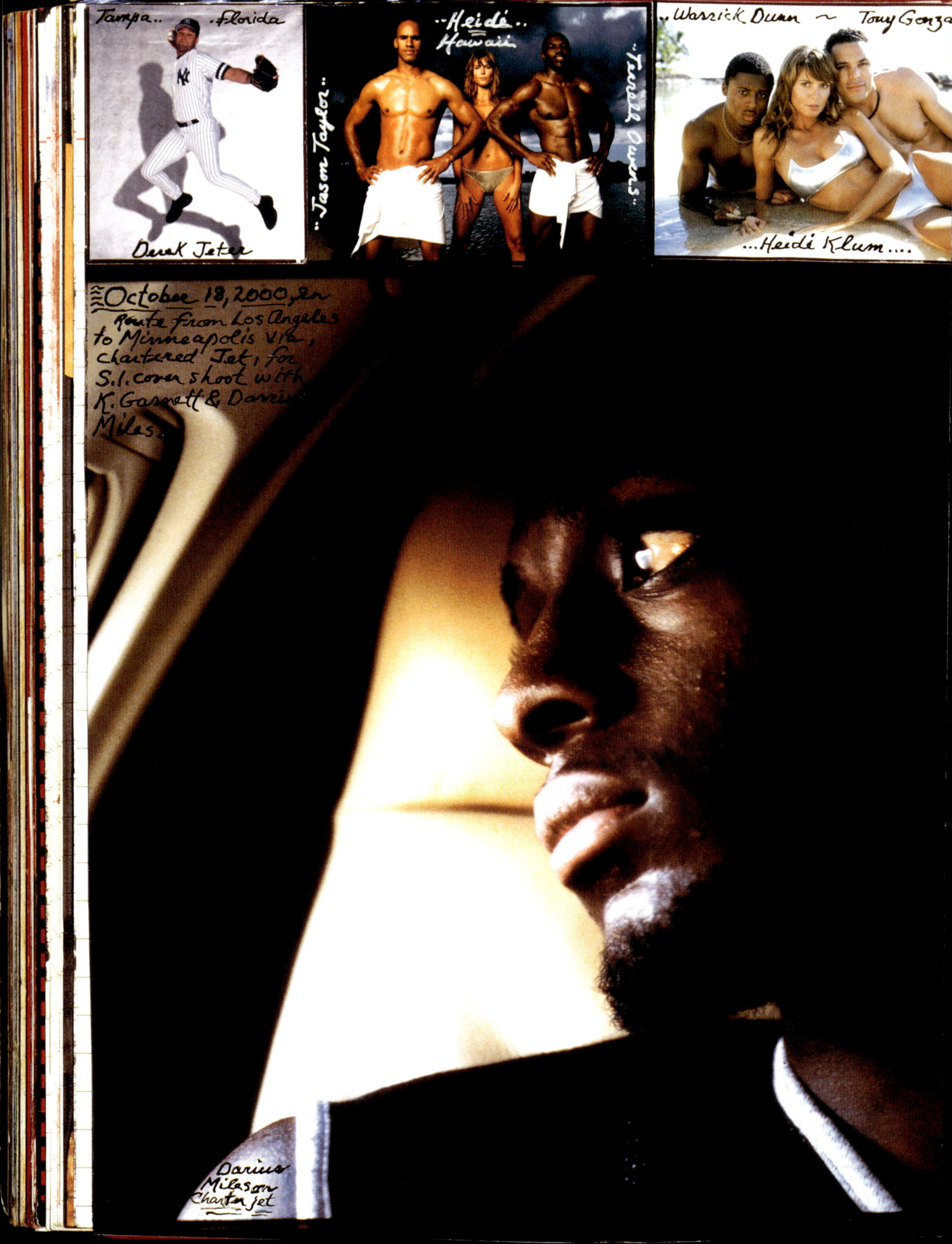
Tampa.. .Florida
Derek Jeter
..Heidi.. Hawaii
..Jason Taylor..
..Terrell Owens..
..Warrick Dunn ~ Tony Gonza
...Heidi Klum....
October 18, 2000, en Route from Los Angeles to Minneapolis via, chartered Jet, for S.I. cover shoot with K. Garnett & Darri
Miles.
Darius Miles on Charter jet

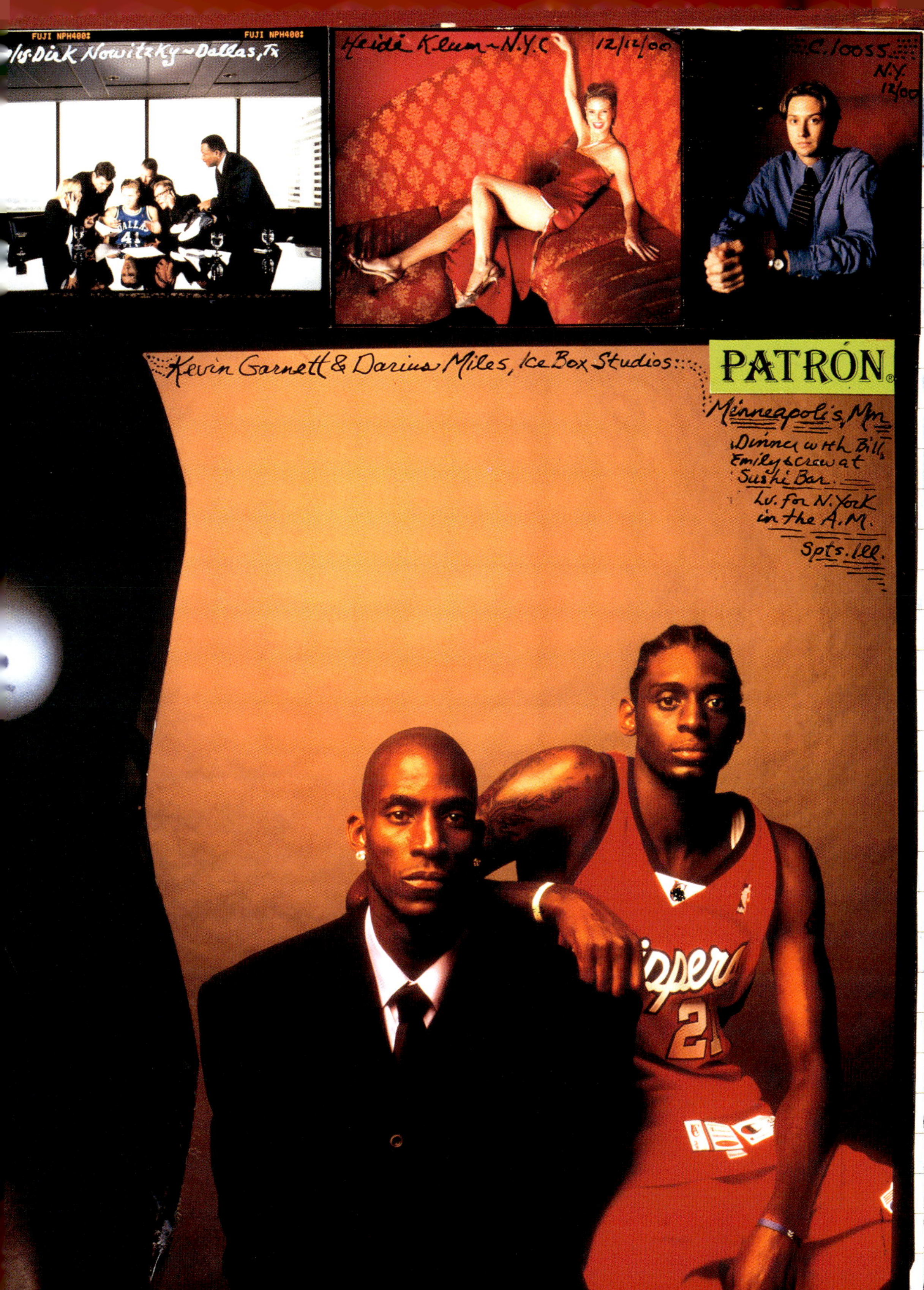
FUJI NPH400
FUJI NPH400
Dirk Nowitzky ~ Dallas, Tx
DALLAS
41
Heidi Klum ~ N.Y.C
12/12/00
C. Iooss
N.Y.
12/00
Kevin Garnett & Darius Miles, Ice Box Studios
PATRÓN
Minneapolis, Mn
Dinner with Bill, Emily & crew at Sushi Bar.
Lv. for N. York in the A.M.
Spts. Ill.
21

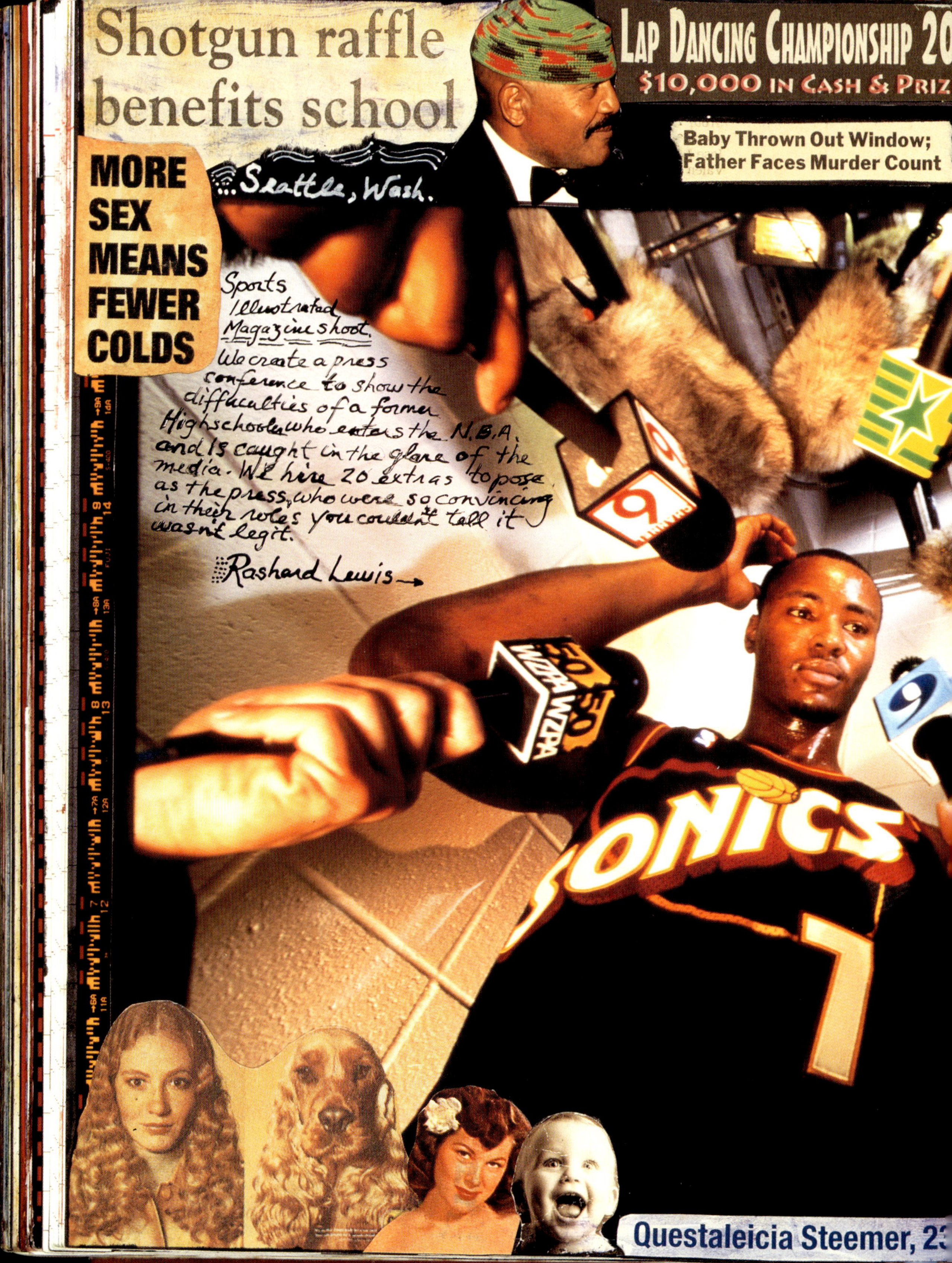

Shotgun raffle benefits school
LAP DANCING CHAMPIONSHIP 20
$10,000 IN CASH & PRIZ
Baby Thrown Out Window; Father Faces Murder Count
MORE SEX MEANS FEWER COLDS
Seattle, Wash.
Sports Illustrated Magazine shoot.
We create a press conference to show the difficulties of a former Highschooler who enters the N.B.A. and is caught in the glare of the media. We hire 20 extras to pose as the press, who were so convincing in their roles you couldn't tell it wasn't legit.
Rashard Lewis →
SONICS
7
Questaleicia Steemer, 23

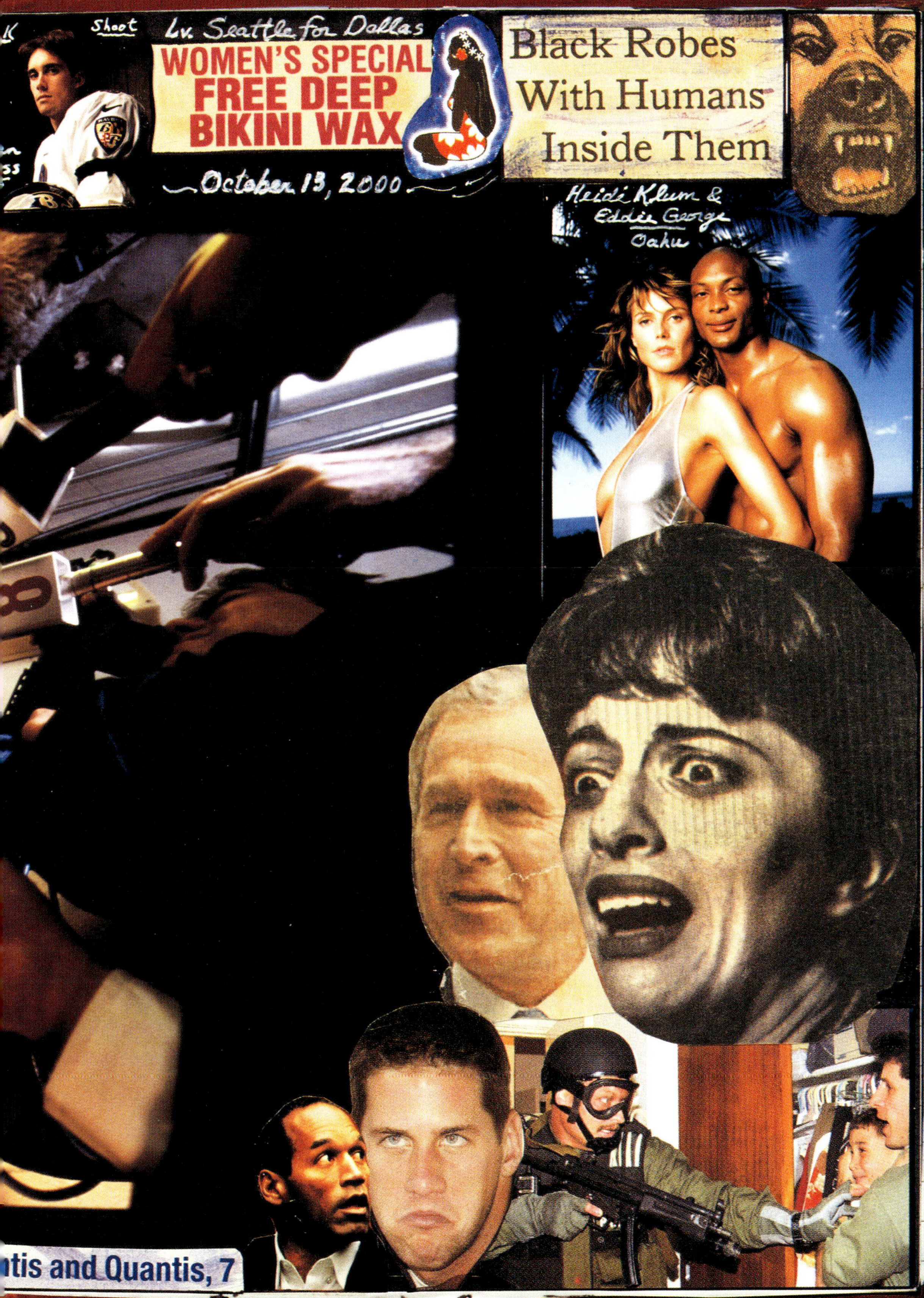
Shoot
Lv. Seattle for Dallas
WOMEN'S SPECIAL
FREE DEEP
BIKINI WAX
Black Robes
With Humans
Inside Them
October 13, 2000
Heidi Klum &
Eddie George
Oahu
tis and Quantis, 7

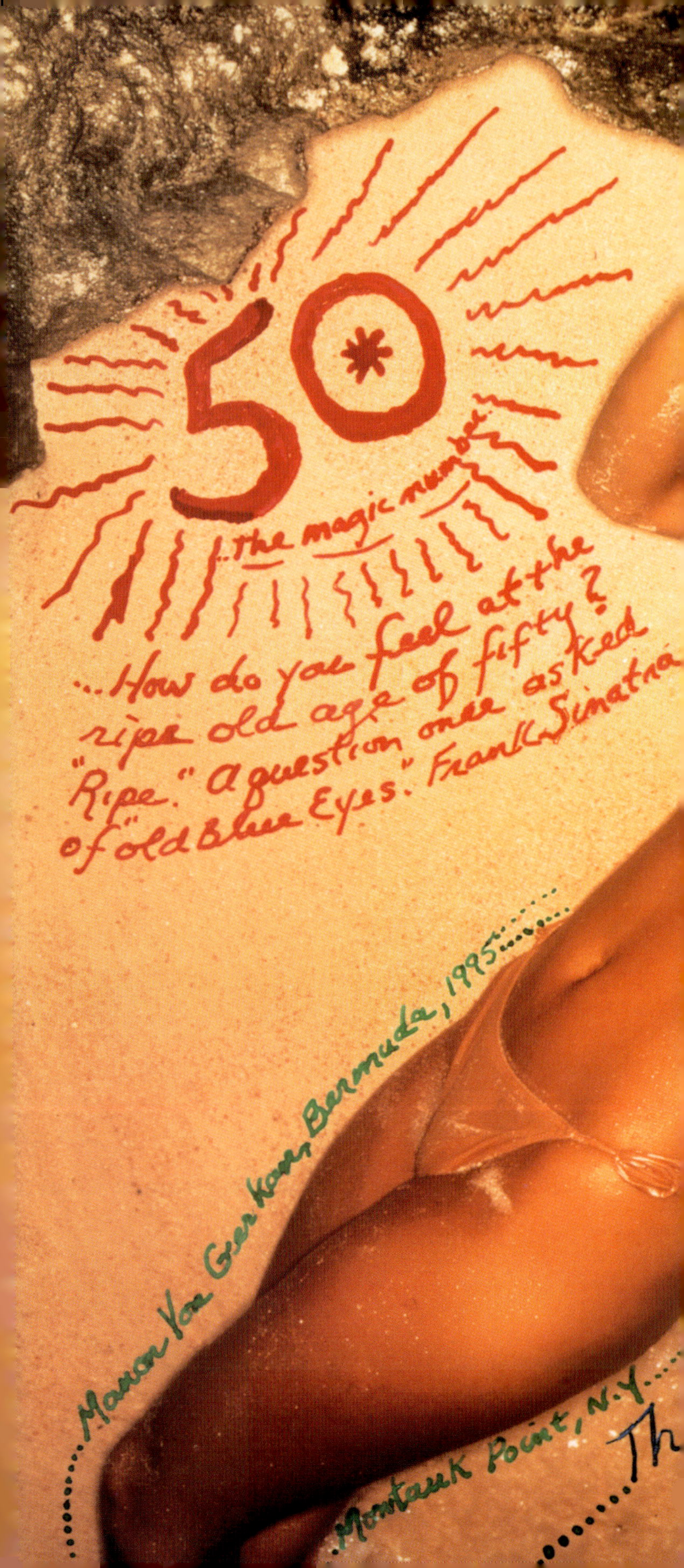

50

...the magic number

...How do you feel at the ripe old age of fifty? "Ripe." A question once asked of "Old Blue Eyes." Frank Sinatra

Manon Von Gerkan, Bermuda, 1995........

Montauk Point, N.Y.....

Th

HARDCORE HAWAIIAN

Kauai

of the century at Caswells, on the eve, November 18th, 2000......

pRest of Birthdays to Brother LEE B.

at a day and night! Stop the presses, turn off

lighthouse, Lee Bieler has made it to the

half century mark. I now have almost no

recall of my historic celebration.

Lee it's not the end but only the

start of another 50 at Ditch.

Love, Eva, Walter, Chris, + B.J.

Montauk

DECEMBER 15 FRIDAY ....Molly Simms.....for Sports Illustrat

2000 350th day – 16 days follow

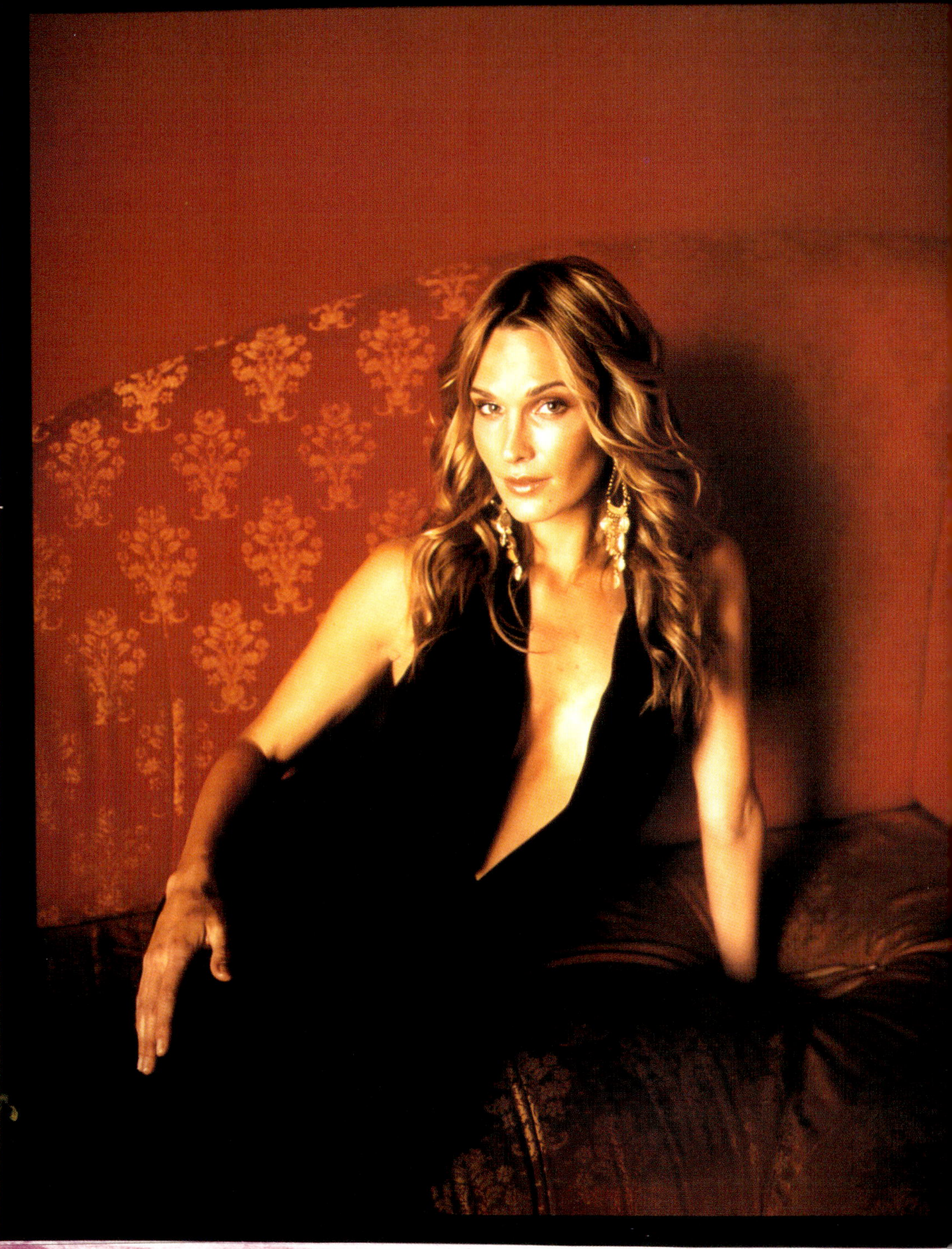

....Photographed at the Ivy Club, N.Y.C....

~S.I. Sportsman of the Year~

2000 351st day – 15 days follow

....Montauk.....Mr. Woods......

the Age of Napster

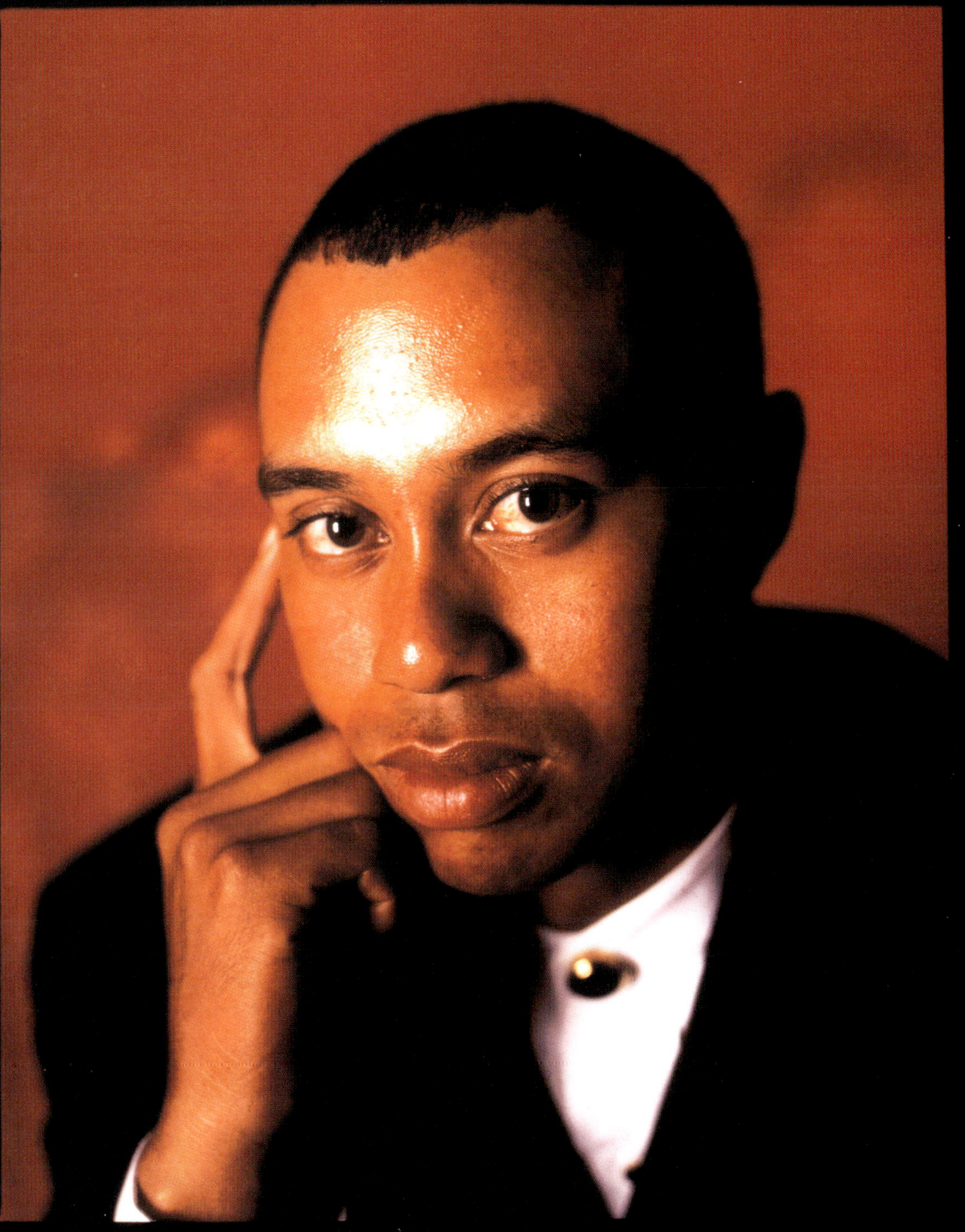

.....Photographed December 12, 2000.....

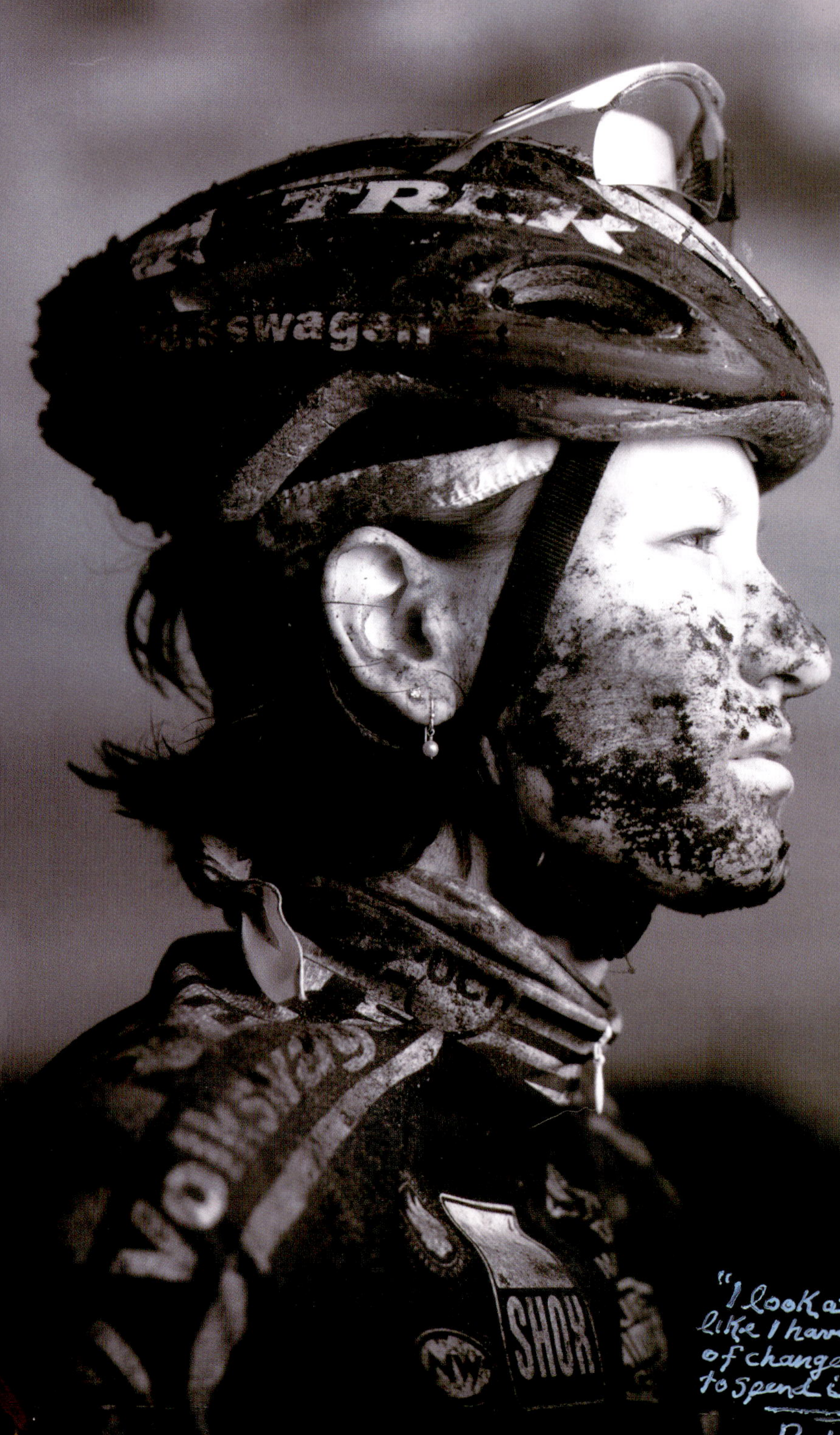

Key Biscayne, Fla..... January 6, 2001..... Power Bar Shoot
SHOX
"I look at race day like I have a pocket full of change, and my job i to spend it all."
... Ruthie Mathes ...
... 2000 Olympic Team

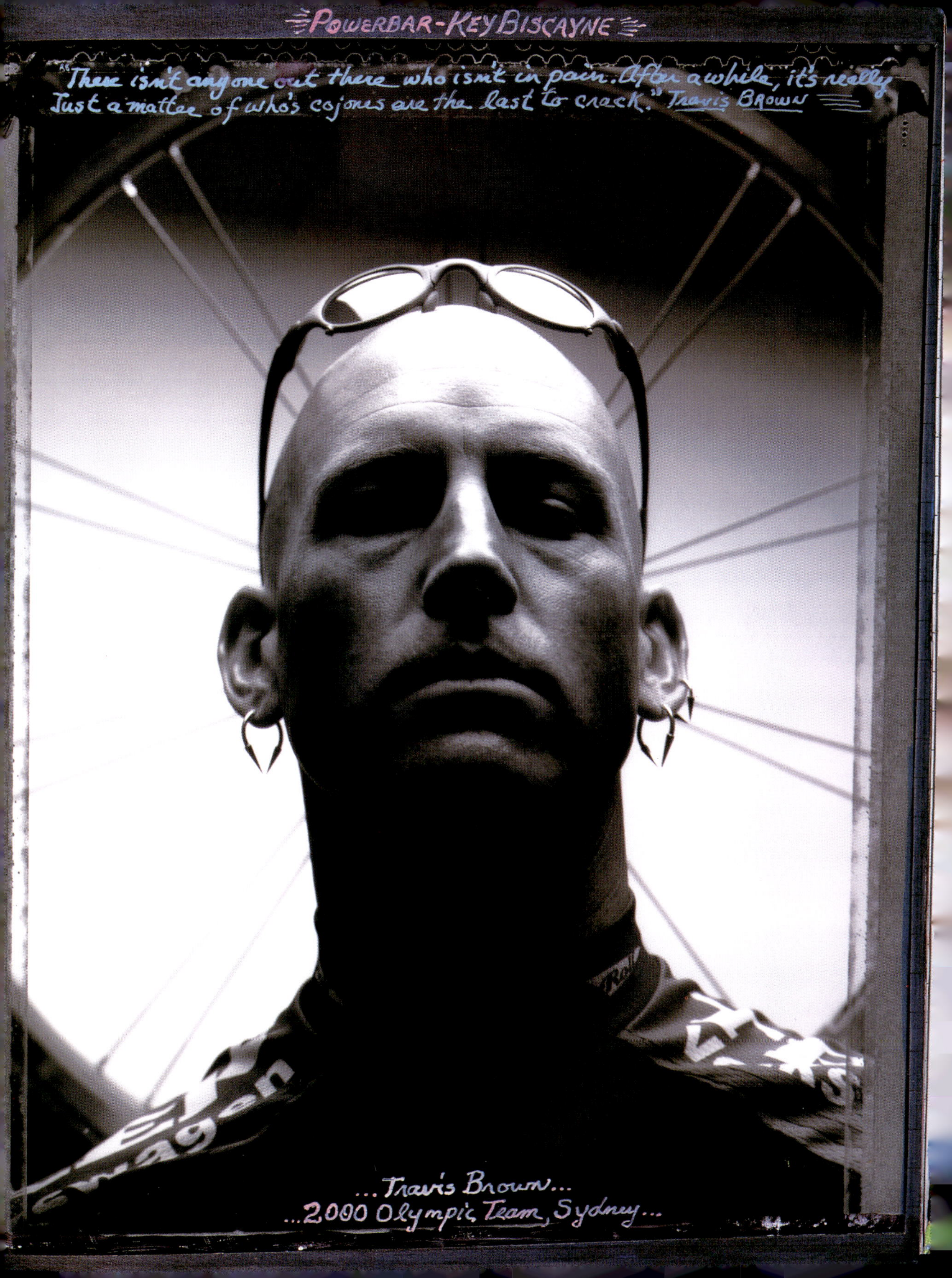

POWERBAR-KEY BISCAYNE

"There isn't anyone out there who isn't in pain. After a while, it's really just a matter of who's cojones are the last to crack." Travis Brown

...Travis Brown...
...2000 Olympic Team, Sydney...

Waikiki, Hawaii .... N.F.L. Probowlers and Heide Klum for S.I. Swimsuit issu

Terrell Owens, Wide receiver
San Francisco 49ers

Lagoon at The Campbell
Estate on the West Side

Young humpback jumps, falls on touris

POLYNESIAN LUAU!! January 31st 2001 ccc Waikiki ccc S.L.

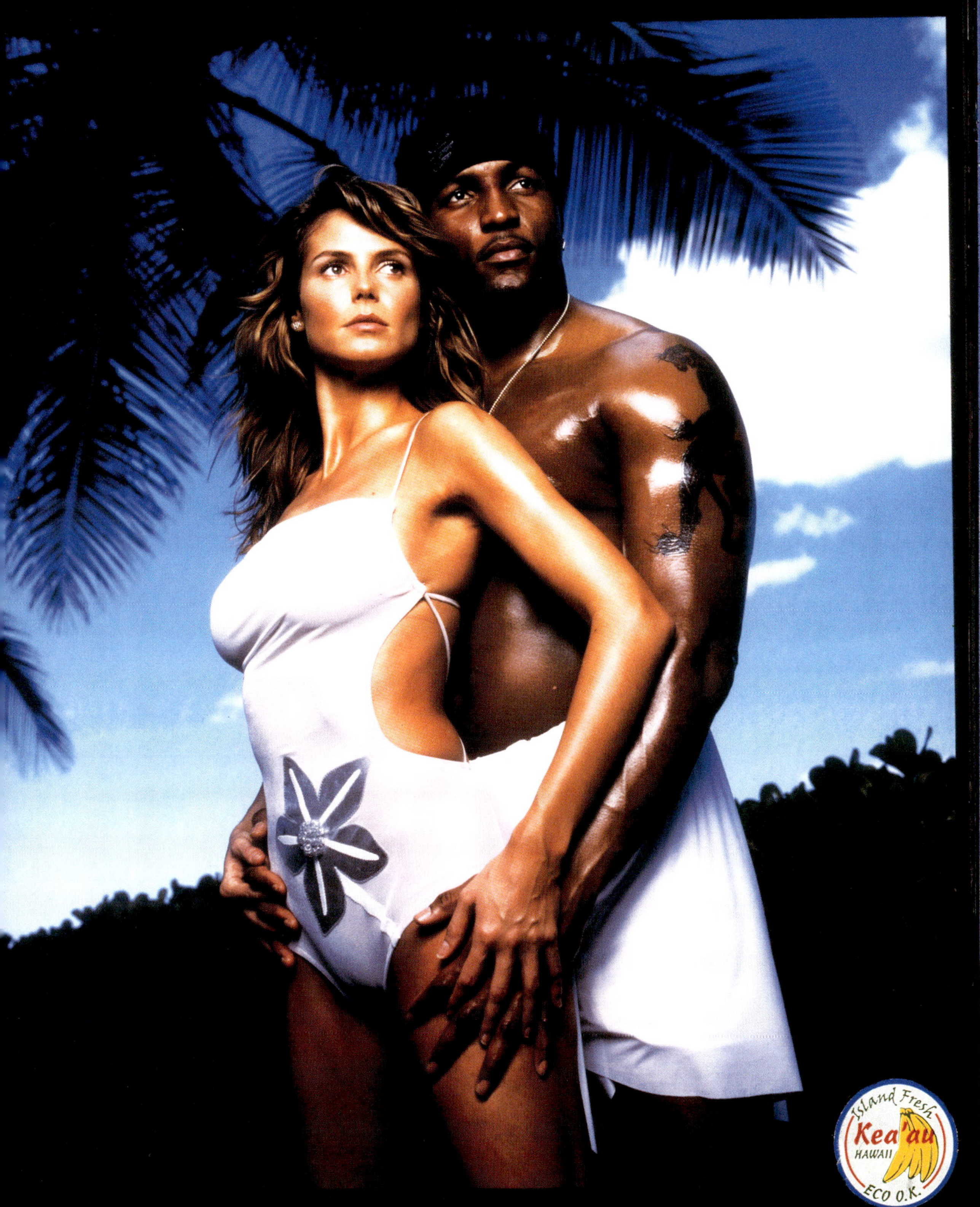

Heide Klum & Ray Lewis ccc Sports Illustrated Swimsuit issue ccc Westside of Oahu

February 3rd, 2001 ~ Sports Illustrated Swimsuit shoot ~ Oahu, Hawaii

Ray Lewis, Baltimore Ravens linebacker, accused murder in twin slaying outside of a club in Atlanta before last years Superbowl is found innocent by a jury of his peers. He returns to football to become the N.F.L.'s most fearsome linebacker. He then plays in this years Super Bowl and becomes the games M.V.P., as his Ravens beat the Giants. He is chosen for the S.I. swimsuit shoot to pose with Heide Klum until the managing Editor gets the news and says he'll never use the photos. So just go through the motions Iooss and we'll tell him later he didn't make the magazine. We will then send him some prints to placate him. Unfortunately he was my best model and became part of my best photograph. I just couldn't treat him that way.

...Shot on the Westside of Oahu...
with Ray Lewis, Terrell Owens,
and Heidi Klum.... for S.I.......
This is the 29th year I've
participated on the
swimsuit story......
I hope there will
be another chance.

Raccoon attack at beach

Free For One Month ... A Full Head of Hair

0308 nerves that controlled his hand and

Baltimore

March 1st, 2001

Sports Illustrated

The great Johnny Unitas, No. 19, my last boyhood hero, still alive, and had never met or photographed. An unusually emotional day for me, memories flashing back to my late teens, traveling to Baltimore to see & photograph my beloved Colts, Johnny U. and Raymond Berry. And me wanting to take a compelling photograph of a man with the once golden arm, now almost useless, unable to even brush his teeth.

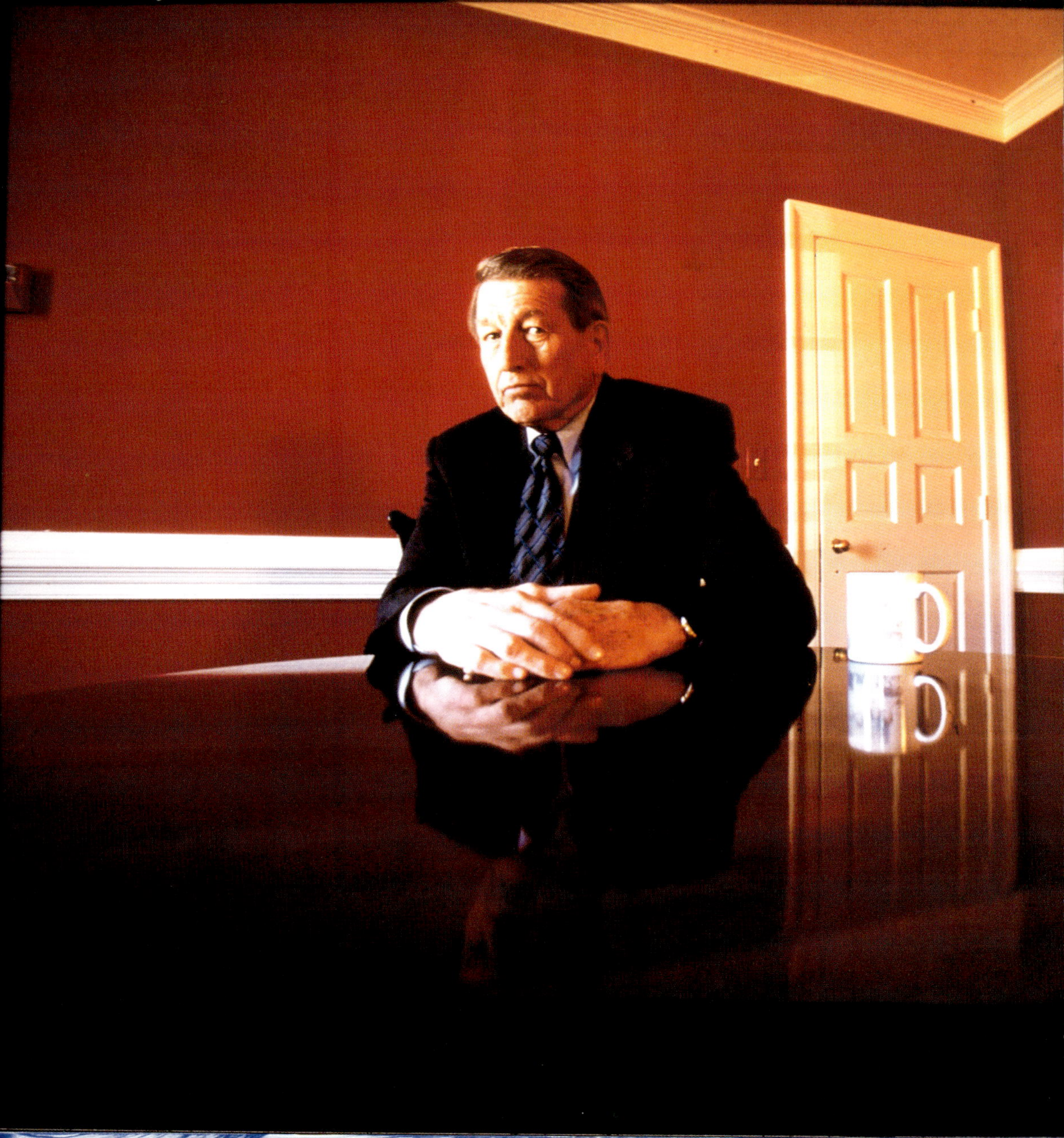

Montauk Pt.

March 2, 2001

~ Living Legend ~ John Unitas ~

Baseball 2001

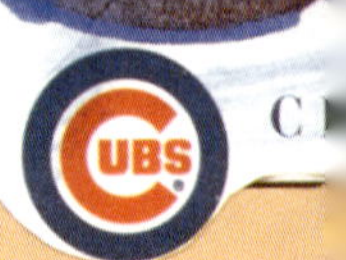

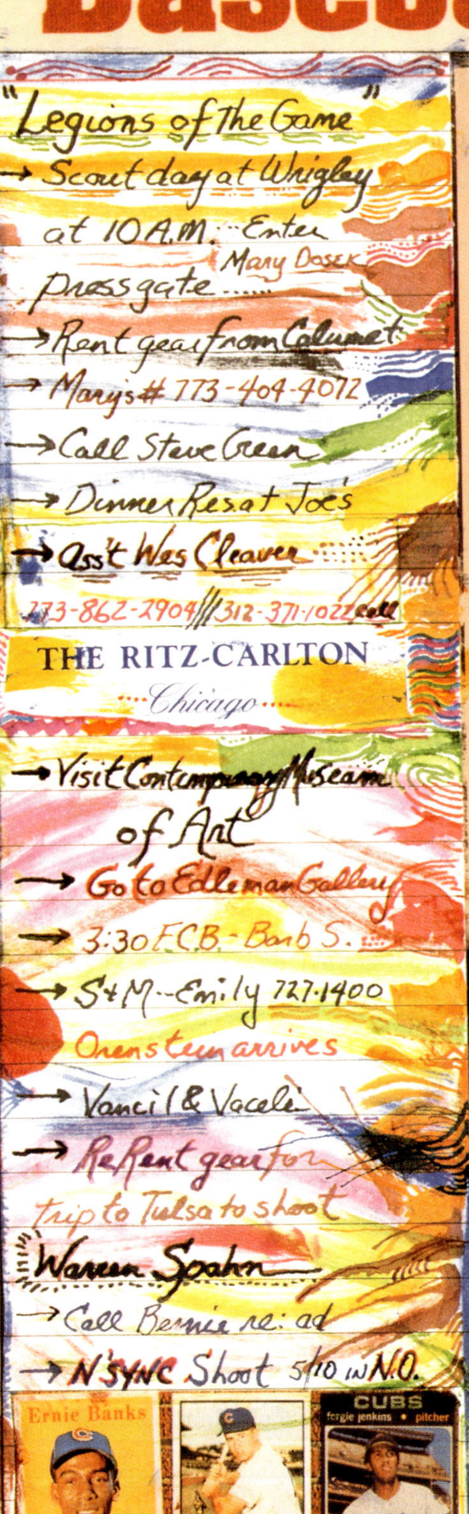

"Until I find a real man, I'll settle for a real smoke."

May 8th, 2001

The Great Ernie Banks at his beloved Wrigley Field.

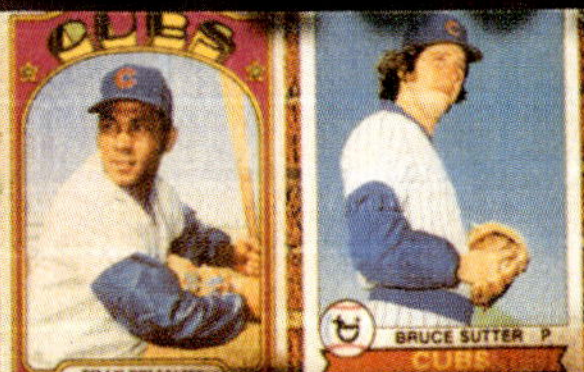

www.cubs.com

SPORTS

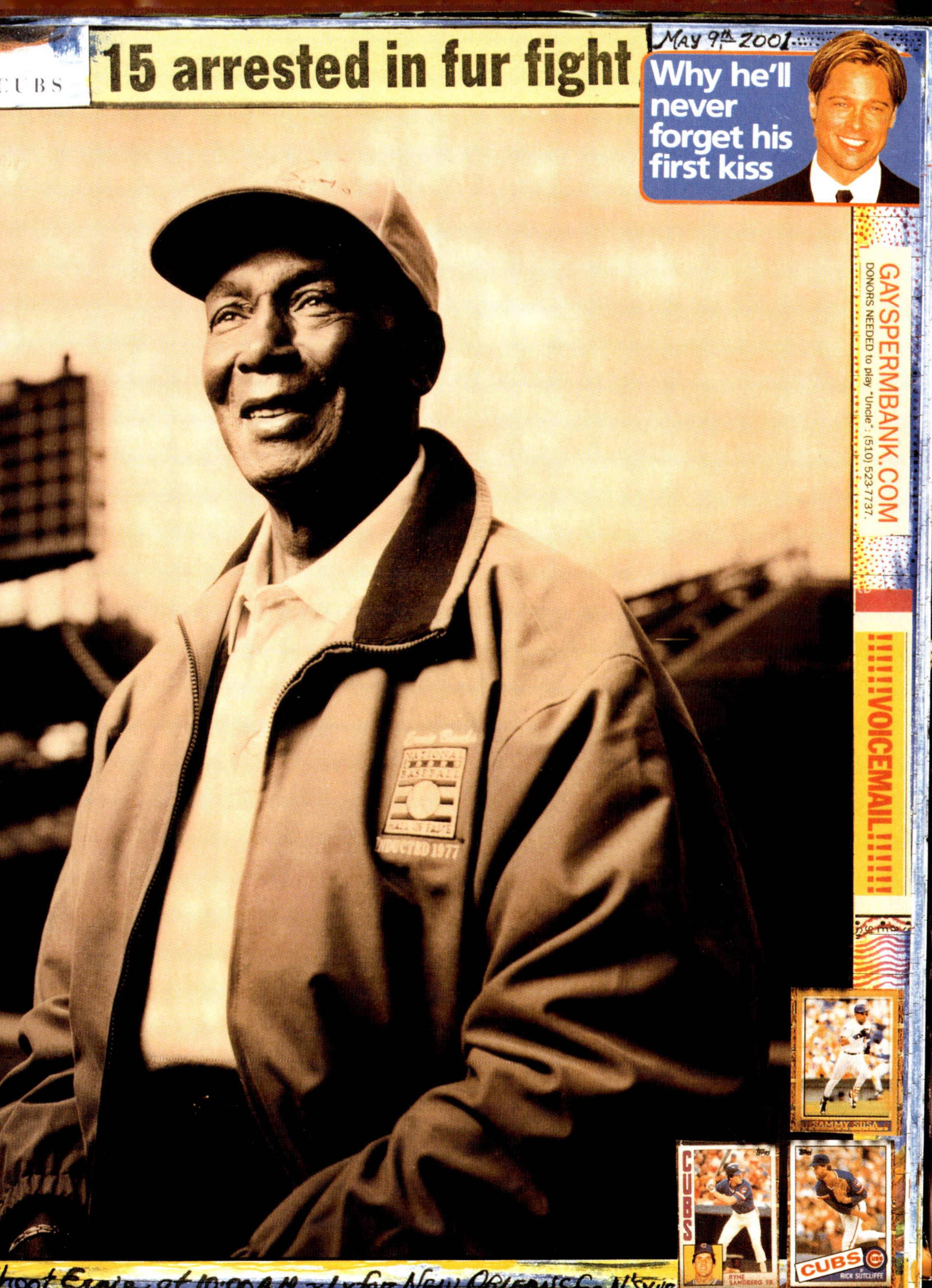

CUBS
15 arrested in fur fight
MAY 9th 2001
Why he'll never forget his first kiss
GAYSPERMBANK.COM
DONORS NEEDED to play "Uncle": (510) 523-7737.
!!!!!!VOICEMAIL!!!!!!
INDUCTED 1977
SAMMY SOSA
CUBS
RYNE SANDBERG 2B
CUBS
RICK SUTCLIFFE
hoot Ernie at 10:00 A.M. ~ Lv for New Orleans for N'Sync

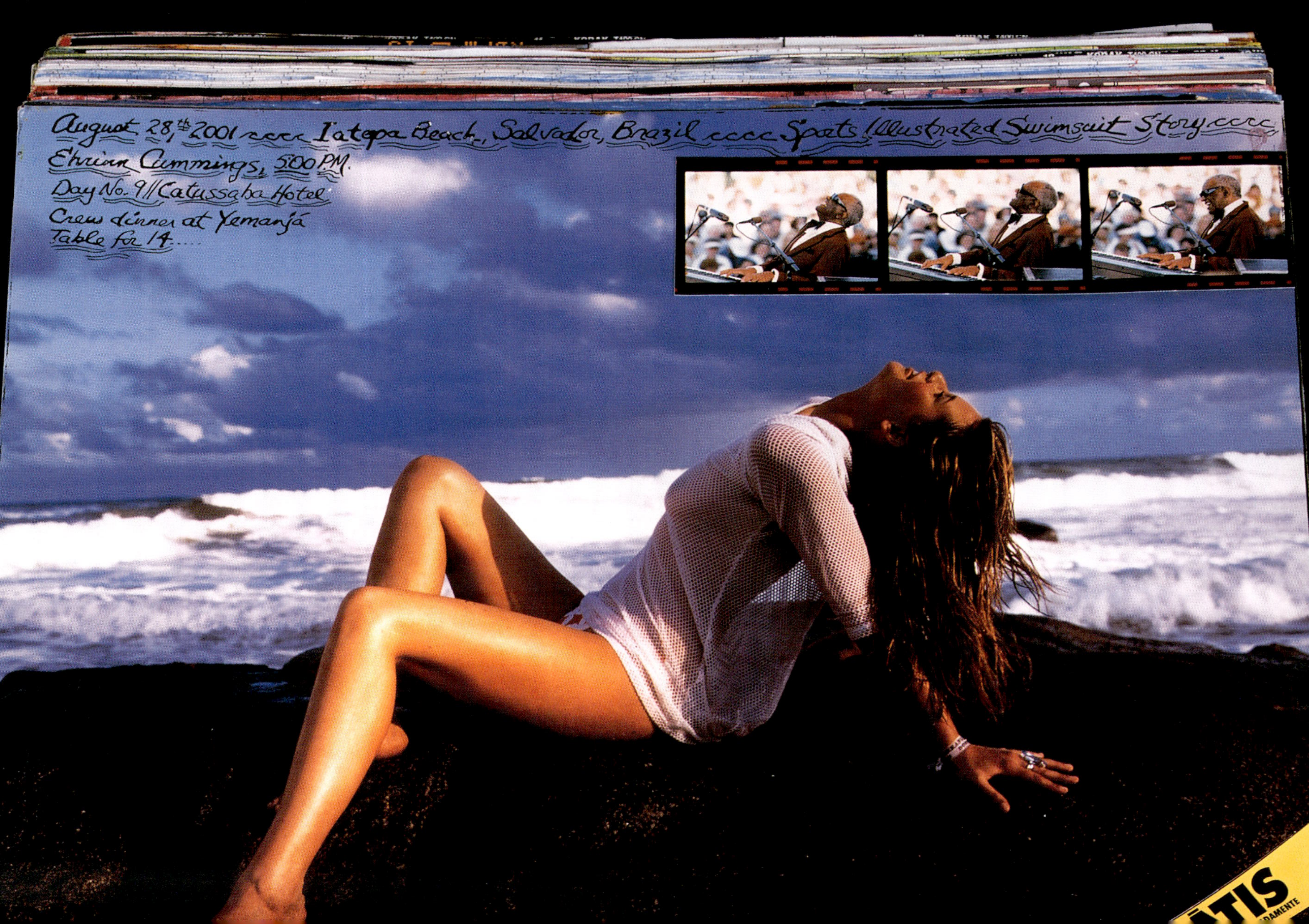
August 28th, 2001 cccc Iatepa Beach, Salvador, Brazil cccc Sports Illustrated Swimsuit Story cccc
Ehrinn Cummings, 5:00 PM.
Day No. 9 // Catussaba Hotel
Crew dinner at Yemanjá
Table for 14....
ÁTIS

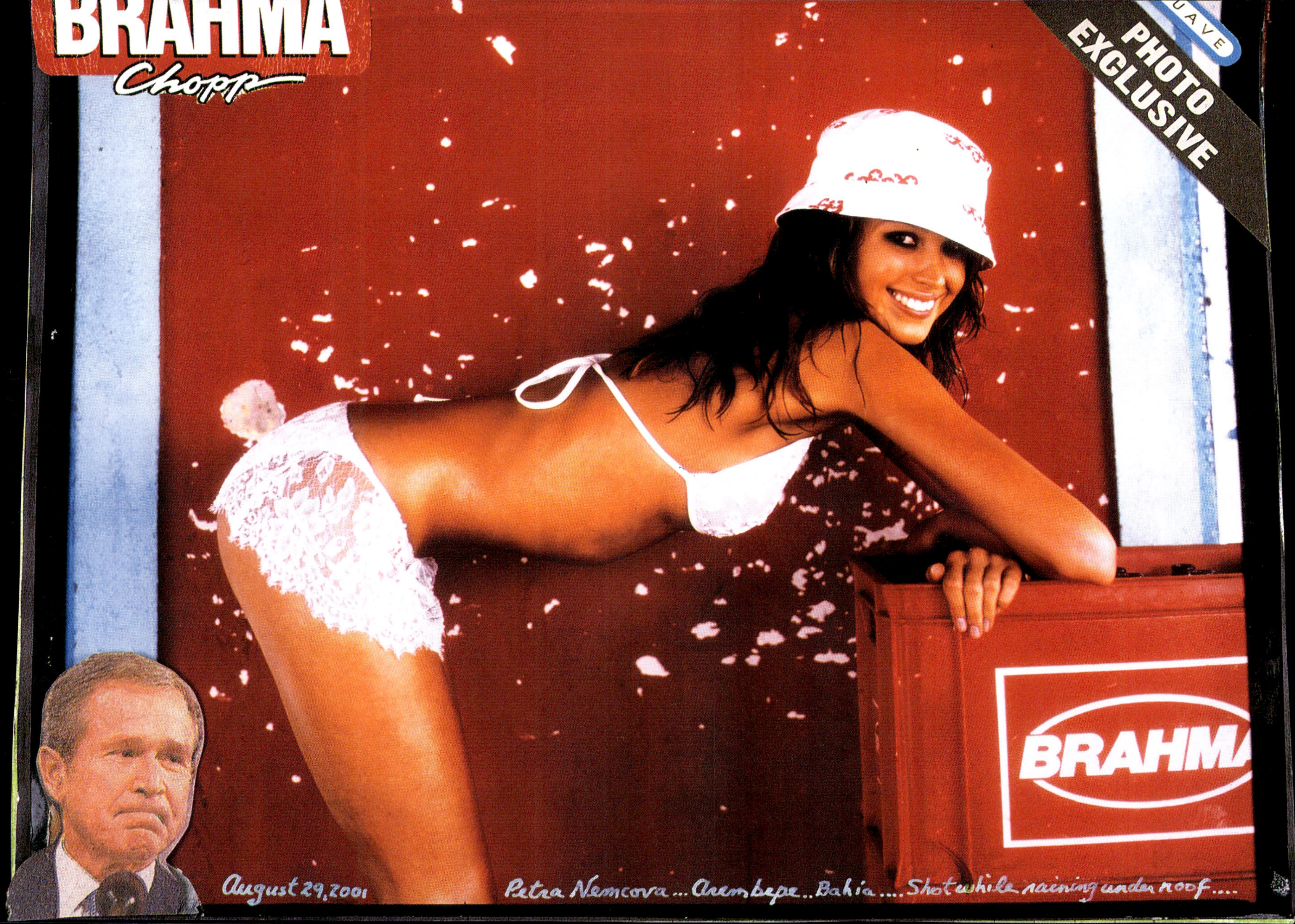

BRAHMA
Chopp

PHOTO
EXCLUSIVE

BRAHMA

August 29, 2001

Petra Nemcova ... Arembepe .. Bahia .... Shot while raining under roof ....

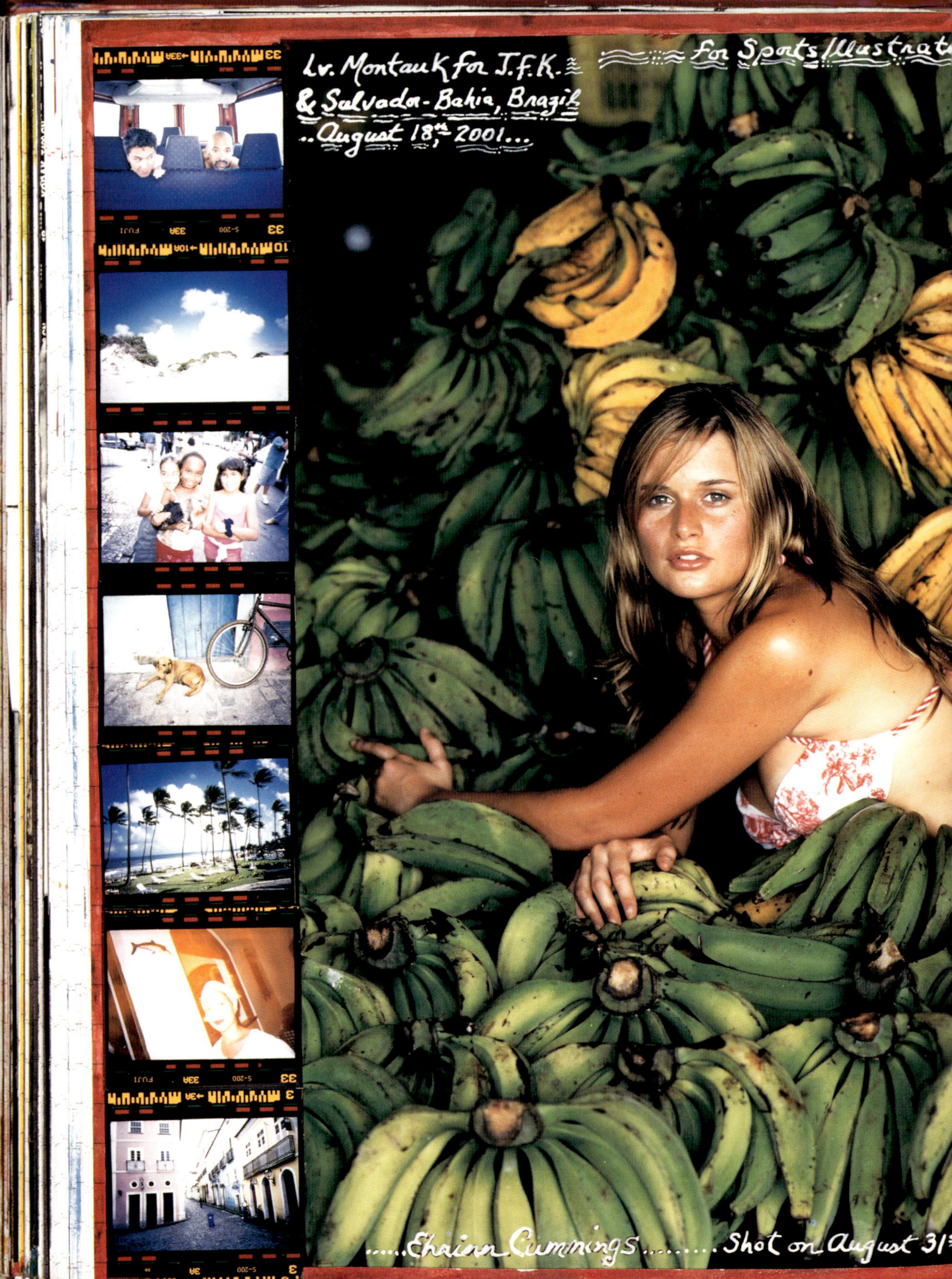
Lv. Montauk for J.F.K.
& Salvador-Bahia, Brazil
..August 18th 2001...
For Sports Illustrat
.....Ehrinn Cummings........Shot on August 31

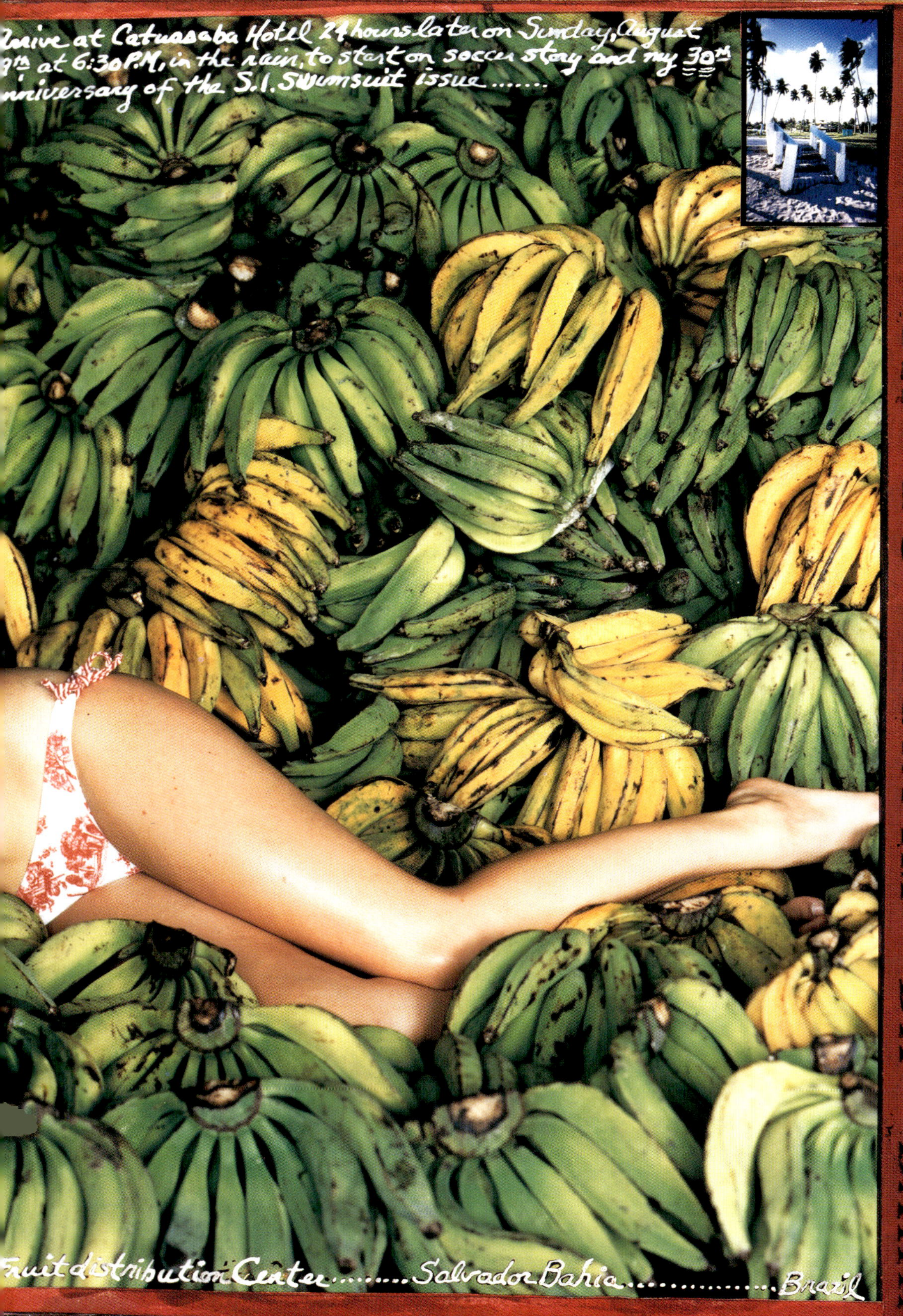

O SENHOR DO BONFIM DA BAHIA

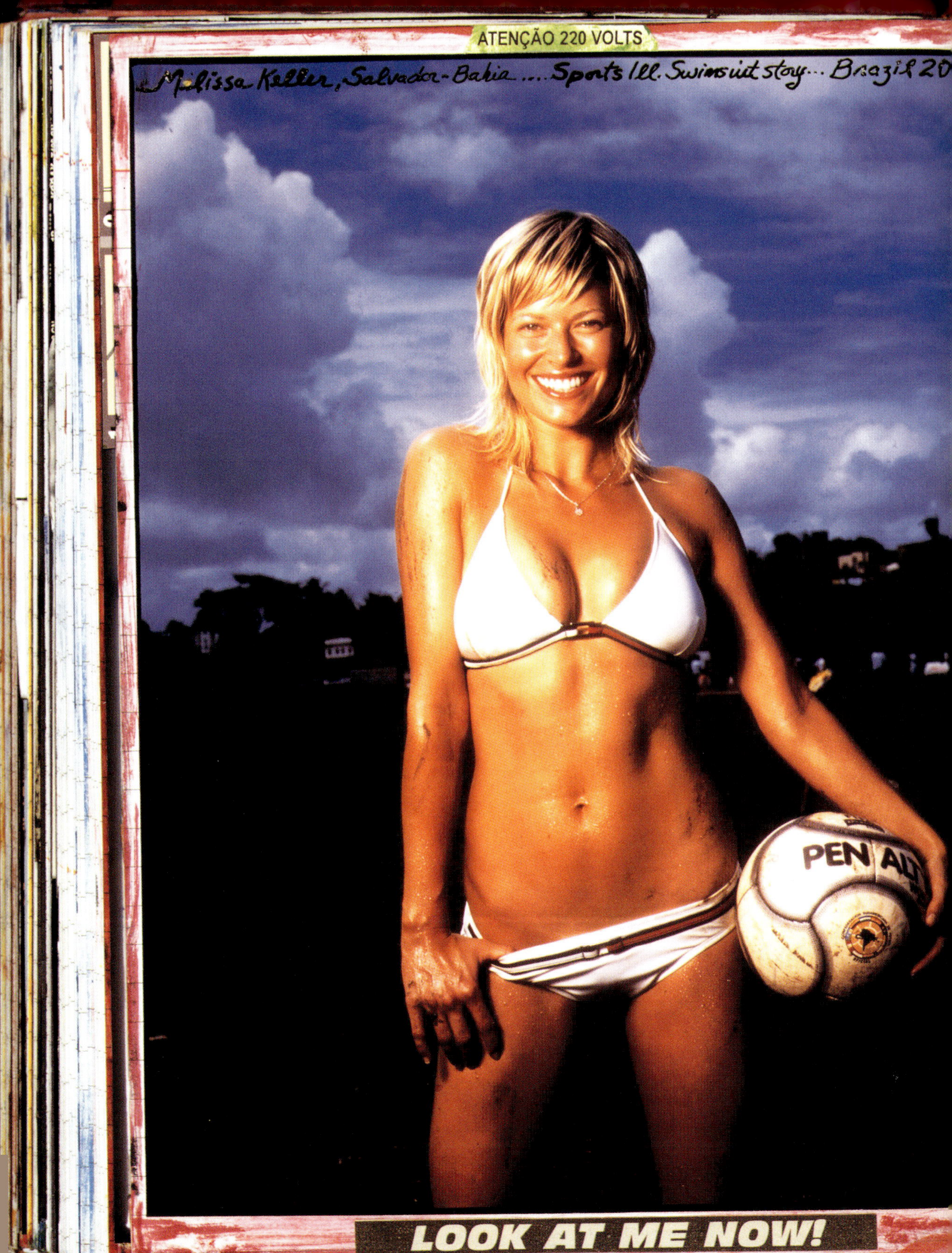
ATENÇÃO 220 VOLTS
Melissa Keller, Salvador-Bahia .... Sports Ill. Swimsuit story... Brazil 20
LOOK AT ME NOW!

August 23, 2001 .. Salvador, Brazil .. for Sports Illustrated .. Soccer Story

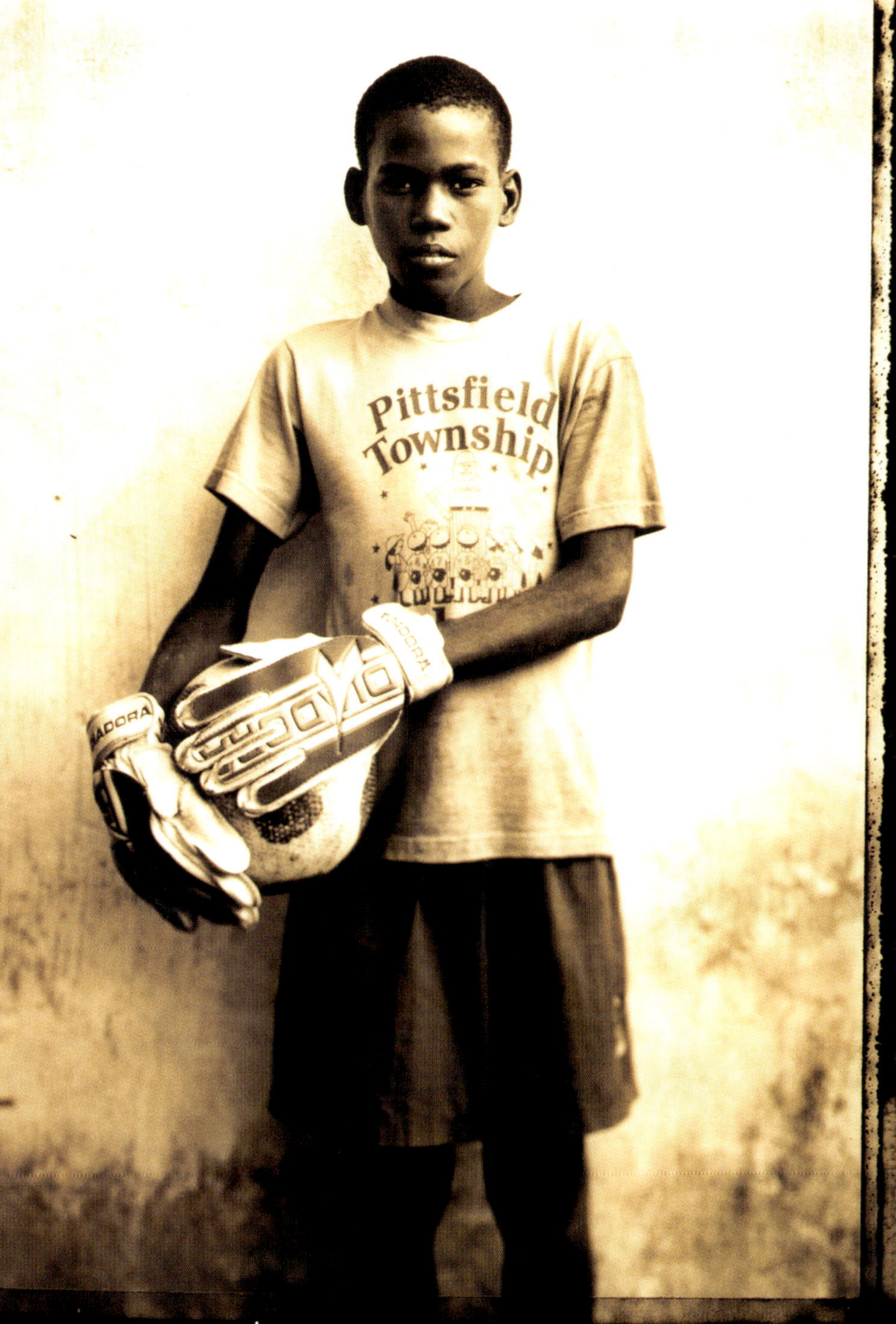

~Rogerio, age 14~

CHECK OUT TIME AT 12:00 AM

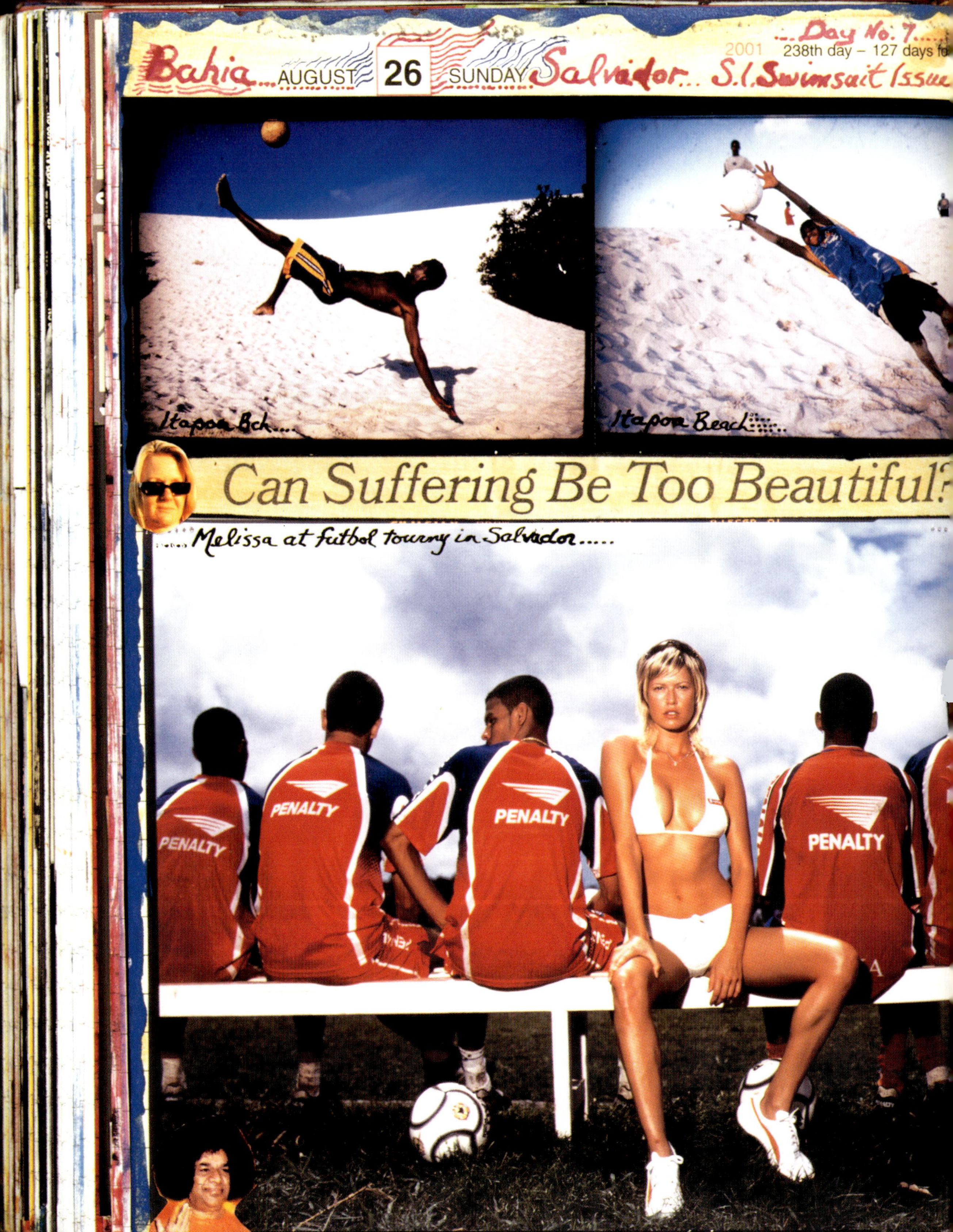
Bahia... AUGUST 26 SUNDAY Salvador... S.I. Swimsuit Issue
...Day No: 7.....
2001 238th day – 127 days fo
Itapoa Bch....
Itapoa Beach....
Can Suffering Be Too Beautiful?
....Melissa at futbol tourny in Salvador.....
PENALTY
PENALTY
PENALTY
PENALTY

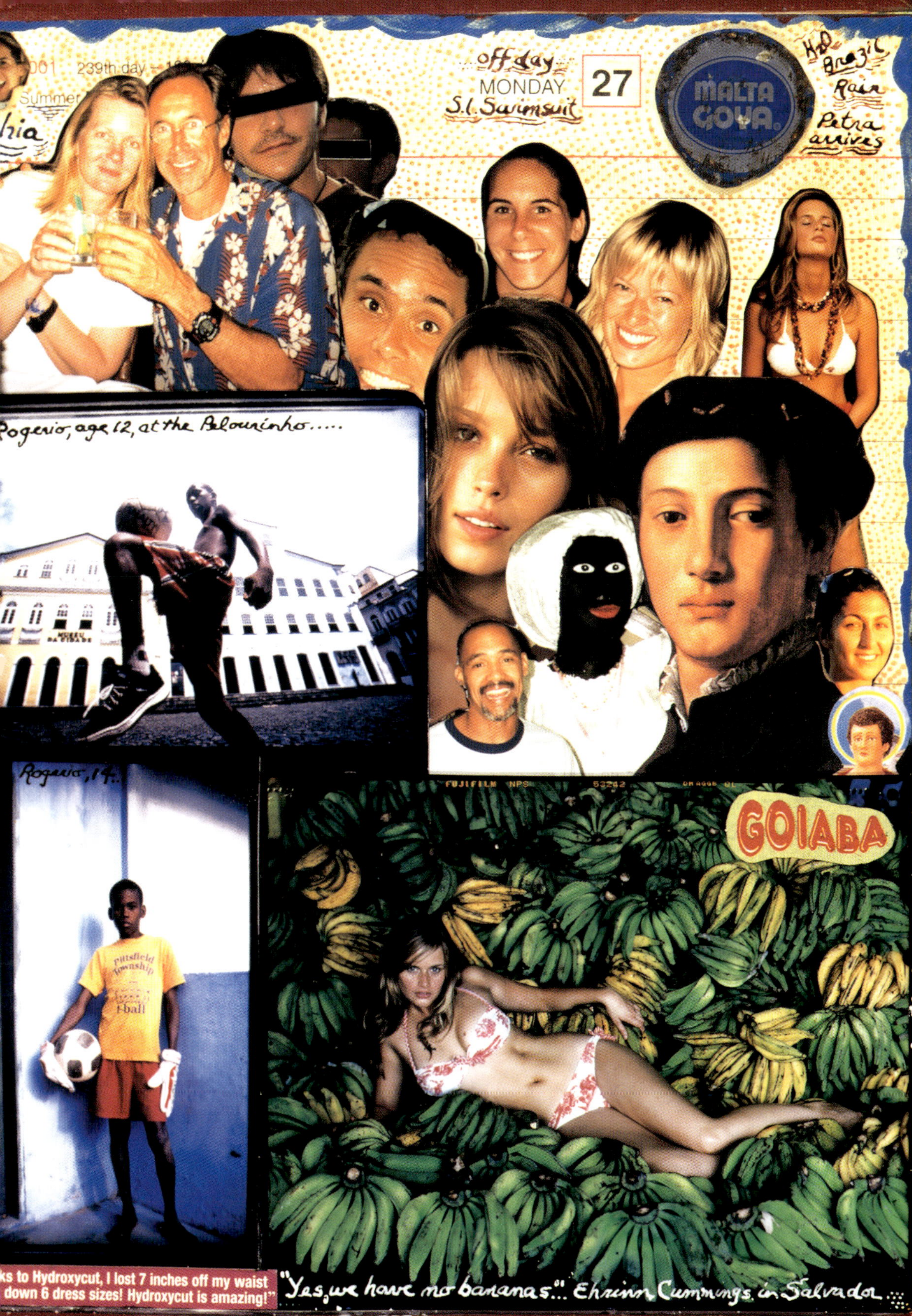

001 239th day
Summer
hia
Off day
MONDAY
S.I. Swimsuit
27
MALTA GOYA
Hot Brazil Rain
Petra arrives
Rogerio, age 12, at the Pelourinho.....
MUSEU DA CIDADE
Rogerio, 14..
Pittsfield Township T-ball
FUJIFILM NPS
GOIABA
ks to Hydroxycut, I lost 7 inches off my waist
down 6 dress sizes! Hydroxycut is amazing!"
"Yes, we have no bananas"... Ehrinn Cummings in Salvador

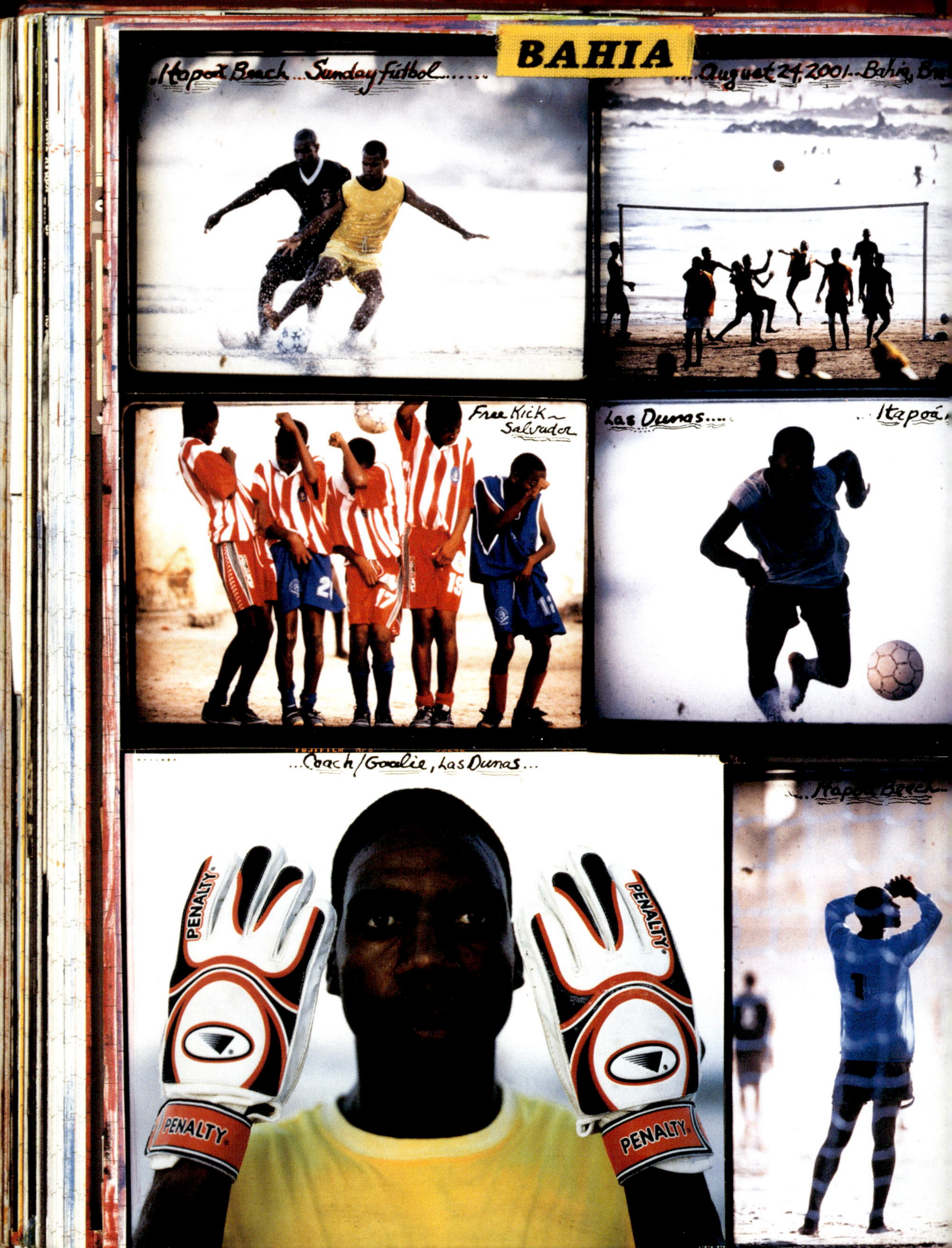
BAHIA
Itapoã Beach ... Sunday fútbol ......
... August 24, 2001 .. Bahia, Bra
Free Kick ~ Salvador
Las Dunas ....
.. Itapoã.
... Coach/Goalie, Las Dunas ...
... Itapoã Beach ...
PENALTY
PENALTY
PENALTY
PENALTY

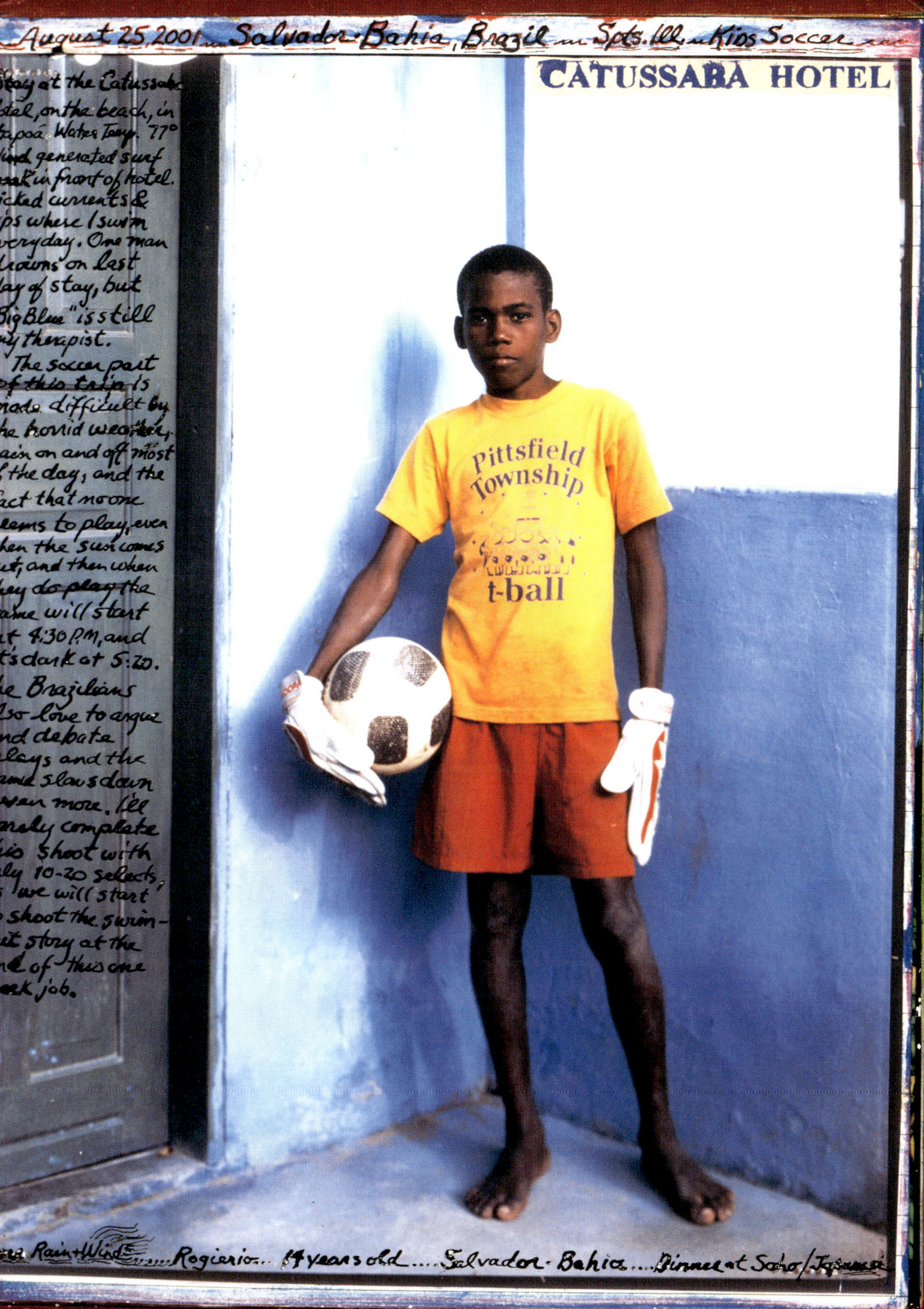
August 25, 2001... Salvador-Bahia, Brazil... Spts. Ill... Kids Soccer...
CATUSSABA HOTEL
Stay at the Catussaba
otel, on the beach, in
tapoá. Water Temp. 77°
Wind generated surf
eak in front of hotel.
icked currents &
ps where I swim
veryday. One man
rowns on last
day of stay, but
Big Blue" is still
my therapist.
The soccer part
of this trip is
made difficult by
he horrid weather,
ain on and off most
f the day; and the
act that no one
eems to play, even
hen the sun comes
ut, and then when
hey do play the
ame will start
t 4:30 P.M, and
t's dark at 5:20.
he Brazilians
lso love to argue
nd debate
lays and the
ame slows down
ven more. I'll
arely complete
his shoot with
ly 10-20 selects,
s we will start
o shoot the swim-
it story at the
nd of this one
eek job.
Pittsfield Township
t-ball
Rain+Wind...... Rogierio... 14 years old.... Salvador-Bahia.... Dinner at Soho/Japanese

8·30·01

...Shoot Melissa at coconut water stand in P.M.–Salvador...

Snore Free Nights
The Very First Night Guaranteed!

Day of the banana

2001 242nd day – 123 days

with Ehrinn, at the fr

distribution center–Sal

A day of classic shots with local color, at two fruit stands, and the photo of the trip... Ehrinn & the banana

VERDE
É VIDA

Ehrinn Cummings, Arembepe Lagoon, at twilight

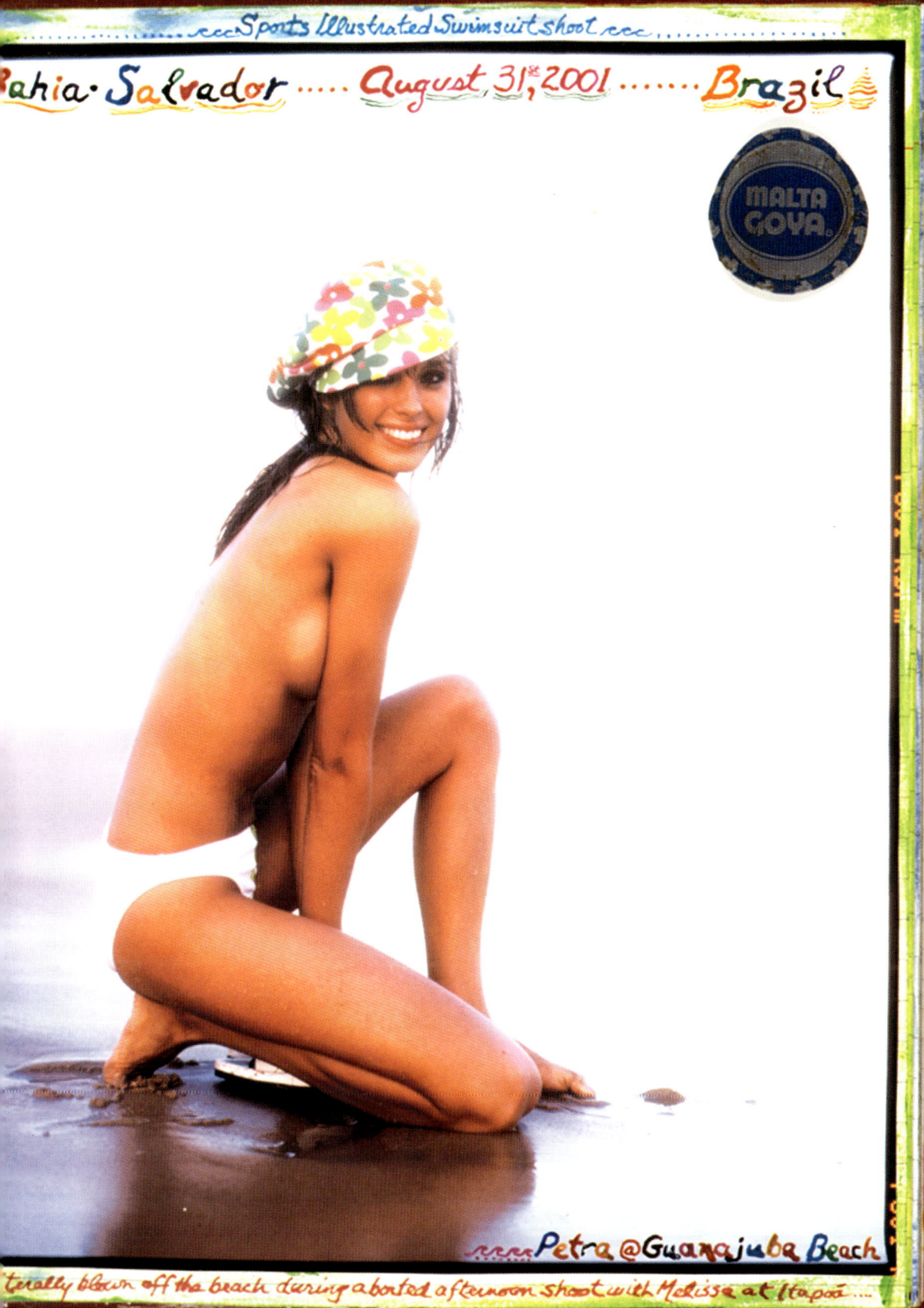

...Sports Illustrated Swimsuit shoot...

Bahia · Salvador ..... August 31st, 2001 .... Brazil

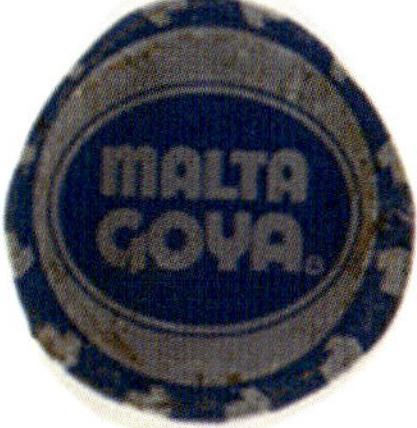

...Petra @Guanajuba Beach

...terally blown off the beach during aborted afternoon shoot with Melissa at Itapoã ...

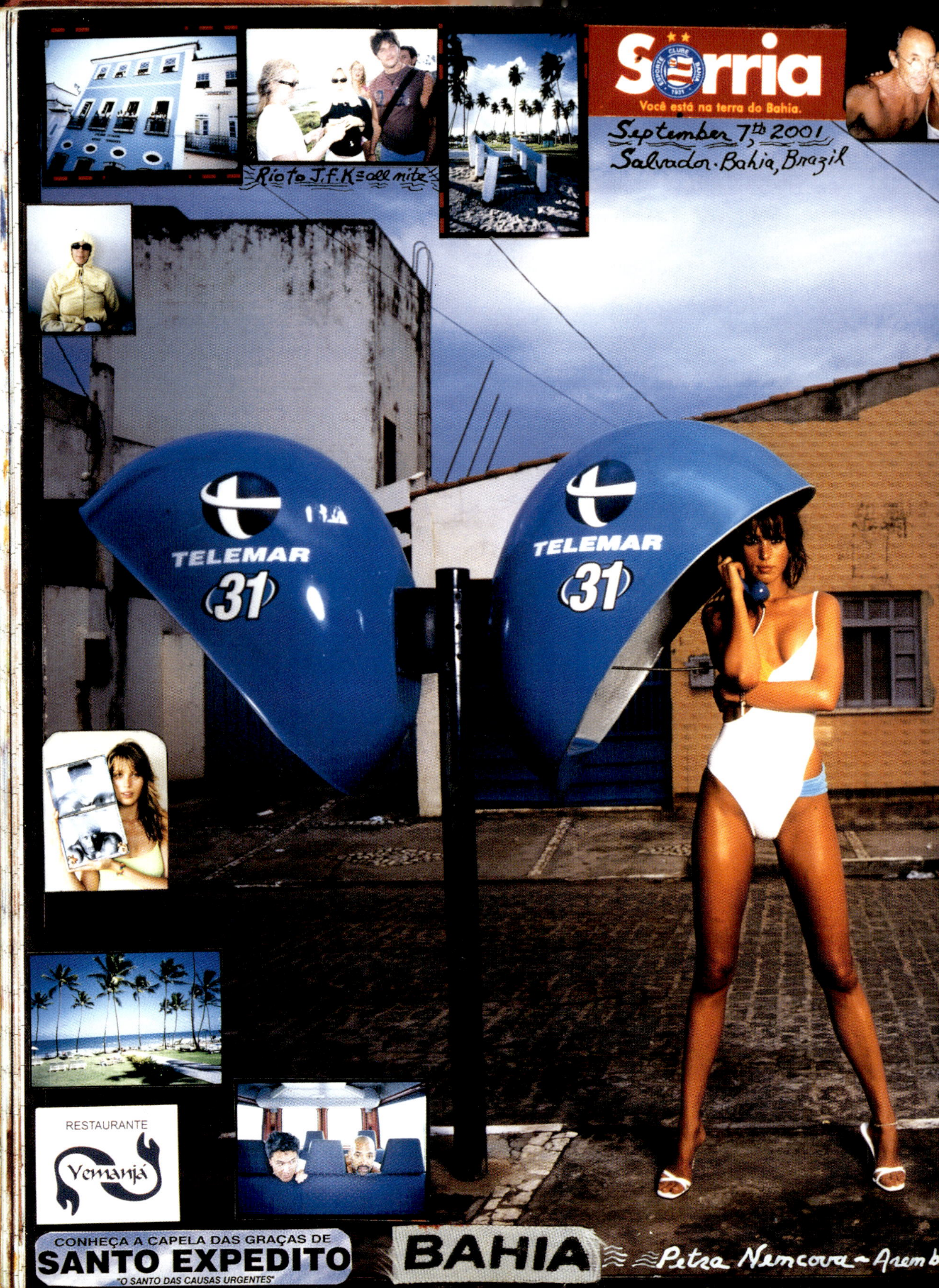
Sorria
Esporte Clube Bahia 1931
Você está na terra do Bahia.
September 7th, 2001
Salvador. Bahia, Brazil
Rio to J.F.K = all nite
TELEMAR
31
TELEMAR
31
RESTAURANTE
Yemanjá
CONHEÇA A CAPELA DAS GRAÇAS DE
SANTO EXPEDITO
"O SANTO DAS CAUSAS URGENTES"
BAHIA
Petra Nemcova - Arem b

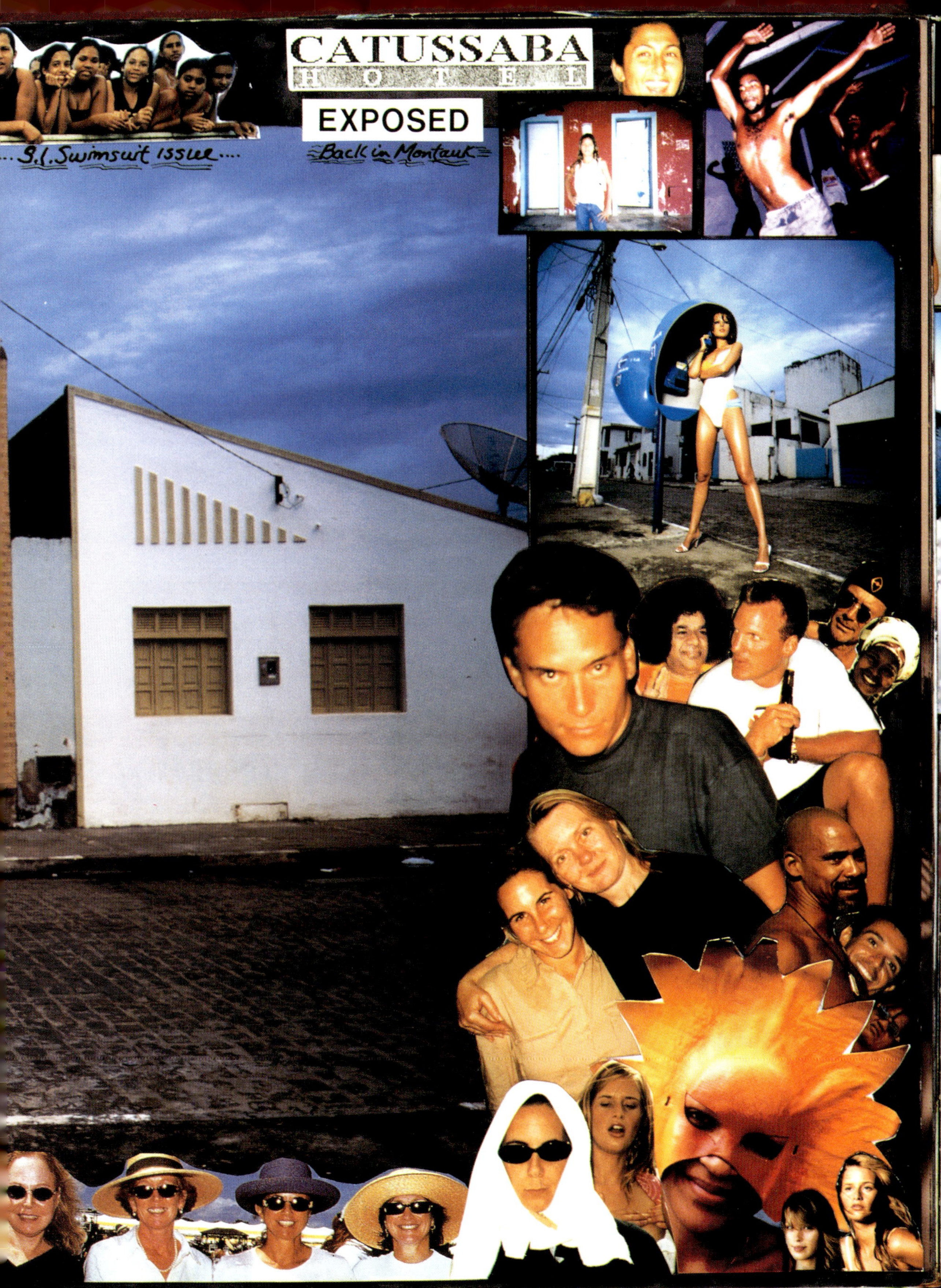
CATUSSABA
HOTEL
EXPOSED
...S.I. Swimsuit issue...
Back in Montauk

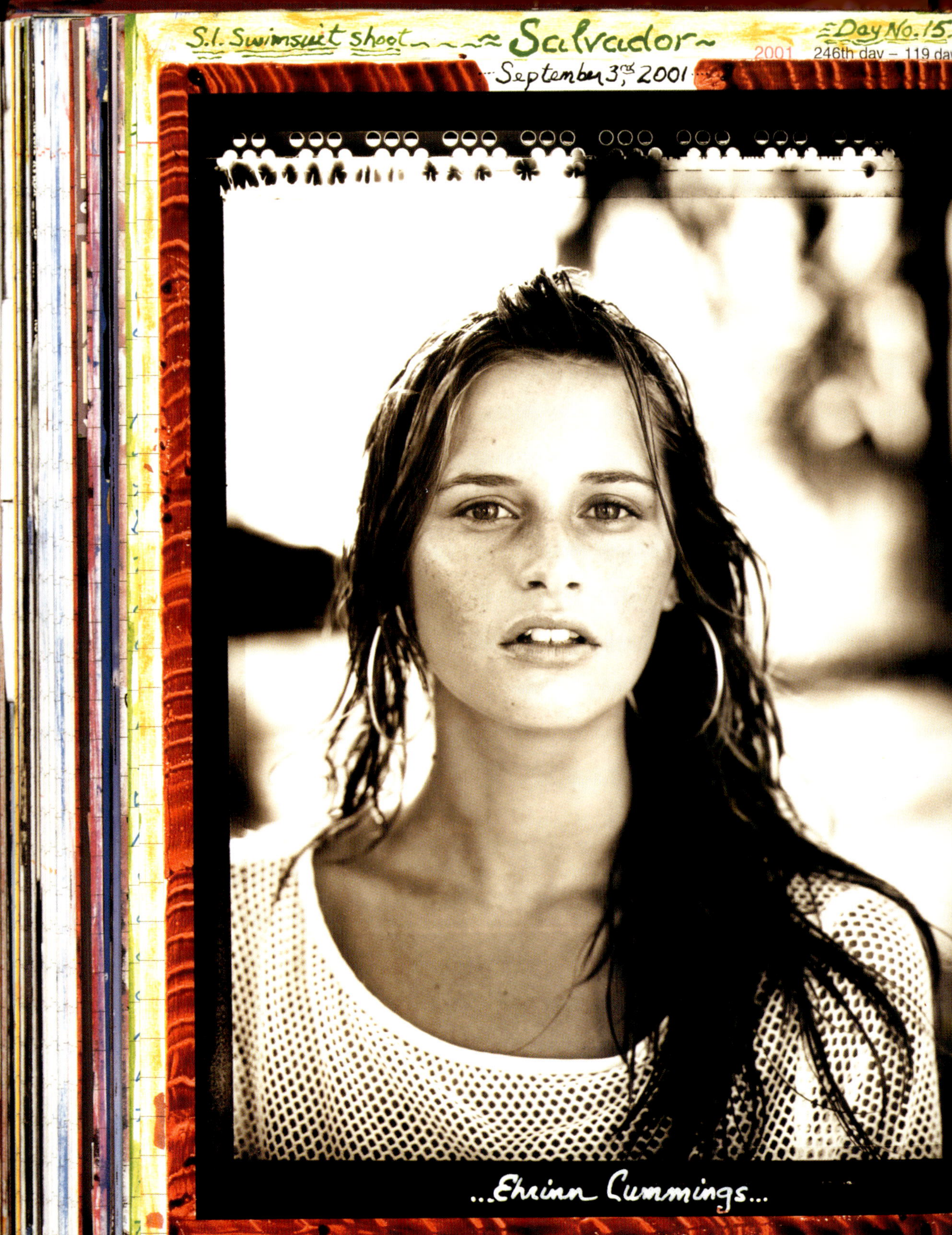
S.I. Swimsuit shoot ~ ~ ~ Salvador ~
Day No. 15
2001 246th day – 119 day
September 3rd 2001
...Ehrinn Cummings...

~Dinner at Trapiche~

~Bahia~

Do dance shot with Shak. in AREMBEPE

2001 247th day – 118 days follow

September 4th, 2001

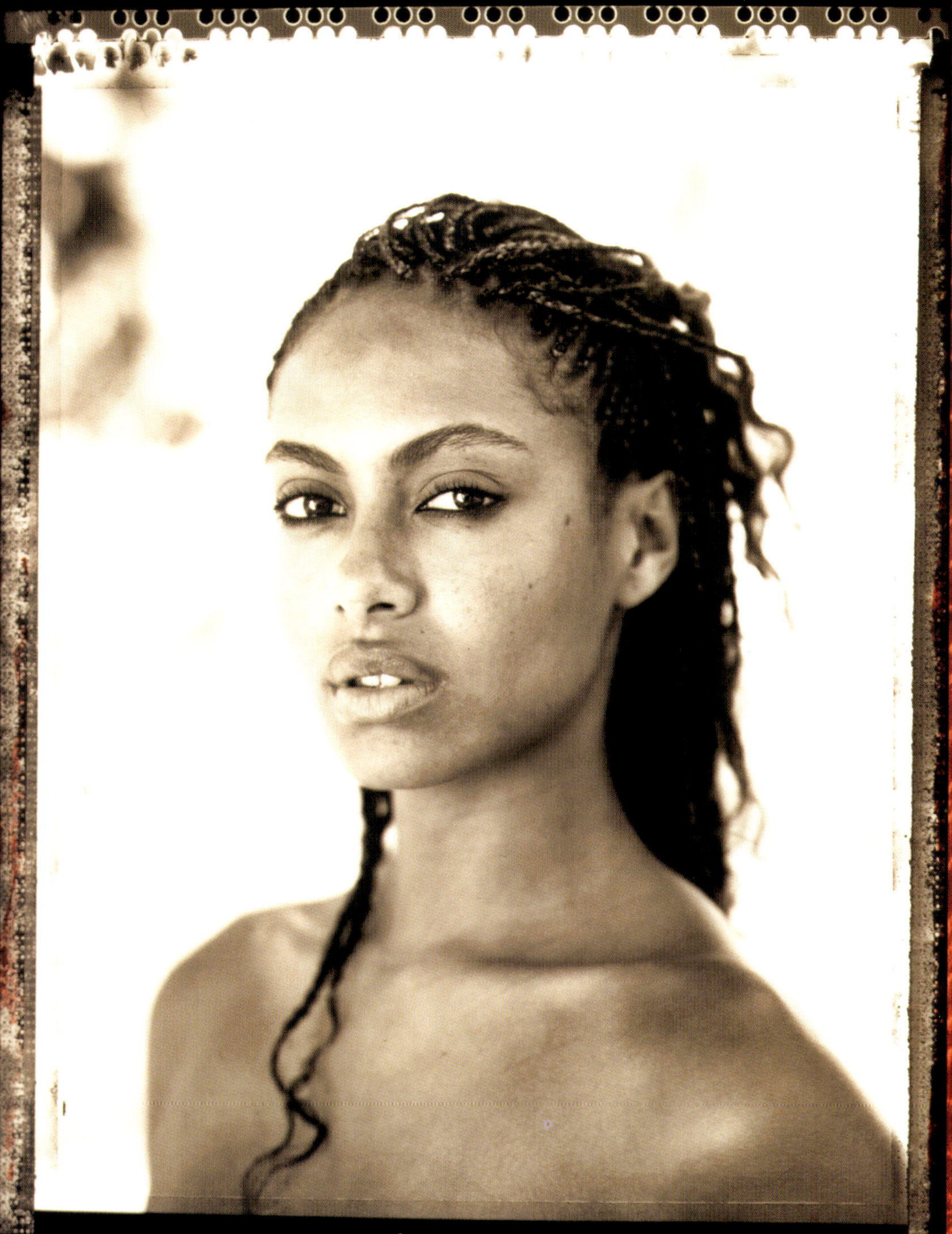

...ShaKara Ledard...

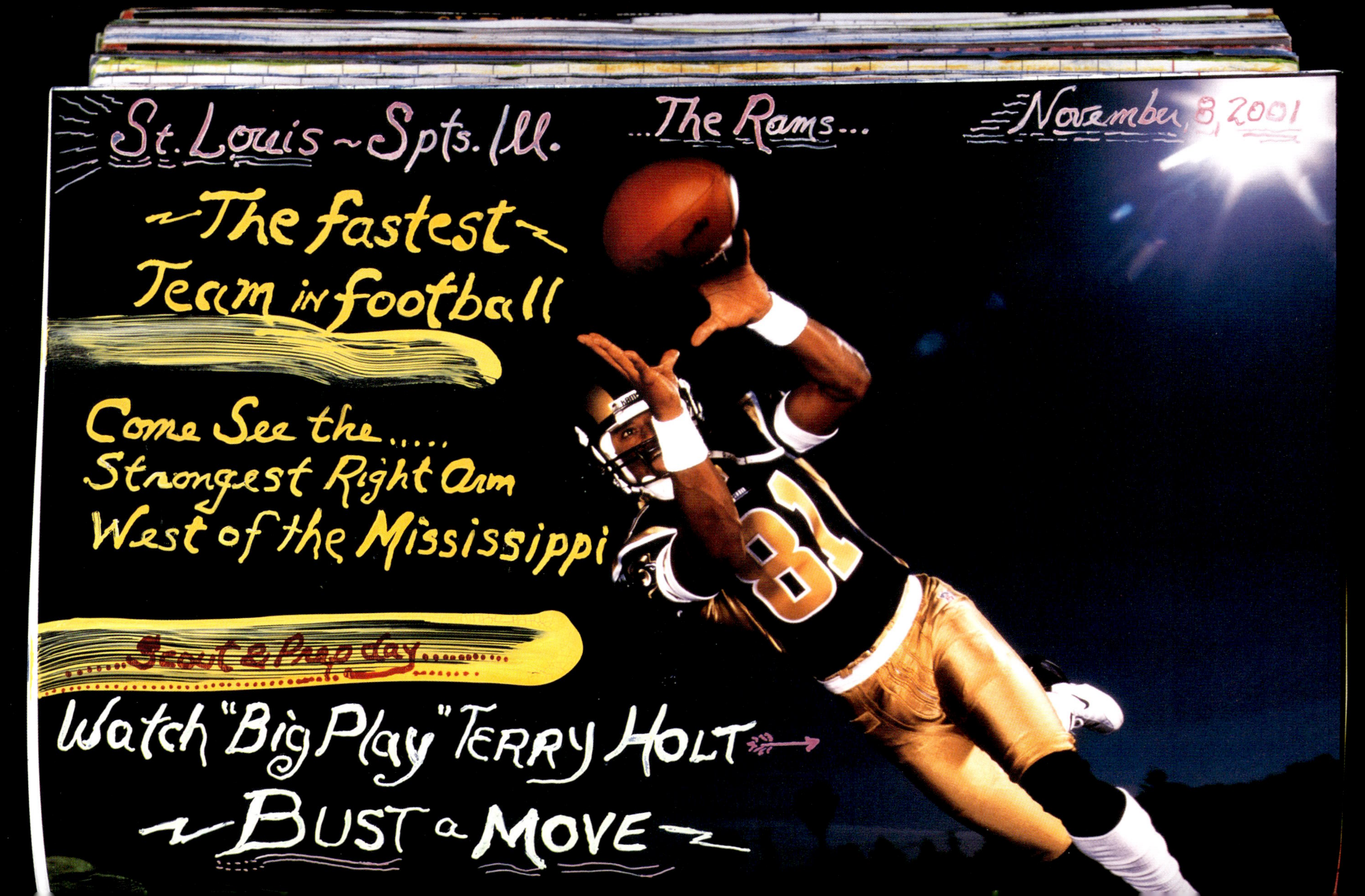

St. Louis ~ Spts. Ill. ...The Rams... November 8, 2001

~The fastest~
Team in football

Come See the.....
Strongest Right Arm
West of the Mississippi

.....Scout & Prep day.........

Watch "Big Play" TERRY HOLT

~BUST a MOVE~